Prais

THE PARAS

"Lacking fear, charismatic in his speech, and armed with solid, straightforward, biologically grounded ideas, Dr. Gad Saad has become somewhat of an internet phenomenon over the last few years. His new book continues in the same vein, warning its readers of the dangers of an unthinking progressive agenda and helping reestablish the general consensus that allows peace to prevail. Has your common sense been thoroughly assaulted? Read this book, strengthen your resolve, and help us all return to reason."

> **—JORDAN PETERSON, PH.D.**, clinical psychologist, professor of psychology at the University of Toronto, and author of *12 Rules for Life: An Antidote to Chaos*

"With disarming humor and withering logic, evolutionary behavioral scientist Gad Saad shows us that self-delusion is an equal-opportunity employer, not defined by race, ethnic background, sexual orientation, political leanings, or level of education. Nothing is taboo. To read *The Parasitic Mind* is to understand why so many people either embrace Saad for his clarity or reject him for holding up a mirror to their inconsistencies."

> **—PAUL A. OFFIT, M.D.**, Maurice R. Hilleman Professor of Vaccinology, Perelman School of Medicine at the University of Pennsylvania, and author of *Deadly Choices: How the Anti-Vaccine Movement Threatens Us All*

"Gad Saad argues that 'nefarious forces have slowly eroded the West's commitment to reason, science, and the values of the Enlightenment' and that these forces act like the weird brain parasites that alter the behavior of mice to make them less afraid of cats, driving human society towards a dark age of irrational prejudice and superstition. His courage, his rationality, and his enthusiasm for that much-neglected thing, the truth, shine through this powerful book."

> **—MATT RIDLEY, PH.D.**, author of *The Rational Optimist* and *How Innovation Works*

"A wonderfully intelligent, witty, and riveting account of the politically correct madness engulfing our society. *The Parasitic Mind* is a must-read for anyone concerned about victim politics, cancel culture, and the assault on reason. Saad not only expertly diagnoses the malady, he also points the way to a cure."

—CHRISTINA HOFF SOMMERS, PH.D., resident scholar at the American Enterprise Institute and co-author of *One Nation Under Therapy*

"A virus is sweeping through our civilization—a mind virus corrupting the brains of students, professors, and the public at large—and *The Parasitic Mind* is the vaccine that will counter this pernicious pandemic. Professor Gad Saad has emerged as a heroic public warrior fighting for reason and science in the search for truth. That he has developed such a fearless following clamoring for a work like this is a testimony to its necessity and why I think its broad readership will help stem the tide of unreason and anti-science."

—MICHAEL SHERMER, PH.D., publisher at *Skeptic* magazine and author of *Giving the Devil His Due*

The Parasitic Mind

THE PARASITIC MIND

HOW INFECTIOUS IDEAS ARE KILLING COMMON SENSE

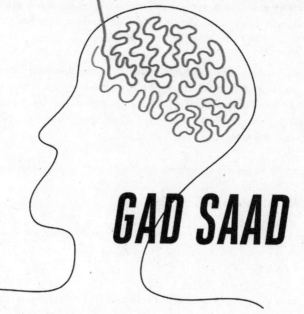

GAD SAAD

Since 1947
REGNERY
An Imprint of Skyhorse Publishing, Inc.

Regnery books may be purchased in bulk at special discounts for sales promotion, corporate gifts, fund-raising, or educational purposes. Special editions can also be created to specifications. For details, contact the Special Sales Department, Regnery, 307 West 36th Street, 11th Floor, New York, NY 10018 or info@skyhorsepublishing.com.

Regnery® is an imprint of Skyhorse Publishing, Inc.®, a Delaware corporation.

Visit our website at www.regnery.com.

Please follow our publisher Tony Lyons on Instagram @tonylyonsisuncertain.

10 9 8 7 6 5 4

Library of Congress Cataloging-in-Publication Data is available on file.

Print ISBN: 978-1-68451-229-4
eBook ISBN: 978-1-62157-993-9

Printed in the United States of America

To Lior, Bahebak

Contents

Preface

When we think of a pandemic, we often conjure images of deadly infectious diseases that spread rapidly across countries causing unimaginable human suffering (like the Black Death, the Spanish influenza, AIDS, or the ongoing COVID-19 crisis). The West is currently suffering from such a devastating pandemic, a collective malady that destroys people's capacity to think rationally. Unlike other pandemics where biological pathogens are to blame, the current culprit is composed of a collection of bad ideas, spawned on university campuses, that chip away at our edifices of reason, freedom, and individual dignity. This book identifies these idea pathogens, discusses their spread from the universities to all walks of life including politics, business, and popular culture, and offers ways to inoculate ourselves from their devastating effects.

In Chapter One, I offer a brief synopsis of the factors that led to my becoming an ardent warrior against these destructive ideas including my experience of two great wars, the Lebanese Civil War (as a child) and the war against reason (as a professor over the past twenty-five years), as well as my life ideals of seeking freedom and truth. In Chapter Two,

I explore the tension between thinking and feeling, and the tension between the pursuit of truth and the minimization of hurt feelings. I argue that it is wrongheaded to create a false tension between our reasoning faculty and our emotions. We are both a thinking and a feeling animal. A problem arises when we apply the wrong system to a given situation (such as letting our emotions guide us in a situation that requires reason, or vice versa). I provide several contemporary examples to highlight this point including the hysterical emotional responses to Donald Trump's election as president of the United States and Brett Kavanaugh's appointment to the United States Supreme Court. In Chapter Three, I posit that freedom of speech, the scientific method, intellectual diversity, and a meritocratic ethos rooted in individual dignity rather than adherence to the ideology of Diversity, Inclusion, and Equity (DIE) are nonnegotiable elements of a truly enlightened society. A fair society ensures that its members have equality of opportunities and not equality of outcomes as mandated by DIE edicts. Chapter Four addresses several anti-science, anti-reason, and illiberal idea pathogens including postmodernism, radical feminism, and transgender activism, the latter two of which are rooted in a deeply hysterical form of biophobia (fear of biology). These idea pathogens destroy our understanding of reality and common sense by espousing such positions as: invisible art is a form of art, all sex differences are due to social construction, and some women have nine-inch penises. Chapter Five examines how the mindset of social justice warriors gave rise to universities that prioritize minimizing hurt feelings over pursuing truth (a continuation of the theme first addressed in Chapter Two), the Oppression Olympics (intersectionality), Collective Munchausen and the homeostasis of victimology (I'm a victim therefore I am), and pious self-flagellating at the altar of progressivism. In this view, warped by outrage and resentment, the world is binary: you are either a noble victim (even if you have to make it up) or a disgusting bigot (even if you've never been one). Choose a side. Chapter Six explores Ostrich Parasitic Syndrome (OPS), a malady of disordered thinking that robs people of their ability to recognize truths that are as obvious as the existence of the sun. Science denialism is one manifestation of OPS but there are many others. Those afflicted with OPS utilize a broad range of strategies to shelter themselves from reality including the use of six degrees of faux-causality wherein countless ills are pinned wrongly on one's favorite culprit (such as "climate change causes terrorism"). I examine how OPS sufferers take imbecilic and at times suicidal positions regarding issues of civilizational import including the root causes of global terrorism, the virtues of open borders, the apparent congruence between sharia law and the United States Constitution, and the supposed racism of profiling. To document the pandemic of disordered thinking without offering a way for people to inoculate themselves against these idea pathogens would be insufficient. So in Chapter Seven while warning readers of various forms of faux-profundity masquerading as truth, I examine how to seek truth via the assiduous and careful erecting of nomological networks of cumulative evidence. Finally, in the last chapter, I propose reasons that cause people to remain passive bystanders in the battle of ideas, and I suggest a course of action to turn the tide. Do not underestimate the power of your voice. Seismic changes start off as small rumbles. Get engaged in the battle for reason and freedom of thought and speech. Your voice matters. Use it.

I am periodically challenged in my dogged efforts to combat the idea pathogens spread by social justice warriors. The criticisms usually take one of two related forms: 1) "Professor Saad, are you not exaggerating the problem? After all, social justice warriors constitute a minority on most campuses." 2) "Dr. Saad, why don't you tackle more important problems? Stop obsessing about some quack outliers. Your time would be better spent elsewhere. Discuss science. Teach us about your areas of scientific expertise." Let me tackle each position in turn with the hope that my responses might compel some people who are quietly watching from the sidelines to join the battle of ideas. On September 11, 2001, nineteen men armed with nothing more than religious fervor and ideological zealotry, killed nearly 3,000 people and permanently altered the New York skyscape if not our collective sense of security. The devastation inflicted by motivated terrorists can greatly exceed their number. Similarly, social justice warriors and their ilk are intellectual terrorists, and they can wreak havoc on reason and our public life, limiting people's willingness to speak and think freely, without ever constituting a majority.

On April 6, 2019, I posted the following message on my social media platforms:

> Some people are truly irredeemably clueless. They post comments attacking me for criticizing the SJW [social justice warrior] mindset instead of supposedly tackling "important" matters. Yes, because having a set of idea pathogens take complete control over the minds and souls of millions of people in academia, government, companies, the media, and the general society in a manner that is akin to religious superstitious dogma is "unimportant." Having anti-science, anti-reason nonsense taught to children in elementary schools is "unimportant." Having governments and universities push policies that are antithetical to individual dignity & a meritocratic ethos is "unimportant." There is NOTHING more important than fighting for freedom of speech, freedom of conscience, and a commitment toward science, reason, & logic over quasi-religious dogma. Those who are incapable of seeing the larger picture are complicit in perpetuating the current zeitgeist of lunacy. That at times I use satire, sarcasm, and humour to battle against the enemies of reason should not detract you from understanding how serious this battle is.[1]

This book is all about that battle.

An associated criticism that I often receive is a form of whataboutism on steroids. People expect that I should dispense my ire and cast my critical eye on the right in equal measure as I do the left. I inhabit the world of academia. This is an ecosystem that has been dominated by leftist thinking for many decades and certainly for the entirety of my professional career. The idea pathogens that I discuss in this book stem largely if not totally from leftist academics. Postmodernism, radical feminism, cultural relativism, identity politics, and the rest of the academic nonsense were not developed and promulgated by right-wing zealots. Runaway selection is an evolutionary mechanism that explains how animals evolve greatly exaggerated traits (like the peacock's tail).[2] I posit that many of the idea pathogens covered in this book are manifestations of a form of runaway selection of insanity spawned by leftist professors. There is an ever-increasing ideological pressure to come up with more egregious departures from reason, as a signal of one's progressive purity. As an evolutionary behavioral scientist, I am as keen to criticize Republican politicians who choose to "reject" evolution as I am Democrats who reject some of its implications. My focus on the left is a mere reflection of the fact that its intelligentsia shape academic culture and the subsequent downstream effects that trickle to the rest of society. I don't need to critique both sides of the political aisle with equal alacrity under the misguided desire to appear impartial. That would be akin to asking a gynecologic oncologist who specializes in cervical cancer why he maintains a strict focus on women. *Come on, Doc, don't be sexist. Please be impartial and also treat men with cervical cancer.* (Actually, this is now a possibility since trans men have cervices.) My goal is to defend the truth, and today it is the left's pathogenic ideas that are leading us to an abyss of infinite, irrational darkness.

Another manifestation of whataboutism occurs when people accuse me of not focusing on *their* preferred issues. "But what about Israel, Professor Saad? Why don't you criticize their policies? What about Trump's position on climate change, Professor Saad? Are you a climate change denier? If you care so much about the state of our educational system, why don't you attack Trump's secretary of education Betsy DeVos?" This is as logical as questioning why a dermatologist is spending her time curing melanoma. *What about childhood leukemia, Doc? Why are you being hypocritical in your clinical practice? You never perform surgeries on ruptured Achilles tendons, Doc. Why the obsessive focus on skin-related medical conditions?* To reiterate, I fight against a particular class of mind viruses. This does not imply that I should address all issues under the sun with equal zeal. This reminds me of creationists who proclaim that in the spirit of fairness, high school students need to be taught evolution and intelligent design as competing theories. Intellectual consistency does not require that I critique the full universe of idiotic ideas. I am a parasitologist of the human mind, seeking to inoculate people against a class of destructive ideas that destroy our capacity to reason.

Upon reading this book, I hope that readers will walk away with a renewed sense of optimism. We may have fallen into an abyss of infinite lunacy, but it is not too late to grab hold of the rope of reason and hoist ourselves back into the warm light of logic, science, and common sense. Thank you for coming on this journey. Truth shall prevail.

CHAPTER ONE

From Civil War to the Battle of Ideas

I am often asked why I am an outspoken academic, willing to tackle thorny and difficult issues well beyond my areas of scientific interest. Given the stifling political correctness that governs academia, it would be advisable from a careerist perspective to be the proverbial "stay in your lane" professor. So why do I stick my neck out repeatedly? As is true of most human phenomena, the answer lies in the unique combination of my personhood (genes) coupled with my personal history (environment). On a personal level, I am a free thinker who is allergic to go-along, get-along group think. The ideals that drive my life are freedom and truth, and any attack on these ideals represents an existential threat to all that I hold dear. I am also the product of my unique life trajectory shaped by two wars. While few people will ever experience the horrors of war, I have faced two great wars in my life: the Lebanese Civil War and the war against reason, science, and logic that has been unleashed in the West, especially on North American university campuses. The Lebanese war taught me early about the ugliness of tribalism and religious dogma. It likely informed my subsequent disdain for identity politics, as I grew up in an ecosystem where the group to which you belonged mattered more than your individuality. With that in mind, let us return to my homeland in the Middle East.

Growing Up in Lebanon

I was born in Beirut, Lebanon, in 1964 and spent the first eleven years of my life in the "Paris of the Middle East." My family was part of the dwindling Jewish community that had steadfastly remained in Lebanon despite the growing signs that Lebanese Jews had a bleak future. My father had nine sisters and a brother, while my mother had six sisters, all of whom, with the exception of one paternal aunt, had emigrated from Lebanon long prior to the outbreak of the civil war in 1975. My maternal grandparents died prior to my birth; my paternal grandparents left for Israel around 1970. A similar immigration pattern occurred within my immediate family. I have two brothers and one sister, all much older than I (the closest to me in age is ten years older). My eldest brother married a Christian woman of Palestinian origin, and they immigrated to Montreal, Canada, in 1974. My sister also moved to Montreal prior to the outbreak of the civil war, both to pursue her studies and to escape the looming dangers. Finally, my other brother who had been crowned Lebanese champion of judo on multiple occasions was forced to flee our homeland due to ominous threats that he should retire (for it was not good optics for a Jew to repeatedly win a combat sport). He heeded that "advice" and moved to Paris, France, around 1973 to continue his studies and judo career. The breathtaking irony is that he eventually represented Lebanon at the 1976 Montreal Olympics. Hence, the Jewish judoka who was no longer welcomed in Lebanon only a few years earlier was "embraced" when it suited the relevant authorities.

Growing up as a Jewish boy in Lebanon had its existential challenges. I vividly recall when the Egyptian president Gamal Abdel Nasser died in 1970, a few weeks shy of my sixth birthday. Nasser's Pan-Arabism (unification of the Arab world) had made him a hero in the region, and as often happens in the Middle East, thousands of people took to the streets to publicly lament his passing. Why would this event constitute an episodic memory for a five-year-old boy? As the angry procession made its way down our street (aptly named *Rue de l'Armée* or The Military's Street), the terrifying chant "Death to Jews" left an indelible mark on me as I cowered in hiding next to our balcony. You see, even in "progressive, modern, and pluralistic" Lebanon, endemic Jew-hatred was always ready to rear its ugly head. All calamities in the Middle East are ultimately due to the diabolical Jew. It rained today. Blame the Jews. The economy is weak. Blame the Jews. Tourism is down. Blame the Jews. You contracted a stomach bug. Blame the Jews. The Christians and Muslims in Lebanon are not getting along. You guessed it, blame the Jews. And contrary to current attempts at revisionist history, this existential disdain for the Jew precedes the founding of modern Israel by 1,400 years. I can still remember sitting around the table on Yom Kippur (the holiest day in Judaism) in 1973 watching the worried look on my parents' faces as word broke that a combined Arab army had attacked Israel on that holy day. Existential genocidal hatred is not something that one magically and suddenly contracts as an adult; rather, it is instilled insidiously and repeatedly in the minds of otherwise pure and innocent children. I was the only one of my four siblings not to attend a Jewish elementary school. I must have been nine or ten years old, in class at the *Lycée des Jeunes Filles*, when the teacher asked pupils to state what they wanted to be when they grew up. Typical responses were uttered uneventfully (policeman or soccer player) until one student said, "When I grow up, I want to be a Jew killer," after which the class erupted in raucous laughter and gleeful claps. I still have the class photos from that era, and that boy's face is forever etched in my memory.

In sharing these stories, I don't wish to imply that our daily lives in Lebanon prior to the civil war were hellish. My parents were well entrenched within Lebanese society. The fact that we were part of the last wave of Jews to leave Lebanon was a testament to my parents' overall attachment to our homeland. Most of my childhood friends were Christian and Muslim (one of whom recently reached out to me, as his daughter was about to start college in Montreal). Any hope of long-lasting peaceful coexistence was shattered once the civil war broke out in 1975. This conflict remains the standard by which the butchery of all other civil wars is gauged. Neighbors who had lived next door to one another for decades became instant prospective enemies. Death awaited us at every corner. If the endless shelling did not kill you (we learned to take cover or not depending on the whistle signature of the bombs), the snipers might if you appeared within their field of vision. Civilians were kidnapped and killed. They were also mowed down while waiting in long bread queues (two of my family members evaded such a death by going out late to buy bread during a ceasefire). Various militia set up roadblocks at which point they'd check to see your internal ID (which had one's religion written on it). If you were of the "wrong" religion, you could be executed. Our religious heritage was written as "Israelite" rather than "Jewish," which meant we had few Muslim friends at roadblocks. Of the innumerable terrifying moments that I experienced during the civil war, one sticks out in my mind as uniquely eerie and ominous.

Prior to the start of the war, my parents had contracted a hand dryer service that provided a roll of washable textile which was installed on the wall of our kitchen. This was a precursor of the subsequent models of disposable hand drying tissues found in public bathrooms. Periodically, the same individual would come to our house to remove the dirty roll and replace it with a clean one (I believe his name was Ahmad or perhaps Mohammad). I thought that this was a rather strange service then, and even more so now as I recount the story. One evening, in the middle of the otherwise endless street-to-street fighting and continuous bomb shelling, I heard a knock at our front door. I walked to the door and asked who was there. The reply came: "It's me Ahmad [Mohammad], the guy who changes your kitchen roll. Open the door, kid." I delayed, and his insistence grew more sinister and forceful: "Open the door now!" I ran to my mother. If memory serves me right, there were four occupants at our house that evening: my mother, my sister (who had returned to Beirut to visit us and was stuck there), a male friend of my parents (who was also stuck at our house even though he lived a short drive away), and myself. My father was not at home; I believe he was outside the country, but I can't remember why he was away. He eventually returned to Beirut and narrowly escaped death on the drive back to our home. My mother approached the door and talked through it with Ahmad who was accompanied by one or more men. The exchange grew tense, and my mother fetched the male friend who was cowering in another room. She hoped he might frighten them away, and I recall the disgust and anger that my mother expressed for this male friend's breathtaking cowardice in refusing to help.

Within the brutality and chaos of the civil war, there remained some semblance of law and order. As a last-ditch effort and against all odds, my mother phoned the police (the Arabic word for the outfit was "sixteen"), and they took the call—remember that this is during a full-blown war. Once they arrived at our house, we opened the door and let everyone into the kitchen. The lead policeman asked the men why they were there and who they were. Ahmad replied: "Oh, my friends and I were in the mountains, and we brought back a basket of pomegranate with us, and so we stopped by to give it to this family." After the policeman (I recall his impressive rifle by his side) checked to confirm the contents of the basket, he stared coldly at Ahmad and said: "Your connection to this family is that you change their hand drying roll, and you decided to brave the street fighting and come in the middle of the night to offer them pomegranate. If I ever find you here again, you'll have serious problems." What happened next still gives me shivers down my spine. Ahmad looked at us and said very coldly and menacingly: "I'll be back for you." We did not stay much longer in Lebanon after that incident, and so Ahmad never had the chance to "visit" us again.

It was clear that we needed to leave Lebanon as soon as possible. The day of our escape from Lebanon was straight out of a shoot 'em up movie. On that fateful day, some armed Palestine Liberation Organization (PLO) militia picked us up at our home. They had been contracted to get us safely to Beirut International Airport; the risk was that they might drive us to a ditch and execute us. The PLO controlled the area around the airport, so there was little chance of clearing the checkpoints if the appropriate militia did not accompany you. One of the armed men asked me if I wanted to hold his machine gun, which I did with excited trepidation. On the way to the airport, I recall my father proclaiming that he had forgotten his money belt at our house and that we needed to return to get it. The militiamen rejected my father's plea, and we proceeded on our precarious journey. The next memory that I have is perhaps one of the most poignant ones of my life: the flight captain declared that we were out of Lebanese airspace, at which point my mother took out a chain with a Star of David (or it might have been a Chai, a Hebrew symbol for *life* or *living*), placed it around my neck, and said: "Now you can wear this, not hide your identity, and be proud of who you are." Several years later, I asked my parents to fill in my memory lapse: Why could I not remember any other details from our drive to the Beirut International Airport? Apparently, as we drove through the various neighborhoods, our militiamen exchanged fire with unsympathetic local militias. We were crouched in the car with luggage over our heads. I have no memory of that incident.

My first impression of Montreal was how cold it was. I had never experienced such a climate. That said, I recall thinking that it was better to face falling snow than falling bombs. I vividly remember being driven by my parents to Iona Elementary School. It was a dark and dreary day. The teacher graciously asked me to stand in front of the class and introduce myself. This was an English school, and I knew very few English words (other than whatever I might have learned while watching spaghetti westerns growing up in Beirut). I began: "Mon nom est Gad Saad. Je viens du Liban." [My name is Gad Saad. I come from Lebanon.] I faced the dreaded collective blank stare. Using my hands, I gestured a machine gun mowing down people while stating "Liban, Liban." I recently ran into a classmate who was present on my infamous first day at school, and he confirmed that this episode was also etched in his mind. It is perhaps poetic that we ran into one another at my daughter's elementary school year-end BBQ.

Even though we had safely arrived at Montreal in 1975, our Lebanese nightmare continued well beyond that point. My parents found it difficult to adapt to their new lives in Canada, and so they did not fully sever their ties with their homeland until 1980. This was the year that my parents made one of their imprudent return trips to Beirut and were kidnapped by Fatah. They were held captive for several days during which time they faced a very unsavory reality. During their disappearance, I was kept in the dark about their circumstances (in a bid to protect me), and only found out what had really happened once my parents were freed (via high-level political figures who intervened on their behalf). One of my high school classmates, who was also Lebanese-Jewish, was fully aware of my parents' kidnapping (his parents and mine were lifelong friends). He later recounted to me that he had found it very odd that I appeared so carefree and joyful during my parents' disappearance. He did not know that I was unaware of their lot as the tragic events were unfolding. As my parents were about to embark on their final flight out of Lebanon, their friends reminded them that while they were very sad to see them go, they should never return. Their sage advice was heeded. The gravity of the situation hit me hard upon being reunited with them in Montreal. I will never forget the trauma in their eyes as well as my father's temporary asymmetric facial paralysis. I also recall being haunted by the possibility that my mother might have been gang raped by her captors.

That I miraculously escaped from Lebanon offered me some temporary respite for the next fifteen years or so. The ugliness of ideological tribalism, however, returned to haunt me on university campuses. But before I get to that, I want to discuss the two life ideals that best explain why I fight against the enemies of reason.

My Life Ideals: Freedom and Truth

I was only ever interested in two possible occupations, professional soccer player and professor. The plan was to pursue my athletic career full throttle and once I retired, I would complete my studies and become a professor. While it is quite rare for professional athletes to complete advanced degrees, Socrates, the captain of the Brazilian national soccer team at the 1982 World Cup, was also a physician. While not an athlete, Brian May, the guitarist of the legendary British rock band Queen obtained a Ph.D. in astrophysics from Imperial College London in 2007 (three decades after abandoning his studies to focus on his musical career). It was certainly not a pipe dream to aspire to both careers. Regrettably, a devastating injury coupled with other life obstacles ended my soccer career, and so, I dove into my studies. I completed an undergraduate degree in mathematics (I recently found out though that mathematics is "racist"[1]) and computer science, which catered nicely to my bent for perfectionism and analytical purity. After all, a mathematical proof is either correct or not. Programming code is either free of bugs or not. Immediately after completing my B.Sc. degree at McGill University, I enrolled in the two-year M.B.A. program at the same institution. During my second year as an M.B.A. student, I was one of a handful of fortunate students picked by Professor Jay Conger for his Group Dynamics course. In each class we delved into psychological principles that illuminated our personal lives. In one of our assignments, we had to identify the scripts that defined our life trajectories (a framework originally developed by psychiatrist Eric Berne, who established the theory and practice of transactional analysis). Berne argued that parents give their children scripts for their lives somewhat in the way that actors receive scripts in order to play their roles. While I concede that parents do wield sizeable influence in shaping their offspring, psychoanalytic theories overestimate such forces while ignoring the unique combination of genes that defines an individual. Some people might indeed be commandeered by life scripts. ("Be a good boy and do us proud. Don't dishonor the family.") Others might be driven by a desire to meet certain guiding ideals and/or objectives. ("Make the world a better place.")

It requires deep (and difficult) self-reflection to consider whether and how one's life has been governed by a recurring life script or by a recurrent assertion of certain ideals. Many realities that you've faced might seem disconnected but upon further scrutiny, you might discover that they are linked via a common script or ideal that you value. One of the benefits of psychotherapy is to precisely identify such patterns for patients. In my case, my life has been shaped by a commitment to two foundational ideals: freedom and truth. The pursuit of these two ideals was not imposed on me by my parents; rather, it is a manifestation of my personhood as inscribed in my genes. I'll address each of these ideals in turn.

The Freedom Ideal

My love of freedom became apparent as a young child being dragged to synagogue in Beirut, Lebanon. I found the rote prayers and herd-like rituals very alienating. My inquisitive nature felt stifled by religious dogma. I found no freedom in religious practice. You simply belonged to the group and mimicked their behaviors. I suspect that many children find religious services unappealing, but I had a more visceral repulsion. My strong individuality, even at such a young age, rebelled at the pressure to conform, and I was delighted to have been the only one of four children in my family never to attend Jewish school. In my forties, my father shared with me his deep regret that I did not receive a Jewish education. I told him that I was thankful that he had not forced such an education on me. My friendships and romantic interests have spanned races, ethnicities, and religions, and I am richer for it. Fast forward to my teenage years when I developed into a very competitive soccer player with the potential to head to Europe to pursue a professional career. I played the number ten position, which is typically reserved for a skillful playmaker who is given free rein to roam the field. Whenever I had a coach who placed constraints on my movements, I was devastated. My playing style required complete freedom of movement, and anything short of that had a deleterious effect on my performance.

The pursuit of freedom is also at the root of my professorial career. This holds true on two very different levels. Academia grants me the freedom to spend my time throughout a given day as I see fit. I often work very long hours, albeit at my discretion as to when and where I do so. Having to attend two or three scheduled meetings in a given week suffocates me, but I'm perfectly relaxed at the prospect of spending twelve hours at a café working on my next book. Having occupational freedom is good for me. People who possess less occupational freedom have higher cortisol levels (a higher stress response). The social epidemiologist Michael Marmot has documented the relationship between individuals' health and the extent to which they possess control over their job responsibilities.[2] More freedom equals better health.

There is a second element of freedom that has defined my scientific career, and that is the freedom to navigate radically different intellectual landscapes. For most academics, the road to glory requires a commitment to hyper-specialization. Develop expertise in a small niche and stay in your lane. Most academics build their entire professional reputations on research of very narrow areas of interest. I do not have the intellectual temperament for such careerist shackles. As a truly interdisciplinary scientist, I traverse disparate intellectual landscapes as long as they tickle my curiosity. This is why I have published in varied disciplines including consumer behavior, marketing, psychology, evolutionary theory, medicine, economics, and bibliometrics. The anti-apartheid activist Steve Biko famously authored a book titled *I Write What I Like*. In my case, I research what I like (and I am thankful to my university for having implicitly supported my broad academic interests). You might imagine that I do not take too well to those who argue that there are some research questions that should never be tackled—forbidden knowledge.[3]

My desire for intellectual freedom is also the reason that I am a professor who is deeply engaged in social media. Unlike the great majority of my highfalutin colleagues who take great pride in being ivory tower–dwellers, I am a professor of the people. I consider it part of my job description to engage with the public. During a recent visit to give a lecture at the Stanford Graduate School of Business, I had a telling conversation with a Stanford colleague who epitomizes the "ivory tower" bias. He was aware that I had appeared on the Joe Rogan podcast (an extraordinarily popular platform) but was clearly disdainful of such public engagement. He seemed to think that one could either publish in leading scientific journals or appear on Rogan's show. I disabused him of this false either-or proposition by pointing out that a complete academic should strive to do both. Many professors forget that their professional responsibility is not only to generate new knowledge but also to seek to maximally disseminate it. Social media offers endless such opportunities by allowing ideas to spread quickly and to a very large number of people. No rational intellectual should oppose such a possibility, and yet many succumb to what I refer to as the *garage band effect*. If you are a struggling band that plays in your parents' garage only to be heard by them and a few annoyed neighbors, you are legit. If your band becomes a smashing success with a number one hit on *Billboard* and now plays in front of large stadium crowds, you're a "sellout." This is precisely the mindset of many academics. They prefer to publish only in peer reviewed journals (play in the garage) and look with derision at appearing on Joe Rogan (number one *Billboard* hits and filled-out stadiums). I reject this intellectual elitism for reasons similar to why Donald Trump leapfrogs the mainstream media and engages the electorate directly via social media. Take the message directly to the people. We have the tools to do so.

The Truth Ideal

Without the necessary freedoms, it would be impossible to instantiate my second life ideal, namely the pursuit of and defense of truth. There is a bidirectional relationship between truth and freedom such that the truth will set you free (John 8:32), and only in being free can one aspire to uncover the truth. Clearly though, few people stay up at night worrying about injuries to the truth. But I do and always have. Growing up, my mother repeatedly warned me that the world did not abide by my punishingly strict standards of intellectual, ethical, and moral purity, let alone follow my pathological commitment to honesty and probity. She was imploring me to recognize that the world was made of multiple shades of grey rather than black-or-white dichromatic coloring (though she did not use these terms). When I am exposed to intellectual dishonesty and ideological dogma, I respond in a manner that is akin to someone being punched in the face. I experience an adverse emotional and psychological reaction that compels me to fight back. While I am a jovial and warm person, I can become a combative brawler when I witness departures from reason that stem either from willful ignorance or from diabolical, ideologically driven duplicity.

The quest for truth should always supersede one's ego-defensive desire to be proven right. This is not an easy task because for most people it is difficult to admit to being wrong. This is precisely why science is so liberating. It offers a framework for auto-correction because scientific knowledge is always provisional. An accepted scientific fact today might be refuted tomorrow. As such, the scientific method engenders epistemic humility. I grew up in a household where this quality was sorely lacking. Several members of my family are classic know-it-alls who seldom exhibit any deference to someone who might possess greater knowledge or wisdom on a given topic. They know more about the heart than the cardiologist, more about teeth than the dentist, more about mathematics than the mathematician, and more about academia than the academic. Also, they were seldom, if ever, willing to admit to being wrong. When it came to epistemic humility, they were not reincarnations of Socrates. I was always deeply troubled by this family dynamic for I viewed their epistemic grandiosity as a deep affront to the truth. A personal anecdote that took place more than two decades ago perfectly captures this reality.

A family member remarked to me that the Ancient Greeks were anti-Semitic Christians to which I gently retorted that they were not Christians. The individual in question insisted that of course they were Christians. At that point, I explained that the time period in question was labelled "BC" in reference to its being "before Christ" (prior to Christianity). Once it was clear to this person that my position was unassailable, what do you think he did? Did he grant me the courtesy of admitting that he was wrong? I have recounted this tale on a few occasions and asked people to guess what his reaction was. No one has successfully cracked that mystery yet. When all hope that he might be proven correct was extinguished, he looked me in the eyes and stated with a straight face, "Yes, I said that they were not Christians, and you said that they were. So I am right." Of course, we both knew that this was a grotesque lie but in his narcissistic and delusional bubble, his perfect record of superior knowledge remained intact.

My mother's admonition about the incongruity between my notions of intellectual and moral purity and the real-world was ironically on full display in my interactions with family members who possess zero epistemic humility. My intellectual probity was repeatedly violated by these individuals who cared only about signaling to the world that they knew more than you did about anything and everything. This family dynamic might explain why I am so offended by individuals who exhibit the Dunning-Kruger effect, that is, a self-assuredness and supreme confidence despite one's idiocy (David Dunning was my professor at Cornell University). Social media is infested with such types. I, on the other hand, am perfectly comfortable admitting to my undergraduate students that I do not know the answer to a posed question. This builds trust because students quickly learn that I care about the veracity of information that I share with them. On topics I know well, I lecture with confidence, on others, such as, say, the pros and cons of legalizing cannabis, I exhibit necessary humility. Confucius was correct: "To know what you know and what you do not know, that is true knowledge."

Given my love for pursuing and defending truth, academia is both the best and worst profession to be in. As I progressed through my university education, I quickly recognized a great paradox: universities are both the source of scientific truths and the dispensers of outlandish anti-truths.

Universities: Purveyors of Truth and Ecosystems of Intellectual Garbage

Once I completed my M.B.A. in 1990, I moved to Ithaca, New York, to continue my education at Cornell University where I obtained an M.S.

and a Ph.D. in 1993 and 1994 respectively. During my first semester, my doctoral supervisor, the famed mathematical and cognitive psychologist J. Edward Russo, suggested that I enroll in Professor Dennis Regan's Advanced Social Psychology course. This course would wield an inestimable impact on my eventual scientific career as this is where I first encountered the extraordinary elegance of evolutionary psychology in explaining human phenomena. Since I was interested in the study of consumer behavior, I had found my academic path. I would combine evolutionary psychology and consumer psychology in founding the field of evolutionary consumption. That said, my doctoral dissertation was on the psychology of decision-making. I examined the cognitive processes that people use when making decisions. Specifically, how do we know when we've acquired enough information to commit to a choice between a pair of competing alternatives? Beyond the incredibly rigorous training that I obtained at Cornell from many of the world's leading psychologists and economists, this is where I was also first exposed to some of the nonsensical gibberish that I critique in this book. I recall taking Professor Russo's doctoral seminar during which he exposed us to the increasing number of postmodernist papers that were being published in the leading consumer research journals. One in particular exemplified this anti-science lunacy. In 1991, Stephen J. Gould (not to be confused with the late Harvard paleontologist) authored a paper in one of the most prestigious journals of the field of consumer research. The paper was titled "The self-manipulation of my pervasive, perceived vital energy through product use: An introspective-praxis perspective."[4] He began the article by lamenting the following: "Much of consumer research has failed to describe many experiential aspects of my own consumer behavior, especially the everyday dynamics of my pervasive, self-perceived vital energy." Narcissist much? He then proceeded in an outlandish exercise of the postmodern methodology of autoethnography (a fancy way of saying he wrote a "dear diary" entry couched in pseudo-intellectual drivel). Here are two passages wherein he shares an "academic" take on his erection and orgasm.

For example, I remember experiencing sensations running throughout my body, including my genitals, so that I felt something akin to sexual feelings through eating. I am not saying that eating feelings were exactly the same as sexual feelings, but that they overlapped. For example, I did not have erections over food, but I did experience excitement akin to sexual arousal in terms of electric feelings and hot-cold flashes that registered from my genitals upwards when I actually did eat something.[5]

Deliberate charging involving an erotic film creates a more intense flow state of excitement so that my heartbeat is noticeable and fast, I feel very warm, and my body is quivering with such intensity that I may actually shake. This state sometimes is heightened even more when my wife and I use certain Asian orgasm control techniques that heighten and prolong pleasure in periods spread over days or weeks (Gould 1991b), and then watch an erotic film to create a culminating crescendo of energy—arousal feeding arousal.[6]

Houston, we have a problem.

Beyond being briefly exposed to postmodernism and associated movements, it became clear to me during my doctoral training that much of the social sciences were bereft of biological-based thinking. Most human phenomena were viewed through the lens of social constructivism (the belief that our preferences, choices, and behaviors are largely shaped by socialization). This struck me as a nonsensical notion. Surely, the environment matters but so does our biological heritage. I left Cornell in 1994 with a newly minted Ph.D. and joined Concordia University in Montreal, Canada, as an assistant professor in the business school. Over the next few years, I settled into my tenure-track position and eventually obtained tenure in 1999. I lived two separate professional realities. Amongst my colleagues in the natural sciences, my attempt to Darwinize the business school was considered laudable. This was not the case with my colleagues in the social sciences, most of whom viewed such attempts with great derision. According to them, biologically-based theorizing was too reductionistic in explaining consumer behavior. And, to postulate that sex differences might be rooted in evolutionary realities was simply "sexist nonsense." I quickly learned that most academic feminists were profoundly hostile to evolutionary psychology. I was respected among evolutionary behavioral scientists and was derided by many marketing scholars. This biophobia (fear of biology in explaining human phenomena) has been a recurring form of science denialism that I've experienced throughout my academic career.

Beyond being purveyors of anti-science (postmodernism) and science denialism (biophobia), universities serve as patient zero for a broad range of other dreadfully bad ideas and movements. In the immortal words of George Orwell, "One has to belong to the intelligentsia to believe things like that: no ordinary man could be such a fool."[7] The proliferation of many of these bad ideas has yielded reward mechanisms in academia that are upside down. The herd mindset is rewarded. Innovative thinkers are chastised. "Stay in your lane" academics are rewarded. Outspoken academics are punished. Hyper-specialization is rewarded. Broad synthetic thinking is scorned. Every quality that should define intellectual courage is viewed as a problem. Anything that adheres to leftist tenets of progressivism is rewarded. Those who believe in equality of outcomes receive top-paying administrative jobs. Those who believe in meritocracy are frowned upon. If they go unchecked, parasitic idea pathogens, spawned by universities, eventually start to infect every aspect of our society.

Idea Pathogens as Parasites of the Human Mind

When asked which animal they fear most, the great majority of people are likely to either mention a large predator (great white shark, crocodile, lion, bear) or perhaps scorpions, spiders, or snakes (humans have evolved a preparedness to learn such phobias). Conspicuously absent from any such list is the animal that has killed by far the greatest number of humans throughout history: the lethal mosquito. I happen to suffer from a deep phobia of mosquitoes. The number of nights that I have kept my wife awake in a hotel room (typically on a Caribbean vacation) as we've hunted an elusive mosquito is considerable. I often remind my wife that this is a perfectly adaptive phobia. It makes a lot more sense to fear the mosquito than to obsess about an attack by a great white shark. Mosquitoes kill by transmitting to their victims one of several deadly biological pathogens including yellow fever (virus) and malaria (parasite). More generally, one of the greatest threats that humans have faced throughout our evolutionary history is exposure to a broad range of pathogens including tuberculosis (bacterium), leprosy (bacterium), cholera (bacterium), bubonic plague (bacterium), polio (virus), influenza (virus), smallpox (virus), HIV (virus), and Ebola (virus). The good news is that we have found ways to temper if not eradicate many of these dangers with improved hygiene and sanitation, vaccines, and at times easy to implement solutions such as mosquito nets.

The central focus of this book is to explore another set of pathogens that are potentially as dangerous to the human condition: parasitic pathogens of the human mind. These are composed of thought patterns, belief systems, attitudes, and mindsets that parasitize one's ability to think properly and accurately. Once these mind viruses take hold of one's neuronal circuitry, the afflicted victim loses the ability to use reason, logic, and science to navigate the world. Instead, one sinks into an abyss of infinite lunacy best defined by a dogged and proud departure from reality, common sense, and truth. While parasites can target and reside in different body parts, neuroparasitology deals with the class of cerebral parasites that manipulate hosts' behaviors in different ways. The animal kingdom is replete with examples of biological pathogens that, once they infect an organism's brain, yield some rather macabre outcomes including a host's reproductive death (parasitic castration) if not actual death (hosts commit suicide in the service of the parasite). Take for example the spider wasp, which engages in a truly morbid behavior. It stings a much larger spider rendering it in a zombie-like state at which point the wasp drags it to a burrow and lays its eggs on it.[8] The offspring eventually devour the hapless spider in vivo. *Parelaphostrongylus tenuis* is a parasite that infects the brains of ungulates (moose, deer, elk) causing afflicted animals to at times engage in circling behavior (going around in a small circle endlessly). This robotic behavior will continue even as looming predators approach the ill-fated animal. A third example of a brain parasite is *toxoplasma gondii*, which when it infects a mouse's brain causes it to lose its otherwise adaptive fear of cats. Finally, *nematomorpha* constitute a class of suicide-inducing parasites that afflict a broad range of insects including crickets, cockroaches, and praying mantises. For example, the Gordian worm gets its host (cricket) to jump into a body of water (which it would usually avoid) so that the parasite can leave its host's body and look for a mate.[9] In the same way that brain parasites have evolved to take advantage of their hosts in the furtherance of their evolutionary objectives, parasitic viruses of the human mind (devastatingly bad ideas) function in a similar manner. They parasitize human minds, rendering them impervious to critical thinking, while finding clever ways to spread across a given population (for example, getting students to enroll in women's studies departments).

Some of the parasitic viruses of the human mind that I tackle include postmodernism, radical feminism, and social constructivism, all of which largely flourish within one infected ecosystem: the university. While each mind virus constitutes a different strain of lunacy, they are all bound by the full rejection of reality and common sense (postmodernism rejects the existence of objective truths; radical feminism scoffs at the idea of innate biologically-based sex differences; and social constructivism posits that the human mind starts off as an empty slate largely void of biological blueprints). This general class of mind viruses is what I have coined Ostrich Parasitic Syndrome (OPS), namely various forms of disordered thinking that lead afflicted individuals to reject fundamental truths and realities that are as evident as the pull of gravity. In a similar vein to how all forms of cancer share a mechanism of unchecked cell division, these mind viruses all reject truth in the defense of a pet ideology. The ideological tribe to which one belongs varies across the mind viruses, but the commitment is always to the defense of one's dogma—truth and science be damned. All is not lost though. OPS need not be a terminal disease of the human mind. Recall that many biological pathogens are defeated by targeted intervention strategies (like the polio vaccine). The same applies to those afflicted with OPS and associated mind viruses. The inoculation against such cancerous mindsets comes in the form of a two-step cognitive vaccine: 1) providing OPS sufferers with accurate information, and 2) ensuring that OPS sufferers learn how to process information according to the evidentiary rules of science and logic.

In his 1976 classic *The Selfish Gene*, evolutionary biologist Richard Dawkins famously introduced the concept of the meme to our public consciousness. Memes are packets of information that spread from one brain to another.[10] In reading this book, your brain is infected by my memes. If you then discuss my ideas within your social circle, my memes are further propagated. Not all memes are created equal though, be it in terms of their valence (positive, neutral, or negative) or their virulence (how quickly they spread). The ice bucket campaign to combat amyotrophic lateral sclerosis (colloquially known as Lou Gehrig's disease) yielded rapidly viral YouTube clips, all in the pursuit of a worthy cause. On the other hand, other memes might take longer to spread (for instance, a death-cult religious belief) though they yield astonishingly dire consequences (convincing people that it is a divine act to fly airplanes into skyscrapers). From this perspective, OPS is a memetic disease of the human mind. When facing a pathogenic epidemic, we call on modern-day dragon slayers, namely infectious disease specialists and epidemiologists to intervene. They defend us against a broad range of monstrous pathogens dead set on infecting us. Part of their job description is to understand where a pathogen originates, the manner and speed by which it spreads, the identity of the first person to be infected (patient zero), and how to eradicate it. This is precisely the approach that must be taken in defeating parasitic viruses of the human mind. Where do these infectiously bad ideas come from? How are they spread? Which ecosystem do they flourish in? How do we inoculate people against their devastating effects? That is the task of this book. It is an exploration of the epidemiology of mind pathogens and the intervention strategies that will allow us to wrestle back reason from the enemies of truth.

Death of the West by a Thousand Cuts

The greatness of the West stems in part from its protection of fundamental freedoms and its commitment to reason and the scientific method (where appropriate). Over the past few decades though, several nefarious forces have slowly eroded the West's commitment to reason, science, and the values of the Enlightenment (see Figure 1 below). Such forces include political correctness (as enforced by the thought police, the language police, and social justice warriors), postmodernism, radical feminism, social constructivism, cultural and moral relativism, and the culture of perpetual offense and victimhood (microaggressions, trigger warnings, and safe spaces on campuses, as well as identity politics). This has created an environment that has stifled public discourse in a myriad of ways. Academics shy away from investigating so-called forbidden topics (such as sex differences or racial differences) lest they be accused of being rabidly sexist or racist. Professors are intimidated into using nonsensical gender pronouns when addressing students lest they otherwise be committing a hate crime (see for instance Canada's Bill C-16). University students demand that they be "protected" from ideas that are antithetical to their own while being warned by administrators about wearing "offensive" Halloween costumes. Politicians are fearful to critique Islam or open-border immigration policies lest they be accused of being bigots. More generally, people are deathly afraid to espouse any opinion that might get them ostracized from the politically correct club (try being a conservative Republican in Hollywood or on a university campus). These trepidations are weakening our culture because we are no longer able to talk with one another using rational and reasoned discourse that is otherwise free from a dogmatic and tribal mindset. In this book, I set out to describe the confluence of forces that are endangering the West's commitment to freedom, reason, and true liberalism (hence, the death of the West by a thousand cuts). Ultimately, any attempt to limit what individuals can think or say weakens the defining ethos of the West, namely the unfettered commitment to the pursuit of truth unencumbered by the shackles of the thought police.

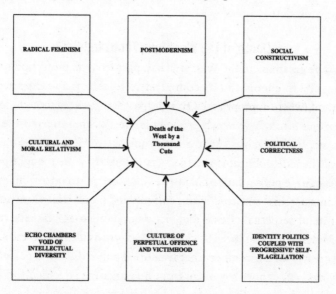

Figure 1. Death of the West by a Thousand Cuts

A few books have addressed the spread of anti-intellectual, anti-reason, anti-science, and anti-liberal sentiment[11] and the specific movements that give rise to them (postmodernism, radical feminism, multiculturalism as a political philosophy, and identity politics).[12] This book weaves together all of these nefarious forces, along with new ones, to explain how they gave rise to the current stifling political correctness, which is enforced by the thought police along with its army of social justice warriors (a recent phenomenon). It offers an up-to-date examination of the current cultural zeitgeist on campuses and in public discourse. Finally, it highlights how these anti-freedom, anti-honesty movements have substantive consequences in the real world. They explain the West's inability to have a frank and reasoned discussion about the place of Islam within our secular, liberal, and modern societies. They also help explain the popular reaction *against* political correctness—and its threats to freedom and honesty—that we saw in the stunning ascendancy of Donald Trump to the presidency of the United States.

Unless we win the battle of ideas, the enemies of reason, along with the mind viruses that they promulgate, will lead our free societies to lunatic self-destruction.

CHAPTER TWO

Thinking versus Feeling, Truth versus Hurt Feelings

"Reason is, and ought only to be the slave of the passions, and can never pretend to any other office than to serve and obey them."
—David Hume[1]

"I always felt that a scientist owes the world only one thing, and that is the truth as he sees it. If the truth contradicts deeply held beliefs, that is too bad. Tact and diplomacy are fine in international relations, in politics, perhaps even in business; in science only one thing matters, and that is the facts."
—Hans J. Eysenck[2]

In describing a debate on the existence of God with Doug Geivett, currently a professor of philosophy at the Talbot School of Theology of Biola University, my good friend and founder of The Skeptics Society Michael Shermer remarked:

Geivett concluded his initial presentation by explaining that we are confronted here with an either-or-choice: Either God exists or He does not; either the universe was created or it was not; either life was designed or it was not; either morality is natural or it is not; either Jesus was resurrected or he was not.

> I opened up my rebuttal by explaining that there are only two types of theories: Those that divide the world into two types of theories, and those that do not.[3]

Shermer's brilliant levity carries an important epistemological message—namely that the pursuit of knowledge does not always neatly fit into clean dichotomies. The penchant of many researchers to map phenomena onto binary realities is what I've coined *epistemological dichotomania*.[4] It stems from a desire to create a workable and simplified view of the world that is amenable to scientific testing. Of note, the dichotomies are at times largely false such as the nature-nurture debate. In the words of the biologist Matt Ridley, "Nature versus nurture is dead."[5] Much of who we are arises from an indissoluble amalgam of our genes and our environments.[6] Furthermore, universal patterns of socialization (nurture) exist in their forms because of biological imperatives (nature). The desire to divide the world into binary forms is at the root of the thinking versus feeling dichotomy, and this creates a false either-or mindset. We are both thinking and feeling animals. The challenge is to know when to activate the cognitive (thinking) versus the affective (feeling) systems.

When you think of perfume commercials, what comes to mind? You are unlikely to see a Harvard chemist in a lab coat explaining the chemical equation of the aromatic recipe used in making the product. Similarly, the brand's name is unlikely to be a technical name such as Anisaldehyde-Eugenol X2000. Instead, the typical perfume commercial sells sex, romance, fantasy, and passion. A beautiful woman with long flowing hair might be shown riding a horse followed by a one-word brand name such as *Obsession*, *Escape*, *Allure*, *Mystère*, or *Désir* (all actual brand names). Perfumes are hedonic products, and as such they must engage our emotions. If one were designing a commercial for a mutual fund, the commercial's content as well as the fund's brand name would be radically different. In this case, given that a mutual fund is a functional and utilitarian product, the commercial must engage the viewer's cognitive system. A beautiful endorser might convince you to purchase a perfume but not to invest in a mutual fund. The Elaboration Likelihood Model posits that consumers use one of two routes of persuasion when processing a message.[7] The central route involves cognitive effort, namely the consumer will carefully evaluate the message's substantive informational content (such as the seven reasons why a particular mutual fund is the best one to invest in). The peripheral route on the other hand relies on the use of non-substantive cues in arriving at an attitude (using an endorser's physical attractiveness in forming an attitude toward investing in a mutual fund). In this case, the peripheral cue is not directly relevant in judging the logical merits of the message. The route that is activated depends on a consumer's motivation and ability to process information. Generally speaking, an attitude wherein the affective and cognitive components are consistent with one another will be more resistant to change (see for example Rosenberg's affective-cognitive consistency model[8]). The negative hysteria surrounding Donald Trump is rooted in peripheral processing ("his mannerisms disgust me"). Trump's detractors should perhaps be spending more effort engaging their central route of persuasion by evaluating his policy positions in a dispassionate and detached manner.

Hierarchy of effects models have been used in marketing and advertising to describe the cognitive (thinking), affective (feeling), and conative (behavioral) stages that consumers go through after seeing or hearing an advertisement. Products that require a high level of involvement (choosing a mutual fund) will have a different sequence of effects from their low-involvement counterparts (buying a candy bar). For the former, the operative sequence is thinking–feeling–behavior: an informed opinion leads to liking the product; hence, its purchase. On the other hand, for impulse products it is feeling–behavior–thinking: a positive feeling leads to an impulse purchase, and the opinion is formed post-purchase. Inherent to the various sequences is the recognition that both cognition and emotions matter in the decision-making process. In other words, we do not need to construe thinking and feeling as antithetical to one another. They are both fundamental components of decision-making. Problems arise when we use the wrong sequence to make a decision. For example, choosing which presidential candidate to vote for should be construed as a high-involvement decision, and accordingly a rational voter should first engage his cognitive system rather than his affective system. And yet, many hysterical anti-Trump voters begin with a visceral emotional hatred of the man and then process subsequent information in a manner that supports their a priori affective position.

The classic saying "don't let your emotions get the best of you," is an apt descriptor of how many people regard sound decision-making. From this perspective, a rational person thinks; an irrational person feels. Classical economists have traditionally thought of human beings as hyper-rational agents who make cost-benefit decisions. The archetype of a good decision-maker is Mr. Spock from *Star Trek*: a hyper-logical agent without emotional distractions. I recall an address by the economist George Loewenstein at the 1995 *International Association for Research in Economic Psychology Conference* in Bergen, Norway, wherein he implored economists to incorporate visceral states such as lust, anger, hunger, and fear into our understanding of human decision-making. In listening to his lecture, I kept thinking: "No kidding! Who doesn't know this?" As a young assistant professor at the time, I was astonished that this should be news to anyone, let alone to sophisticated economic psychologists. It seems self-evident to me that it is perfectly rational to be an emotional being, when one's emotions are applied in the proper context.

Emotions such as happiness, fear, lust, disgust, or envy serve as solutions to recurring evolutionary challenges that our ancestors have faced.[9] Take romantic jealousy. Which of the following two scenarios is more emotionally painful for you to imagine: Your spouse committing sexual infidelity or committing emotional infidelity? Evolutionary psychologist David Buss and his colleagues showed that men respond more harshly to sexual infidelity (as this raises a fear of uncertain paternity about children), while women are more upset by emotional infidelity (as this serves as a greater predictor of a man's lack of commitment to a long-term union).[10] Men and women respond to infidelity according to the mating challenges of their sex. The triggered emotions are perfectly rational when viewed through an evolutionary lens.

In his 2011 bestselling book *Thinking, Fast and Slow*, Nobel laureate Daniel Kahneman argued that humans are endowed with two systems of thinking: System 1 composed of fast, intuitive, automatic, unconscious, emotional, and instinctive processes; and System 2 made up of slow, deliberate, analytical, logical, and conscious processes. It is hardly surprising that humans are endowed with the capacity to use a broad range of cognitive and affective strategies when making decisions. Nor is it surprising that people differ in the extent to which they rely on feelings versus thinking when making choices.[11] The problem arises when domains that should be reserved for the intellect are hijacked by feelings. This is precisely what plagues our universities: what were once centers of intellectual development have become retreats for the emotionally fragile. The driving motto of the university is no longer the pursuit of truth but the coddling of hurt feelings.

Truth versus Hurt Feelings

On October 15, 2017, with Wikipedia as my research tool, I conducted a quick, and obviously informal, analysis of university mottos. I found that there were one hundred twenty-eight matches for the word *truth*, forty-six matches for the word *wisdom*, sixty-one matches for the word *science* and zero matches for the words *emotion* or *feeling*. For example, Harvard's motto is *Veritas* (truth) and Yale's is *Lux et veritas* (light and truth). These venerable institutions of higher learning were not founded on an ethos of *feelings* but on the dogged pursuit of *truth*. And yet, across all our institutions—from universities to the media to the judicial system to the political arena—truth is increasingly taking a back seat to feelings. This is true in the United States, it is true in Canada, and it is true across most of the western world.

An extraordinarily chilling and instructive example of this dreadful trend occurred in the Netherlands in 2010. Geert Wilders, a Dutch parliamentarian, was charged with a slew of crimes for having the temerity to criticize Islam and its growing influence in his country. Any freedom-loving reader should be appalled that criticism of a religion is now considered hate speech in many Western countries. As part of his defense strategy, Mr. Wilders sought to call on expert witnesses to validate the veracity of his stated public positions. The response from the prosecutor's office (*Openbaar ministerie*) was truly breathtaking: "It is irrelevant whether Wilders's witnesses might prove Wilders's observations to be correct. What's relevant is that his observations are illegal."[12] In a free society, people should have the right to criticize a religion; they should have the right to do so, and of course their criticisms are themselves open to criticism; that is the essence of freedom of speech and thought. In this case, the prosecution was beyond Orwellian, stating flatly that *telling the truth could be illegal.* This mindset is increasingly prevalent in academia, and it falls under the rubric of forbidden knowledge (see the recent case of Noah Carl who dared to support researchers' right to study the relationship between race and intelligence).[13]

In August 2017, I made my fifth appearance on *The Joe Rogan Experience.* For those of you unfamiliar with the podcast, it is a conversational marathon that typically lasts just shy of three hours. During our conversation, Joe asked me about the scientific pursuit of potentially sensitive topics. Here is the relevant excerpt:

> **Me:** When I was on Sam Harris's show you know earlier this year about six or seven months ago, he asked me: "Is there any research question that you would not tackle in your scientific career, that is too taboo?" And my answer is "no." As long as you address the question honestly and objectively there is nothing that should be off limits. Because then it becomes very easy to say "sex differences, we shouldn't study that because it might marginalize one sex or the other. Race differences, we shouldn't study them for the same reasons" and so on. That becomes forbidden knowledge. No. The highest

ideal that any honest person should pursue is the pursuit of truth.... So don't be encumbered by political correctness, just pursue the truth. And I think that one of the reasons that Jordan Peterson's message and my message have resonated now with a lot of people is because at least they see that we are ascribing to that ideal to the best of our abilities.

Rogan: What if that truth hurts your feelings?

Me: Fuck your feelings.

Rogan: [Gasping] Oooohhhh!

There are two fundamental ethical orientations that guide people's daily behaviors: deontological and consequentialist ethics. The former is an absolutist view of ethical standards (it is never correct to lie) whereas the latter evaluates the ethical merits of an action based on its consequences (it is at times acceptable to lie to spare someone's feelings). The reality is that most people operate under both systems. For example, if your wife asks you if she looks overweight, you will likely utter "no" without flinching, whatever you actually think. On the other hand, most people consider it morally wrong under all circumstances to make sexual advances on children. A deontological view regarding the pursuit of truth asserts that it is never justified to violate or suppress the truth. A consequentialist perspective asserts that the truth must at times be altered, fudged, or suppressed to avert such bad consequences as hurt feelings. Much of the lunacy that we see from the "progressive" camp is a result of consequentialism when it comes to the truth.

Any human endeavor rooted in the pursuit of truth must rely on facts and not feelings. Legal proceedings constitute one such domain. We do not establish the innocence or guilt of defendants using feelings; rather, we rely on a broad range of available facts in making a case. The threshold for establishing guilt is set purposely high: the cumulative evidence must be beyond a reasonable doubt to convict someone. The evidentiary threshold for uncovering scientific truths is even more stringent than those expected within the legal arena.

One problem we face today is that consequentialists make a virtue of having emotions cloud our judgments, not only to avoid hurt feelings but because emotion is seen as a sign of authenticity. As British prison psychiatrist Theodore Dalrymple observed: "[I]s it not the case that we live in an age of emotional incontinence, when they who emote the most are believed to feel the most?"[14] Remember though that one's heartfelt outrage seldom says anything about the truth or falsehood of one's position.

Donald Trump Is Going to End the World

When Donald Trump won the 2016 U.S. presidential election, I was bewildered at the mass psychogenic hysteria that engulfed my academic colleagues and the great majority of folks within my social circle. The stock market was going to crash and never recover. Trump was going to abolish democracy. Minorities were going to be endangered. He was about to usher in a nuclear holocaust. His supposed ties to white supremacists would marshal a new wave of genocidal anti-Semitism across North America. I decided to satirize this profound idiocy by releasing a clip on my YouTube channel showing me hiding under the table (in my study) to avoid being caught by Trump's Jew-hating death squads.[15] I have since released several other installments of "hiding under the table" clips, including one upon the confirmation of Justice Brett Kavanaugh to the U.S. Supreme Court, and another shortly prior to hosting Professor Rachel Fulton Brown on my show. She had the "audacity" to write a blog post that lauded white men (since they were instrumental in leading the charge in founding the emancipatory freedoms that we now possess in the West, including women's rights).[16] This led to her being accused of being a white supremacist and a merchant of hate by many of her colleagues, including Professor Dorothy Kim, who was supposedly existentially threatened by Brown's remarks since Kim is a "person of color."[17]

What explains such irrational hysteria especially when promulgated by supposedly sophisticated academics? I've argued that Donald Trump represents a deep and visceral aesthetic injury to the sensibilities of those who reside in the highfalutin ivory tower. Trump is the antithesis of the restrained diplomat who delivers polished and seemingly eloquent messages of platitudinous hope. Can you think of a recent U.S. president who was a world champion at delivering such messages and who was revered by the intelligentsia as the last and final messiah? Perhaps a hint might prove helpful: that president won a Nobel Peace Prize largely for having enriched the world with his message of love, peace, and hope. The nominations deadline for the prize was eleven days after he was inaugurated. As such, his Nobel Prize was awarded for "accomplishments" that he achieved prior to becoming president. Some people win Nobel Prizes by being held prisoner for twenty-seven years in their quest to fight apartheid (Nelson Mandela). Others win it for sporting a winning, radiant smile of sunny hope. They are equally worthy winners, and if you think otherwise you are a racist. Barack Obama is majestic in his personal style. He is tall, thin, and elegant. His elocution and speech cadence are melodious. He is polished in a way that appeals to those who become drunk by merely smelling the cork of a wine bottle (an Arabic expression). Donald Trump on the other hand is a brash and cantankerous brawler. The unhinged "progressives," best exemplified by the utterly deranged Robert De Niro, are irrevocably and perpetually outraged by him. They are viscerally disgusted. They possess no theory of mind that might allow them to place themselves in the shoes of the nearly 63 million Americans who voted for Trump. Perhaps the ensuing analysis might help them see the light.

Subsequent to the historic political upset that shook the world, I witnessed innumerable people, many of whom are supposedly rational and educated individuals, aping Hillary Clinton's "deplorables" position. According to this viewpoint many of the nearly 63 million people who voted for Donald Trump are racist, toothless, redneck simpletons who sleep with their siblings. Of course, nowhere was this perspective more rampant than in the halls of academia. It is bafflingly moronic that sophisticated intellectuals could actually believe such nonsense. I offer an alternative account to explain Trump's victory using principles from behavioral decision theory.[18] In short, if your average voter had five key issues in mind, scored each candidate on them, and weighted them in order of importance, it was easy to understand how perfectly reasonable and rational people might have voted for Donald Trump without being deplorable bigots. Or take a much simpler decision process, the Lexico-graphic Rule, which states that a voter will solely examine the issue most important to him and choose the candidate who scores higher on it. It is perfectly conceivable that if a voter were using this rule, he could have voted for Trump in a multitude of possible ways.[19] Those who viscerally hated Trump could not see that on issues ranging from immigration policy to tax policy to regulatory policy to trade policy to foreign policy to the appointment of federal judges, Trump took positions that appealed to many thinking Americans who wanted, for instance, stronger border enforcement, an "America First" foreign policy and trade agreements, "constitutionalist" judges, and deregulation and tax cuts. Trump cam-paigned on these policies, while Hillary's campaign focused on the evil of the Orange Man Bad (and his supporters). Those suffering from Trump Derangement Syndrome cannot see that for 63 million Ameri-cans, voting for Trump was an obviously rational decision.

The Brett Kavanaugh Debacle

Oftentimes when I comment about American politics, I remind people that I'm Canadian and do not have a dog in that fight. My posi-tions are always based on first principles and are not in the least bit biased by a desire to be loyal to any political tribe. As an impartial observer of the Brett Kavanaugh affair, I was bewildered by the duplicity of Demo-crat politicians and their eagerness to dispense with a presumption of innocence as a non-negotiable legal standard (in a twist of gargantuan Democratic hypocrisy, the outlandish #BelieveAllWomen tenet appar-ently does not apply to the more credible accusation recently levied against Joe Biden). Several decades of scientific research have cast doubt on the accuracy of eyewitness testimony and the accuracy of human memory in legal settings.[20] And yet, Democrat politicians were perfectly willing to ignore first principles (including a presumption of innocence) and a large corpus of scientific evidence and instead were decidedly eager to unequivocally believe testimony about an event that may or may not have taken place nearly four decades earlier. Political tribalism fueled by emotional indignation superseded logic, science, and reason. Once it became evident that the FBI could not uncover any corroborative evidence in support of Christine Blasey Ford's accusation, the Democrats moved the goalposts. The new deal-breaker regarding Kavanaugh's candidacy was his supposed lack of "judicial temperament." He was too emotionally labile, too unhinged to be a sober member of the highest court in the land. In other words, his detractors were now arguing that he did not possess the appropriate disposition to be a Supreme Court justice. His righteous indignation and justifiable disgust were not attributed to the situation at hand but were wrongly placed on the shoulders of his innate character. This is precisely what psychologists refer to as the fundamental attribution error, namely exaggerating the extent to which an individual's internal traits (his personality) are responsible for an observed reality while failing to take the circumstances into account. In the case of Kavanaugh, he was accused of horrifying crimes (without any concrete evidence) that were devastating to his personal and professional reputation. Imagine his having to explain these accusations to his wife and young daughters. His irate impatience when interacting with some of the Democrat senators was not properly attributed to the grotesque injustice that had been levied against him, but to his "volatile" personality. I doubt that this misattribution was anything but willful on the part of his detractors.

I have faced a similar misattribution whenever I've rolled up my sleeves and gone after someone forcefully on social media (typically on Twitter). I let loose and accordingly engage in rhetorical sparring that at times can be quite spicy, albeit nearly always in the spirit of fun jabbing. It always amazes me when some buffoon writes me to share his surprise at my "belligerent" disposition after having seen how restrained, polite, and warm I appear in countless other settings. Well, how I might respond if accosted by violent muggers in a dark alley is radically different from how I behave when affectionately tucking my young children to bed. My personality does not magically change across the two scenarios; the situation does. Returning to the Kavanaugh case, no fair-minded individual could fail to attribute his understandable anger to anything but the situation at hand, and yet the Democrats placed the full blame on Kavanaugh's "intemperate" temperament. In a ploy that would make Sigmund Freud beam with pride, the Democrats managed to project their emotional hysteria onto Kavanaugh.

I'm Outraged! I'm Offended!

In 2005, Lawrence Summers, then president of Harvard University, delivered a lecture at the National Bureau of Economic Research Conference on diversifying the science and engineering workforce.[21] During his talk, he intimated the possibility that intrinsic sex differences might explain why women are underrepresented in these disciplines. Notwithstanding the fact that there are robust findings in the scientific literature that supported his contentions, he had committed a fatal error. To argue that men and women might exhibit dispositional differences is blasphemous within most halls of academia. Despite the fact that world-renowned Harvard psychologist Steven Pinker defended Summers's positions, he was forced to resign from Harvard. Shortly after Summers's lecture, *The Harvard Crimson* (a student newspaper) asked Pinker, "Were President Summers's remarks within the pale of legitimate academic discourse?" to which the psychologist brilliantly replied "Good grief, shouldn't everything be within the pale of legitimate academic discourse, as long as it is presented with some degree of rigor? That's the difference between a university and a madrassa."[22] Incidentally, that there are fewer female faculty members in STEM fields is hardly due to sexist hiring practices. The exact opposite holds true as evidenced by the 2:1 preference exhibited by both male and female faculty members for prospective female hires (in comparison to equally well qualified male candidates).[23] And yet, the victimhood narrative persists, unencumbered by facts.

In July 2017, I delivered a lecture at the prestigious *Talks at Google* series in Mountain View (the main Google campus) on my scientific work at the intersection of evolutionary psychology and consumer behavior.[24] Shortly thereafter, the now infamous Google memo written by James Damore went viral. In it, Damore argued that innate sex differences might explain why women were less likely to be interested in a career in high tech. Some thought that Damore had attended my Google lecture and that it might have emboldened him to release the memo. Alas, he confirmed to me that he was away in China when I had delivered my talk. Shortly after the memo went viral, Damore and I had our first communication, which was to set up a chat on my show. In a truly Orwellian moment, I was advised that if I wanted my Google lecture to be seen on the Internet, I should wait until it was uploaded on the Google platform before I interviewed Damore.[25] In any case, Damore was fired by Google despite the fact that Google had expressly solicited comment on their diversity policies—and notwithstanding that Damore's positions were well supported by the scientific literature.[26] If the truth hurts, it must be suppressed for the sake of diversity, inclusion, equity, and of course community cohesion.

Still, apparently not all academics have received the memo that scientific data cannot be used to question a politically correct narrative. Alessandro Strumia, a professor of physics at the University of Pisa and a fellow at CERN (the European Organization for Nuclear Research) learned this lesson the hard way.[27] He delivered a lecture at an inaugural event organized by CERN titled "Workshop on High Energy Theory and Gender." He presented several bibliometric analyses that questioned the prevailing victimhood narrative in physics, namely that women were discriminated against. For example, he found that across eighteen countries, men had an extraordinarily higher number of citations than women when being hired for the same position (ratios of male-to-female citations across the countries varied from 2.96:1 to 12.5:1). It would be perfectly reasonable to challenge his conclusions if one had competing data to present, but he was condemned, essentially, as a blasphemer and meta-phorically burned at the stake. Several thousand scientists under the obnoxious banner of *Particles for Justice* signed a statement condemning Strumia.[28] Their statement of condemnation contained countless mis-representations unbefitting of supposedly unbiased and objective scien-tists including the following lead sentence [bold in original] of the second paragraph: **"We write here first to state, in the strongest possible terms, that the humanity of any person, regardless of ascribed identities such as race, ethnicity, gender identity, religion, disability, gender presenta-tion, or sexual identity is not up for debate."** This is a grotesquely dishon-est tactic as Strumia did not question anyone's humanity let alone mention any of the listed identities.

A powerful and brilliant rebuttal letter to that statement was penned by a physicist and published in Areo Magazine.[29] The letter is precisely what one might expect of an intellectually honest and non-hysterical academic. It lays out the logical and scientific errors in the statement as well as many of the mischaracterizations of Strumia's positions. It also conceded, even-handedly, that Strumia had, on occasion, been less than collegial. The long rebuttal was published anonymously because the author felt that "…anonymity is the wisest course. Although I am a genuinely liberal person, and although I have striven to be fair and con-scientious, I fear attaching my name could harm my career and my relationships. I know there are many other physicists who were also put off by the polemical nature of the response, and who would at least be willing to discuss these things privately, but the social atmosphere is toxic right now."

That this physicist felt the need to publish his rebuttal anonymously is the most important take away from this whole debacle. While I com-mend the author for writing such a trenchant reply, I admonish him for lacking the testicular fortitude to channel his inner Martin Luther: *Here I Stand.*[30] I have weighed in on countless occasions about the Strumia case, including inviting him for a chat on my show and have commented about matters that are extraordinarily more fear-inducing than this matter (such as critiquing Islam), and I've never done so under the cloak of anonymity.[31] An honest signal of one's commitment to truth, reason, and justice must be costly for it to carry any weight. Still, one can understand the temptation of anonymity. A new journal, *The Journal of Controversial Ideas*, has announced that it will permit authors to publish their works under pseudonyms.[32] The journal has many leading academics on its board, but that such a journal is required in supposedly free societies in the twenty-first century speaks volumes about the extent to which we are approaching the abyss of infinite intellectual darkness.

That darkness will not be lightened by humor because jokes and levity are also forbidden by "progressives" in academia. Sir Tim Hunt, a 2001 Nobel Prize winner, was giving a toast at the 2015 World Conference of Science Journalists in Seoul, South Korea, when he jokingly referred to the emotional predicaments that take place in mixed-sex labs: "Let me tell you about my trouble with girls. Three things happen when they are in the lab. You fall in love with them, they fall in love with you, and when you criticize them, they cry." He then facetiously recommended same-sex labs to eliminate such pitfalls. The tsunami of outrage was swift and deadly. He was forced to resign from University College London and from the European Research Council.[33] It did not matter that many leading female scientists came to his defense, as did Richard Dawkins, a scientist and one of Britain's leading public intellectuals.[34] The reputation of this extraordinarily accomplished scientist who had been a champion of women's participation in science for several decades was shattered because of flippant comments made during a toast. That his own wife is a prominent scientist and a feminist did not give pause to the perpetually faux-outraged and their lust for blood.

Lazar Greenfield is a distinguished surgeon with a long list of scientific and clinical accomplishments. While serving as editor-in-chief of *Surgery News*, he authored an editorial in 2011 discussing research that women exposed to sperm via unprotected coitus had lower depression scores than their counterparts who engaged in protected sex.[35] Greenfield concluded with a quip: "So there's a deeper bond between men and women than St. Valentine would have suspected, and now we know there's a better gift for that day than chocolates." Cue the Taliban of faux-outrage. This monster had to pay for his unforgivable humor. He was forced to resign as editor of *Surgery News* as well as step down as president-elect of the American College of Surgeons.[36] Steven Platek, whom I know well, and who is one of the three authors of the paper that Greenfield had cited, penned a reply letter on behalf of his collaborators: "How can someone be asked to resign for citing a peer-reviewed paper? Dr. Greenfield was forced to resign based on politics, not evidence. His resignation is more a reflection of the feminist and anti-scientific attitudes of some self-righteous and indignant members of the American College of Surgeons. Science is based on evidence, not politics. In science knowing is always preferable to not knowing."[37] But today in academia, progressive ideology trumps scientific facts.

Matt Taylor is another scientist who crossed paths with the perpetually offended and rabidly outraged. In 2014, while being interviewed during a livestream about a breathtaking accomplishment of human ingenuity, he wore a rather obnoxious and frankly inappropriate shirt that included drawings of scantily clad women in various poses.[38] Taylor had been working for the European Space Agency as an astrophysicist and was part of the team that landed the Philae probe on a rapidly moving comet located nearly 300 million miles away from our planet. The scientific and engineering expertise needed to pull off such a feat is truly astounding. This should have been his crowning moment. Alas, he is more likely to be remembered for his sartorial crime and his subsequent sobbing apology than for a truly momentous achievement. Of note, the shirt was made by Elly Prizeman, a female friend who had given it to Taylor as a gift. When interviewed about the matter, she replied: "Everyone is entitled to have an opinion. We would all be very boring if we felt the same way about everything. I can see both sides of the coin in this debate, but as it is a style I am into, I don't see it as offensive. But that is

just my view. It is up to us to empower ourselves. We can achieve anything we want to if we have the skills and put our minds to it."[39]

The angry feminists who are willing to ruin the career of an accomplished scientist because of his idiotic shirt choice are also the ones likely
to argue that the male gaze is a form of "visual rape." They are the ones
who posit that the patriarchy promulgates a beauty myth that compels
women to beautify themselves. When parasitized by such a conspiratorial
and delusional mindset, the bikini becomes a sexist tool of the patriarchy
whereas the burqa is liberating and freeing since it averts the male gaze.[40]
To satirize this astonishing departure from reason I began to use the
#FreedomVeils hashtag in reference to this garb. Religious attire such as
the hijab, niqab, and burqa that stem from profoundly patriarchal societies and are imposed on millions of women, are liberating according to
many Western feminists. Bikinis, which under second-wave feminism
might be construed as empowering if used in the pursuit of sexual liberation, apparently are manifestations of the West's patriarchal misogyny.
To recapitulate, bikinis, cosmetics, and miniskirts are bad. Shirts with
whimsical drawings of scantily clad women are a capital offence. The
burqa, niqab, and hijab represent feminist liberation from the male gaze.
No satire can compete with progressive buffoonery.

During my appearance on Sam Harris's podcast, I recounted how
my wife and I had taken our daughter to play at a local children's park.
Standing in the middle of the play area were some individuals so fully
covered in black niqabs that we could not tell if they were women, men,
or any of the 873 "genders" that now constitute the rich fluidity of "gender expression." The image was so jarring that we decided to leave. Since
sharing this story, I have been derided by some Western bien-pensants
for our "silly" overreaction. After all, what could be more engaging and
fun than walking into a play area with a very young child and having
ghosts in ominous black robes stare at your child? Surely only racist
bigots would feel uncomfortable at such a symbol of secularism, moder-
nity, and true liberalism. Of course, I am being sarcastic because this is
the only possible way to process such suicidal stupidity. Vision is the

dominant sense for humans. We have evolved a highly specialized visual system that permits us to read a broad range of nonverbal cues including facial features. Once a person's identity and humanity are hidden behind black robes of "freedom and liberation," it is only natural for most sane people to feel uneasy about such a reality. And yet the virtue signalers mock, deride, and condemn those who exhibit perfectly rational responses to an otherwise disturbing stimulus.

Clear-thinking people know that there is a place for both emotions and intellect, for humor and seriousness, and understand when to activate their emotional versus cognitive systems as they navigate life. But people who have fallen prey to idea pathogens have lost control of their minds and their emotions—and those pathogens are spreading rapidly and threatening our freedom.

CHAPTER THREE

Non-Negotiable Elements of a Free and Modern Society

"But the peculiar evil of silencing the expression of an opinion is, that it is robbing the human race; posterity as well as the existing generation; those who dissent from the opinion, still more than those who hold it. If the opinion is right, they are deprived of the opportunity of exchanging error for truth: if wrong, they lose, what is almost as great a benefit, the clearer perception and livelier impression of truth, produced by its collision with error."
—*John Stuart Mill*[1]

What are the essential features that a society must possess in order to be truly liberal and modern? Niall Ferguson, the Harvard historian, proposed "Six Killer Apps" that define the greatness of the West, namely competition, scientific revolution, property rights, modern medicine, consumer society, and work ethic.[2] In this chapter, I offer a more distilled set of factors. I posit that the guaranteed right to debate any idea (freedom of speech and thought) coupled with a commitment to reason and science to test competing ideas (the scientific method) are what have made Western Civilization great.

Social Media Companies and Free Speech

Many people in the West have a poor understanding of the concept of free speech. Whenever I mute or block someone on social media, a cacophony of fools will accuse me of being a free speech hypocrite for "silencing their voice." They do not understand that I have the right to walk away from their online taunts, insults, and idiocy. To do so is not "restricting" their speech but expressing my right to avoid listening to them. This is an obvious point, and yet many people are confused by it. A second mistake is the mindlessly aped line: "Social media companies are not the government. They have the right to choose which content will be carried on their platforms." In a sane world, this would be a laughable position to hold, and yet it is endlessly repeated without any reflection on its nefarious implications. Google, YouTube, Facebook, and Twitter have more global control over us than all other companies combined. It is not hyperbole to say that they have more collective power, in terms of the information they control, than all the rulers, priests, and politicians of history. If knowledge is power, then these social media giants are nearly all-powerful when they decide which information we can have and whether we can be allowed a social media platform. Big tech companies routinely ban right-leaning commentators, but of course this is all an unfortunate "algorithmic coincidence." What could be more sinister?

Another tool that online companies use to repress free speech is going after your wallet. Of the 1,000+ clips on my YouTube channel, roughly one-third have been demonetized (albeit some are monetized again once I file a request for a manual review). Many of my clips are demonetized prior to my even posting them publicly. In other words, an algorithm automatically demonetizes my clips as a default setting. In other instances, money exchange portals such as Patreon and PayPal, which are used by online content creators to solicit financial support, have banned individuals whom they feel have violated one of their tenets of acceptable speech. Carl Benjamin (a.k.a. Sargon of Akkad), an influential YouTuber on whose show I have appeared on two occasions, was booted from Patreon. The company had uncovered a clip where he used the "N-word" as a means of mocking racists. Despite this context and the fact that the clip had not been produced on the Patreon platform, a key feature of their terms of use (and hence not supported by his patrons), they deleted his account. This caused a gigantic backlash against Patreon. My good friends Jordan Peterson and Dave Rubin left the platform in protest, and many people pledged to boycott the company. But the boycott indirectly punished many other content creators who lost a huge amount of revenue (it cost me more than two-thirds of my financial support). As a libertarian, I am a fervent proponent of small government. I despise the never-ending and ever-increasing governmental encroachments into our daily lives. But it seems obvious that these online companies must be regulated as utilities.[3] Just as your electricity or phone line is not shut off if the electric company or phone company doesn't like what you say, social media platforms should not be in the business of monitoring and punishing speech.

Self-Censorship Is the Greatest Scourge to Free Speech

As a result of my public engagement, I have become a global confessor for students and academics suffering under the political correctness that dominates our universities. A common theme in these first-person testimonies is the necessity of self-censorship lest one be punished for violating progressive orthodoxy. The fear is so great that professors thanking me for my defense of classical liberal values often request that I not share their identities (which I never do without their permission). Imagine for a moment how chilling this is. Below I share excerpts of a few representative emails sent to me:

> I'm a 47-year-old white male who because of an injury made a choice to return to school.... In the first year, to maintain full-time status, I was forced to take another social justice–Black Lives Matter course. Students are not allowed to challenge or question the course content because that's considered disrespectful and may disrupt someone's safe space. I believe I'm a respectful student with good attendance and whose

marks are in the mid-eighties. That said, after a few weeks of the one-sided syllabus, I'm considering dropping out of the program and leaving school entirely. This leftist academic world is a little too much for me.

The reason I am contacting you is because, as an honors cognitive student, part of my requirement is to complete 12 credits of research. However, because of purely political reasons (I am apparently a violent, misogynist, racist Trump supporter), I have not only lost my job at a very prestigious behavioural neuroscience laboratory at [redacted], but my name has been removed from a publication on research I personally conducted, and the lead researcher has told me he would never work with me ever again.

I very much appreciate your courage to fight the cancer that is taking over American academia. People like me feel cheated at their attempt to pursue a tenure track career. It only takes a glimpse at the job offerings that the Modern Languages Association publishes each year, to understand that what is expected from recent graduates like me is political activism, and I refuse to mix that with my academic interests.

I will save you my long stories of dealing and suffering career-wise from politically correct nonsense from the directions of feminism, gender ideology, trans-extremism, and Islamo-philia. I am trying to keep a lid on things for now, as my wife is a very promising academic but hasn't secured a position yet. I know if I started voicing my thoughts and arguments on social media, she'd be completely shut out of the academy.

As a fellow professor who has been frustrated by the discourse within academia on issues such as political correctness, moral relativism, and social justice, I'd like to thank you for speaking up the way you have been from within academia.... I have nevertheless been frustrated by the conformism and group think I see and hear around me. I see otherwise very reasonable and capable people abandoning reason and cowing to the narrative of the regressive left on many social issues.

When I told this professor to engage and debate these issues openly, the professor replied:

These are all things which I would like to get involved in once the tenure decision is behind me (about one year to go). As upsetting as it is, one fears expressing unpopular social ideas prior to tenure. In the meantime, please keep fighting the good fight for freedom of speech and against thought policing and orthodoxy.

These are not emails sent to me from dissidents in North Korea, Yemen, or the former Soviet Union. Ideological Stalinism is the daily reality on North American college campuses. Any freedom-loving person should be appalled by this, and yet most academics yawn in complicit apathy and cowardly inaction. They are too worried about their selfish, careerist considerations to weigh in on these matters. They are happy to tell me privately that they support my efforts but "please, Dr. Saad, don't share my name. I don't want people to know that I share your views." Why should people in a free country be afraid of saying what they believe? Think about that, and you will know the direction that the "progressives" want to take us.

Free Speech=Nazism?

On August 22, 2017, Ryerson University was scheduled to host an event titled "The Stifling of Free Speech on University Campuses" organized by Sarina Singh (a Sikh woman of color, to use the parlance of social justice warriors). Ms. Singh worked for two decades as a social worker until she decided to quit her occupation, as she could no longer handle the pernicious anti-science, illiberal progressive dogma that had infested her field. Four speakers were scheduled for the event: Dr. Jordan Peterson; Dr. Oren Amitay, a clinical psychologist and lecturer at Ryerson University; Faith Goldy, a somewhat polarizing journalist; and me. I was going to speak about how freedom of speech is the source from which all our freedoms flow. I was also planning on reading first-person testimonies of students and professors terrorized by the thought police on their campuses.

Are you able to guess what transpired next? In a twist of Orwellian irony, an Antifa-like outfit shut down the event. Rather than standing up to these intellectual terrorists and enemies of reason, Ryerson University cited "security concerns" as their justification for cancelling an event meant to highlight the importance of free speech on university campuses. The lunacy does not end there. The organizers of the shutdown had created a Facebook page with a Nazi swastika declaring that they did not tolerate Nazis, white supremacists, and anti-Semites in "their" city (they added Islamophobes and transphobes for good measure). I am an olive-skinned Lebanese Jew who escaped execution in Lebanon, and yet I am apparently an anti-Semitic Nazi. Dr. Amitay is Jewish, and his family suffered during the Holocaust. He is married to a Japanese woman, and he has an adopted black, gay brother. What a racist transphobic Nazi! Our identities and personal histories did not cause these violators of human dignity to take stock. They simply doubled down on their positions. We were Nazi peddlers of hate.

This recent debacle is hardly an isolated event. The American-based Foundation for Individual Rights in Education (FIRE) documented 192 disinvitation efforts (attempts to stop invited speakers) at American universities for the period 2000 to 2014, and this dreadful pattern is growing.[4] The "success" rate of such attempts varied between 38 percent and 44 percent, a truly breathtaking affront to the First Amendment of the American Constitution. Disinvitation efforts are nearly three times more likely to take place if the "offending" speaker is seen as belonging on the political right. Since the 2014 report was released, there have been many more leftist-led disinvitations and disruptions of a broad range of speakers including former CIA director John Brennan (at the University of Pennsylvania), the political scientist Charles Murray (at Middlebury College), equity feminist Christina Hoff Sommers (at Lewis & Clark College), feminist icon Camille Paglia (at the University of the Arts), and Nobel Laureate James Watson (at New York University and the University of Illinois at Urbana-Champaign). The status of freedom of speech on Canadian universities is hardly better. The Justice Centre for Constitutional Freedoms's 2017 Campus Freedom Index evaluated the health of free speech at sixty Canadian universities along four variables: 1) university policies; 2) university practices; 3) student union policies; and 4) student union practices, using the grades A, B, C, D, and F.[5] Of 240 possible grades (60 universities x 4 grades per university), Canadian universities garnered six As and thirty-eight Fs. American and Canadian universities are hardly bastions of free speech. Instead, they are echo chambers for the left. Deviate from the herd at your peril.

I Believe in Free Speech, but...

It is now part of the West's zeitgeist that we should not utter anything that might offend, anger, or insult anyone who is a "minority" or a "progressive." This was not always the case. The 1988 Salman Rushdie affair was a landmark in this new era of restricted speech. When his book *The Satanic Verses* was released, it immediately drew the ire of many members of the ummah (the global Islamic community) who viewed it as blasphemous to their religion and prophet. Ayatollah Khomeini, then the Supreme Leader of Iran, issued a death sentence against Rushdie. Rushdie was forced to live under police protection. The novelist made a guest appearance on Larry David's highly popular television series *Curb Your Enthusiasm*, mocking his own predicament by explaining why women are keen on having sex with a globally wanted man. Two passages from an article Rushdie wrote in 2005 make the succinct case for freedom of speech. "The idea that any kind of free society can be constructed in which people will never be offended or insulted, or in which they have the right to call on the law to defend them against being offended or insulted, is absurd." Moreover: "The moment you say that an idea system is sacred, whether it's a religious belief system or a secular ideology, the moment you declare a set of ideas to be immune from criticism, satire, derision, or contempt, freedom of thought becomes impossible."[6]

Progressives consider it laudable to criticize, mock, or insult all religious beliefs—except for the one untouchable faith. To attack Islam in the West is "Islamophobic," "racist," and "bigoted." If a Republican politician says he believes homosexuality is wrong because of his Christian faith, progressives are quick to express their outrage and horror and will organize protests accordingly. If ISIS members throw gay men off rooftops based on specific fatwas, the same progressives are deafeningly silent. After all, who are we to criticize the practices of the Noble Religion? It is apparently arrogant cultural imperialism to impose our values onto others, especially if they are members of the untouchable faith. In 2005, the Danish newspaper *Jyllands-Posten* published twelve cartoons that caricatured Muhammad, the prophet of Islam. Violence erupted around the world resulting in the deaths of around 200 individuals. Several years later, Jytte Klausen authored a book on the controversy titled *The Cartoons that Shook the World*. The publisher, Yale University Press, decided against publishing the caricatures in a book about the caricatures![7] Most major media outlets were equally cowardly and refrained from printing the cartoons on their platforms. Nearly ten years later, the *Charlie Hebdo* massacre occurred in Paris. This satirical magazine had blasphemed against Islam, and so Muslim terrorists attacked its employees, brutally massacring twelve people and seriously injuring several others.

Christianity is repeatedly criticized and mocked, and yet Christians do not respond with such violence, or anything like it.[8] In 1987, Andres

Serrano's photo titled *Piss Christ* depicting a crucifix in the photographer's urine won an award that was partly sponsored by the National Endowment of the Arts (an agency of the United States government). Many Christians were clearly upset by it, but they did not lead violent protests. In a 2009 episode of *Curb Your Enthusiasm*, Larry David (co-creator of *Seinfeld*) visits the home of an employee, and while using the bathroom inadvertently splashes urine on an image of Jesus Christ in the restroom. The employee, unaware of David's mishap, interprets it as a divine tear. It is difficult to imagine a more offensive story line to the more than two billion Christians in the world, and yet no one was killed as a retaliation against this puerile humor. The Austrian film *Paradise Faith* featured a woman masturbating with a crucifix, and yet it won a jury prize at the 2012 Venice Film Festival.[9] *The Book of Mormon* is a highly successful musical that makes fun of various practices of the Mormon religion. It has won a Tony Award and has grossed more than $500 million on Broadway alone. And yet no Mormon explosion of anger and violence has taken place. Contrast these tame reactions to what happened in 2012, when an ineptly produced short movie titled *Innocence of Muslims* triggered mass protests in many countries resulting in more than fifty deaths and a death fatwa being issued on the film's producer, director, and actors. There was even a debate within the upper echelon of the United States government as to whether the 2012 attack on an American compound in Benghazi, Libya, resulting in the death of four Americans including a U.S. ambassador, was a violent response to the film.

Holocaust deniers engage in perhaps the most egregious form of offensive speech. They constitute an affront to human decency, as they reject the well-documented historical fact that millions of Jews were systematically exterminated. Of all possible falsehoods, the denial of the Holocaust is an unrivaled murder of the truth. And yet, I, a Jewish man who escaped religious persecution in Lebanon, support the right of Holocaust deniers to spew their vile and inhumane garbage. It is difficult to imagine a greater manifestation of what it means to be a free speech absolutist. If you truly understand the meaning of free speech, then you must agree with the following: "There is simply no better alternative than to allow those with unpopular views to express them and to allow those wishing to hear them to do so."[10]

The "I believe in free speech but" crowd violates the foundational ethos of what it means to have free speech. Usually, what comes after the "but" is an appeal to refrain from hurting people's sensibilities and feelings. The general idea is that we must weigh our freedom of speech against the right of others to not be offended. No! Freedom of speech is precisely meant to protect the most obnoxious, offensive, and disgusting speech. It does not exist to ensure that you only levy beautiful compliments at me. Occasionally being offended is the price that one pays for living in a truly free society. Your feelings might get hurt. Grow a pair and move on. Needless to say, being a free speech absolutist comes with the usual provisos including that screaming "fire" in a theater, inciting violence against others, and engaging in defamatory and libelous discourse are not protected speech, but the opponents of free speech are trying to contort these commonsense restrictions to suit their own purposes. One of the ways that the West is losing its will to fight for freedom of speech is by enacting hate speech laws. Several prominent European figures have been prosecuted under the broad shoulders of hate speech including the Dutch parliamentarian Geert Wilders mentioned earlier, the president of the International Free Press Society Lars Hedegaard, and Austrian activist Elisabeth Sabaditsch-Wolff. In all these cases, these individuals and many others got into legal trouble for criticizing Islam. Under the watch of Prime Minister Justin Trudeau, Canadian parliamentarian Iqra Khalid introduced Motion 103, which originally stemmed from E-411 (a petition to the House of Commons) initiated by Samer Majzoub. Both the petition and the motion (neither of which is a law) sought to combat "Islamophobia" (which is a nonsensical concept). In a free society, people have every right to mock, condemn, criticize, despise, and fear any ideology.

Perhaps the most chilling attempt to quell the right of individuals to criticize religions (and by that, I mean one particular religion) has come from the Organization of Islamic Cooperation (the OIC, composed of fifty-six countries and the Palestinian territories). They constitute the largest voting bloc of the United Nations, and as such it is perhaps not surprising that Israel receives far more official UN condemnations than all brutal regimes in the world combined. The OIC has repeatedly attempted to get Western nations to adopt the Cairo Declaration on Human Rights in Islam, which would oblige signatory nations to punish anyone who criticizes Islam. This repeated quest to impose Sharia-like restrictions on free speech regarding Islam is receiving a sympathetic hearing in the West including from former secretary of state Hillary Clinton and former president Barack Obama who famously stated in an address to the United Nations assembly that "the future must not belong to those who slander the prophet of Islam." On the contrary Mr. President, the future must belong to those who criticize, mock, ridicule, and satirize all prophets, ideas, religions, and ideologies.

Satire as the Surgeon's Scalpel

"Wherever there is objective truth, there is satire."
—*Wyndham Lewis*[11]

"How much truth is contained in something can be best determined by making it thoroughly laughable and then watching to see how much joking around it can take. For truth is a matter that can stand mockery, that is freshened by any ironic gesture directed at it. Whatever cannot stand satire is false."
—*Peter Sloterdijk*[12]

"Ridicule is the only weapon which can be used against unintelligible propositions. Ideas must be distinct before reason can act upon them."
—*Thomas Jefferson*[13]

Satire is a strategy I frequently employ to critique idea pathogens. To make it effective, as Mary Wortley Montagu said, "Satire should, like a polished razor keen, / Wound with a touch that's scarcely felt or seen."[14] This is precisely why totalitarian rulers have always outlawed satire directed at them and their ideologies. If an idea is veridical, it should be anti-fragile. It should be capable of withstanding ironic, satirical, and sarcastic attacks. If it is too brittle to do so, it is undoubtedly a falsehood. Satirists have recognized this for millennia, as evidenced by the works of Horace, Aristophanes, Juvenal, Lucian of Samosata, Al-Ma'arri, Voltaire, François Rabelais, Jonathan Swift, Oscar Wilde, Mark Twain, Ambrose Bierce, and George Orwell. I would also include comedians like Lenny Bruce and George Carlin, the television show *South Park*, and magazines like *Mad* and *Charlie Hebdo*.

On July 16, 2018, the noted evolutionary scientist and atheist Richard Dawkins tweeted: "Listening to the lovely bells of Winchester, one of our great mediaeval cathedrals. So much nicer than the aggressive-sounding 'Allahu Akhbar.' Or is that just my cultural upbringing?"[15] I replied: "Dear Richard, Arabic is my mother tongue. When properly translated, 'Allahu Akbar' means 'We love all people but hold a special fondness for Jews, women, and gays.' Don't worry. It's a message of love, tolerance, and liberalism."[16]

Newsweek, initially not getting the joke, said I had criticized Dawkins for his "bigotry," before eventually realizing that I had been sarcastic. My satirical powers, however, reached all the way to Pakistan, where I managed to bamboozle *The Express Tribune* in an article written to condemn Dawkins's "Islamophobia" (they deleted any mention of me and my tweet when they realized that I had tweeted in jest).[17] At times, my satire is so powerful that it fools even those who have followed me on Twitter for a while. Donald Trump Jr. had weighed in on Alexandria Ocasio-Cortez's unfortunate use of the term "concentration camps" in reference to the detention centers at the U.S. border with Mexico. Specifically, he posted a tweet that included clips from actual Holocaust survivors to drive home the point that her comparison was foolish if not grotesque. In my attempt to satirize the left's routine false equivalence between their opponents and Nazis, I replied to Trump Jr.'s tweet as follows: "No way Donald. @AOC is a woman of color in Trump's MAGA country. She faces much greater daily threats than those Holocaust survivors ever did."[18] The average three-day-old pigeon should be able to pick up such outlandishly obvious satire. Apparently, Charlie Kirk, a conservative pundit and founder of Turning Point USA, did not receive the memo. He tweeted:

WOW

@GadSaad a Professor who is teaching youth in Canada at the John Molson School of business [sic] – says that @AOC is in MORE DANGER than holocaust survivors ever were

This is who is teaching our children

This is the face of liberal education

SICK!

RT!

I ended up receiving innumerable angry tweets from people, all of whom were apparently immune to the powers of satire. Note that Kirk behaved like a leftist social justice warrior: he was outraged and so mobilized an e-mob against me and took aim at the school where I teach. He eventually deleted his tweet, though without offering me an apology.

But perhaps my greatest satirical ruse occurred when PJ Media listed one of my quotes amongst its twenty worst quotes of 2018.[19] Now that is an accomplishment of the highest order! Here is the quote: "To all Noble Undocumented 'immigrants': We apologize for our bigotry and racism. It is Nazism to not allow you to vote in our elections. After all, national borders is Nazism. Nationhood is Nazism. In a just world, everyone should get to vote in any district. #WeApologize"[20] I contacted the author of the piece—who apparently was unable to distinguish political satire from real political lunacy—and he eventually removed me from his "worst quotes" list.

The takeaway point is this: Free societies do not recoil at the power of satire. They recognize that all beliefs and ideologies are fair game. Once we delimit what can be satirized, we are no longer living in a free society.

Identity Politics Are Antithetical to Science

In Fall 2018, I organized and hosted a symposium on evolutionary consumption at my university. A few days prior to the symposium, I received an email from a female colleague in another department at my university, telling me she could not attend and then chastising me for my "oversight" of not including more women speakers. Here is my reply:

> Many thanks for your email. I am sorry that you won't be able to make it.
>
> As to your point, I do not subscribe to identity politics and certainly not in science. If the symposium at hand necessitated that most speakers be women, so be it. If in this case, the number of male to female speakers is not "balanced" so be it. I did invite another female speaker but she was unavailable. I did not choose my speakers as a function of whether they ovulate or not. I chose them based on their fit with the topic at hand, their availability, etc.
>
> The US government released data across five races and four educational attainment levels (Associate's degree, Bachelor's, Master's, and doctorate). As such, there were 20 cells to analyze. In EVERY single cell, women outnumbered men. Are you

going to push for greater gender parity across the cells because it is difficult to imagine a more "biased" reality?

I should add that we do not know whether any of the male speakers self-identify as women so perhaps the gender parity is more balanced than might first appear.

In any case, thank you for writing in. I hope that we'll have a chance to interact again.

I have yet to receive a reply from my colleague. Of note, I visited her university website and saw that she had posted a photo of herself with her nine lab members, all of whom were women. Lest you think that this incident is an outlier, Joe Rogan was recently chastised by the progressive organization Media Matters for having many more male guests than female ones.[21] The Canadian government's allocation of endowed research chairs at Canadian universities (known as Canada Research Chairs) must now abide by an "Equity, Diversity, and Inclusion Action Plan" that ensures that more "women, Indigenous peoples, persons with disabilities and members of visible minorities" are appointed as chairholders. Universities that do not abide by this action plan will have funding withheld. Even the Nobel Prize has been infected with this destructive mindset. An article published in *Nature* (one of two premier science journals) chastised the Nobel committee for the gender disparity in science laureates (3 percent of whom have been women) and went on to add that the great majority of winners have operated in Western countries.[22] The recognition of scientific excellence ought to be driven by meritocratic ideals, and yet it is increasingly contaminated by identity politics.

In April 2017, the inaugural March for Science rally was held across hundreds of cities around the world to reaffirm the importance of science (in part as a response to Donald Trump's supposed anti-science agenda). On January 30, 2017, I visited a key mobilizing website for the event and found this mission statement:[23]

At the March for Science, we are committed to centralizing, highlighting, standing in solidarity with, and acting as accomplices with black, Latinx, Asian and Pacific Islander, indigenous, non-Christian, women, people with disabilities, poor, gay, lesbian, bisexual, queer, trans, non-binary, agender, and intersex scientists and science advocates. We must work to make science available to everyone and encouraging individuals of all backgrounds to pursue science careers, especially in advanced degrees and positions. A diverse group of scientists produces increasingly diverse research, which broadens, strengthens, and enriches scientific inquiry, and therefore, our understanding of the world.

If you are a white Christian heterosexual male scientist, tough luck, buddy. Following a wave of criticism from several high-profile academics including the Harvard psychologist Steven Pinker and yours truly, the latter statement was revised albeit it remained a manifestation of anti-science gibberish.

By definition, science is, or should be, an apolitical process. Scientific truths and natural laws exist independent of researchers' identities. The distribution of prime numbers does not change as a function of whether the mathematician is a white heterosexual Christian man or a transgendered, Muslim, differently sized (obese) individual. The periodic table of elements is not dependent on whether a chemist is a Latinx queer or a cisnormative Hasidic Jew. Oh, you are a non-binary bisexual chemist? Well this completely changes the atomic numbers of Carbon, Palladium, and Uranium. All satire aside, science is liberating precisely because it does not care about your identity. It is the epistemological means by which we seek to understand the world using evidentiary rules that are unbiased. There is no other game in town, no other way of knowing. This leads me to another virulent mind pathogen that has spread within the university ecosystem: the idea that science is a white colonial way of knowing. In fall 2016, South African students at the University of Cape Town known as "fallists" (who believe science must fall) gained worldwide attention when they argued that it was imperative to decolonize one's mind from the shackles of white colonial science. Sorry Albert Einstein, Charles Darwin, Isaac Newton, and Galileo Galilei: You are not people of color. Your work cannot be fully trusted. Back to the drawing boards. Readers might be tempted to think that this is hardly something to worry about. After all the South African quacks in question are undoubtedly an anomaly. Surely, this form of anti-science idiocy could not spread. Or could it? There is a growing push across Canadian universities to indigenize the curricula. This is meant as a conciliatory response to past historical grievances against the indigenous people. According to such a view, the scientific method is only one of many ways of knowing. Other forms of knowing, including those that might belong within the folklore and mythology of indigenous people, are peddled as equally valid forms of discovery. I'm here to tell you that, no, they are not. Of course, indigenous people do have unique insight about the flora and fauna of lands on which they've lived for generations. And it is perfectly reasonable to presume that such content-specific local knowledge is extremely valuable and worthy of learning and sharing. However, the *manner* by which scientific information is codified within the pantheon of human knowledge is not culture-specific. Patrick Beauchesne, a Quebec deputy minister, was recently severely rebuked for daring to question how indigenous knowledge might be evaluated against scientific knowledge (when conducting environmental impact studies). Apparently, he was guilty of supporting a "hierarchy of knowledges."[24] The scientific method is the universal epistemological framework for understanding the world around us. Science does not care about the privileged position of "ancestral wisdom," "tribal knowledge," and "the ways of the elders." There are no revealed truths in science. There is no Lebanese-Jewish way of knowing any more than there is an indigenous way of knowing. All claims about the natural world must pass through the evidentiary prism of the scientific method.

There are several other ways by which the indigenization of academia is taking place. Indigenous land acknowledgement statements are often made at the start of formal academic events (such as graduation ceremonies) wherein speakers start off by acknowledging that the attendees are on hallowed grounds whose provenance belongs to indigenous people. A more forceful version of this new ritual is to proclaim that the attendees are trespassing on stolen lands. In fall 2017, I delivered an invited lecture at the University of Regina titled "Death of the West by a Thousand Cuts: Forces that Impede the Free and Rational Exchange of Ideas."[25] The introducer began by reminding the audience of Treaty 6 signed between the Canadian Crown and various indigenous peoples in 1876, and added that we were on the lands of the Métis. At university convocations, masters of ceremony will often start off by making such land acknowledgements. Put yourself in the shoes of the thousands of graduating students who must sit silently while having the cloak of historical guilt placed on their shoulders. They have worked hard for many years to arrive at this point. This is their moment. It is their time in the spotlight. And yet, they are catapulted into historical grievances that have nothing to do with any of them. The reality is that innumerable existing lands have belonged to someone else at some point. This is a defining feature of history. It is an indelible part of *Homo sapiens*. Should we adopt a global standard wherein any and all ceremonies must begin with a forensic historical accounting of all peoples who laid claim to a given land? If so, Jews should insist that all future events that take place in Saudi Arabia start off by recognizing the historical rights of the Banu Nadir, the Banu Qaynuqa, and the Banu Qurayza, Jewish tribes that existed in the region prior to the ascent of Islam.

The indigenization process is not restricted to university curricula and university ceremonies. It has attacked the fundamental means by which academic works are evaluated, namely the peer review process. It might be worthwhile to step back and briefly explain how it works. Academic journals are managed by an editor in chief, associate editors (at times), and an editorial board of academic experts in the field in question. The peer review process begins when the editor receives a paper for consideration, and quickly establishes whether it is of the necessary quality and within the focus of the journal. If these conditions are not met, the editor will "desk-reject" the paper, which means he will not send it out for review. Otherwise, a suitable number of reviewers are sent the paper for their academic evaluations (usually this consists of two or three experts from the editorial board but at times the editor might ask an expert who does not sit on the board to review the paper; this is known as an ad hoc reviewer). Once all reviews are submitted to the editor, a decision letter is sent to the authors with typically one of four possibilities. The journal will: 1) accept the paper; 2) ask the authors to make minor revisions and resubmit the paper; 3) ask the authors to make major revisions and resubmit the paper; or 4) reject the paper. This process can go on for several rounds of review consisting of several years of intense expert scrutiny. As such, once a paper is published in the academic literature, it has typically gone through an extensive evaluation. Peer review is hardly perfect (great papers are at times rejected; poor papers are accepted), but it is a necessary and integral element of the vetting of human knowledge. It might surprise you to know that it is a "racist" process despite the fact that it is typically double-blind (reviewers and authors do not know one another's identities). This was the claim made by University of British Columbia law professor Lorna June McCue in 2016.[26] Specifically, McCue who is an indigenous woman, asserted that peer reviewed works were incongruent with the oral traditions of her heritage, and as such the university was being discriminatory against her ancestry. Astonishingly, her case was heard in front of the British Columbia Human Rights Tribunal, and it decided that the university had not discriminated against Professor McCue. Someone should have advised all Jewish Nobel laureates long ago that they did not have to bother writing things down since Judaism also stems from a rich oral tradition.

The contemporary progressive mantra considers it laudable to argue that different races, cultures, or religions possess distinct ways of knowing. However, not too long ago, the idea that people of different races or classes possessed distinct ways of thinking and reasoning, was reserved for racists and other miscreants. Ludwig von Mises, a leading figure of the Austrian School of Economics and a staunch defender of classical liberalism, coined the term polylogism to capture this exact folly. Mises differentiated between

Marxian polylogism and racial polylogism. In the former case, an individual's method of thinking was determined by his social class while in the latter case, race was the guiding factor. Mises was well aware of the illogical nature of this premise when he remarked: "A consistent supporter of polylogism would have to maintain that ideas are correct because their author is a member of the right class, nation, or race. But consistency is not one of their virtues. Thus the Marxians are prepared to assign the epithet 'proletarian thinker' to everybody whose doctrines they approve. All the others they disparage either as foes of their class or as social traitors."[27] Current social justice warriors engage in similar ideological thinking. "I disagree with you" is thus replaced with disparaging labels: climate change denier, white nationalist, New Atheist, white supremacist, Alt-Right, and so on, demonizing dissenters from progressive orthodoxy as nefarious and evil.

Polylogism is an anti-science notion, as Mises well knew. "[Mises] had highlighted the wider significance of polylogism, characterizing it as a 'romantic revolt against logic and science' and pointing out that it 'does not limit itself to the sphere of social phenomena and the sciences of human action. It is a revolt against our entire culture and civilization.'"[28] The scientific method liberates us to pursue truth, regardless of who we are. Similarly, evolutionary psychology, a discipline viscerally despised by many progressives, is expressly anti-racist in that it recognizes that underneath many of our surface differences, human minds were borne of the same evolutionary forces irrespective of our racial or ethnic backgrounds. Environmental forces (or culture) do affect our thinking styles, reasoning, and decision making, but these effects are not immutable elements of one's race or ethnicity. There is no "black mind" or "white mind," no "white male way of knowing" or "indigenous way of knowing," there is only one truth, and we find it through the scientific method.

The Ideological Conformity of Diversity, Inclusion, and Equity

Progressives seem to believe that if they say the words "diversity, inclusion, and equity" often enough, all problems will be solved. But of course only certain types of diversity, inclusion, and equity matter. Diversity based on race, ethnicity, religion, sex, sexual orientation, and gender identity are foundational sacraments in the Cult of Diversity. On the other hand, intellectual and political diversity are heretical ideas that need to be expunged. If Saudi Arabia's state religion is Islam, the official quasi-religion of Western universities is Diversity, Inclusion, and Equity (or DIE for short). An ever-growing number of academic administrators are hired to ensure that the DIE cult reigns supreme. Mark J. Perry, a professor of economics at the University of Michigan–Flint, has estimated that the University of Michigan has 93 employees on its payroll to uphold the tenets of DIE for a total yearly cost of more than $11 million.[29] The top DIE administrator within that list receives a yearly compensation of $396,550, more than the combined salary of four faculty members at most American universities. Bloated administrative payrolls are already a disastrous financial reality at most universities; adding endless DIE bureaucrats is only making it worse.

In the never-ending need to uncover illusory racists lurking in every crevasse, members of the DIE cult have benefited from the use of the Implicit Association Test (IAT), which is supposed to measure people's latent biases. In other words, even when you proclaim that you are not a racist and have never harbored a single racist thought in your life, the IAT will prove otherwise. It is similar to the infamous principle of Lavrentiy Beria (head of Joseph Stalin's secret police): "Show me the man and I'll find you the crime." In this case, show me the person (undoubtedly a heterosexual white Christian male), and the IAT will show you a hateful racist. The reality is that the IAT has very poor predictive validity,[30] diversity training based on identifying supposed unconscious biases is likely ineffectual,[31] and the IAT's scientific value continues to be a hotly debated topic,[32] so it is grossly imprudent to use it in corporate and educational settings as though it were settled science.

But the DIE zealots insist that all those under their dominion must be full converts to the progressive faith. A growing number of universities now require as part of the faculty hiring and promotion process that one demonstrates adherence to DIE principles. Take for example UCLA's Office of Equity, Diversity, and Inclusion. It released a report explaining that faculty members should submit a statement (as part of the standard evaluation of academic personnel) wherein they highlight their "past, present, and future (planned) contributions to equity, diversity, and inclusion."[33] In the same way that Ba'ath Party members swore their allegiance to former dictator Saddam Hussein and North Koreans publicly sang with great fervor their undying love for their now deceased, albeit glorious, Dear Leader Kim Jong-il, academic personnel must now prostrate themselves at the altar of DIE. Failure to do so might bring the death of one's academic career. Let me share a personal anecdote that speaks to this growing reality. I was contacted by a female student (who happened to be an apparent fan of my work) who was a member of the John Molson Women in Business Club. They were interested in inviting me to speak at an event about how men could serve as allies to women in the workplace. I held a Skype chat with the woman to learn more about the session. She told me she wanted me to share strategies that I might have used in my career to support and advance women. I reminded her that I treat each person with equal dignity irrespective of their sex or other immutable characteristics, and that I have always judged people based on their individual merits. I also pointed out that the dean of our business school is a woman, as is the associate dean of research (since holding my chat with her, our department has appointed a woman as our chairperson). I conceded that women had faced discrimination in the past but pointed out that the current situation is very different, as the data show that women are currently doing quite well vis à vis men and are surpassing them in many academic fields. Instead of promoting a false victimhood narrative, I offered to deliver a lecture on my scientific research on sex differences. The committee decided against inviting me.

I could have played along and delivered the requested lecture on the need for men to be better allies to women. But my commitment to truth and adherence to reality meant I could not do so in good conscience because it is terribly condescending and patronizing to pretend that women need men to serve as their allies. This is a form of infantilism that should not exist in a meritocratic system.

But, of course, in academic institutions it reigns supreme. Francis Collins, the director of the National Institutes of Health, has stated that before accepting a speaking engagement, he would examine the conference's commitment to eradicating all-male panels.[34] To my chagrin, his position was endorsed by Simon Baron-Cohen, a leading cognitive neuroscientist.[35] The virtue-signaling of such high-profile male "allies" should really be seen as an insult to female scientists who do not need to be coddled and protected from meritocratic standards. They do not need so-called "affirmative action."

Totalitarian ideologies insist on conformity, and there are many ways to impose a herd mindset on a population. Take for example the imposition of sartorial norms in Mao Tse-tung's Communist China or within the ultraorthodox Hasidic sects. Everyone looks the same. To stand out as an individual is to explicitly proclaim that you are more important than the collective. How do the DIE bureaucrats impose conformity? In the academic world, you are free to dress as you'd like, but your thoughts and beliefs are subject to the intellectual conformity of the progressive ideology. Numerous studies have explored professors' political affiliations, and the findings are truly astonishing. A 2005 study conducted across eleven California universities uncovered a 5 to 1 Democrat-to-Republican ratio.[36] Perhaps not surprisingly the most lopsided ratio was that of UC-Berkeley (8.7 to 1 ratio). When broken down by departments across universities, thirty-nine out of forty-two listed fields had a greater ratio of Democrat professors. Not surprisingly, fields laden with social justice activism were the most lopsided (Sociology had a 44 to 1 ratio). In a 2016 study of professors' voting registration at forty leading American universities across five disciplines, the Democrat-to-Republican ratios were 4.5 (economics), 33.5 (history), 20.0 (journalism), 8.6 (law), and 17.4 (psychology).[37] The total across the five disciplines was an 11.5 to 1 ratio favoring Democratic professors. A detailed examination of law professors at American universities found that only 15 percent were classified as conservative (based on data from political donations), and the liberal lopsidedness was differentially acute across legal subspecialties.[38] As might be expected, legal specializations laden with social justice activists were ranked as the most liberal. These were, in decreasing order: Feminist Legal Theory, Poverty Law, Women and the Law, Critical Race Theory, Immigration Law, and Disability Law. Finally, a recent study of professors' political registrations at fifty-one out of the sixty top liberal arts colleges in the United States uncovered a 10.4 to 1 Democrat-to-Republican ratio.[39] If the two "outlier" military colleges are removed, the ratio increases to 12.7 to 1. Incredibly, twenty institutions had a proportion of Republican professors that, statistically speaking, was zero. Of note, the more prestigious a school is, the more lopsided the Democrat ratio (21.5, 12.8, 12.4, and 6.9 across tiers 1, 2, 3, and 4 respectively).

The economist Thomas Sowell, who happens to be one of the original slayers of social justice warriors back in the 1960s and 1970s, famously quipped: "The next time some academics tell you how important 'diversity' is, ask how many Republicans there are in their sociology department."[40]

Samuel J. Abrams, a professor of politics at ultra-liberal Sarah Lawrence College, recently penned a *New York Times* opinion piece wherein he reported his survey findings of 900 administrators tasked with the management of student life on campuses.[41] He found that the ratio of liberals-to-conservatives among this group was 12 to 1 (well in line with similar skewed ratios for the professoriate). In his closing paragraph, he opined: "This warped ideological distribution among college administrators should give our students and their families pause. To students who are in their first semester at school, I urge you not to accept unthinkingly what your campus administrators are telling you. Their ideological imbalance, coupled with their agenda-setting power, threatens the free and open exchange of ideas, which is precisely what we need to protect in higher education in these politically polarized times." This is a plainly sensible position, and yet the hysterical reaction from students and staff at his college was what we've come to expect from these adult toddlers. Threatening and insulting notes were left outside his office demanding that he first apologize and then resign.[42] The college's president accused him of lacking compassion and of making people "feel unsafe" on campus.

Whenever I discuss studies that document the extreme liberal bias on university campuses, I am invariably told: "Professors are educated, intellectually sophisticated, and smart. So of course, they are liberal. It's a self-selection bias. Intelligent people are liberal. Universities are comprised of intelligent people; therefore, most of them are inevitably liberal." Self-selection, however, is not what drives the liberal bias on university campuses, but rather systemic politically-based discrimination. A study of social and personality psychologists documented the paucity of conservative faculty members (only 6 percent of the surveyed sample).[43] Of note, a sizeable number of faculty members admitted that they would discriminate against conservative colleagues when reviewing their papers or grant applications, when deciding whether to invite them to a symposium, and when making hiring decisions. The more "liberal" a faculty member was, the more likely he was to endorse this sort of brazen discrimination. Given the rampant discriminatory bias against them, is it any surprise that conservative students and professors feel unwelcome in the academy and that most conservative graduate students and faculty members are likely to hide their political leanings?

The "academics are smart and hence they are liberals" premise is faulty for a second reason. The implicit but erroneous implication is that conservatives are largely science deniers. But science denialism is found amongst liberals at least as much as it is amongst conservatives. Yes, some conservatives reject evolution for religious reasons, but many progressives reject evolutionary psychology because it contradicts many of their secular ideologies including radical feminism. The human instinct to protect one's beliefs from the indignity of being challenged transcends an individual's political orientation.[44] It is a frailty of the human spirit, and as such, it is not restricted to liberals or conservatives. Few people possess the intellectual courage to expose their most cherished positions to opposing perspectives. The human ego is brittle and frail.

The "academics are smart and hence they are liberals" canard is devastatingly wrong for a third but equally important reason. If a conservative ecology professor rejects the theory of evolution—a scientific truth that is as incontrovertible as the existence of gravity—this is obviously a problem. One's political or religious beliefs cannot supersede accepted scientific knowledge (though we must remember that such knowledge remains provisional and open to falsification). But there are many issues on which there can be conflicting, yet perfectly reasonable and valid, positions that lend themselves to debate. What should a country's foreign, fiscal, and immigration policies look like? What are the pros and cons of the death penalty? Is universal healthcare a viable and sustainable program? There are countless issues of substantive political, societal, and economic importance where university students stand to benefit greatly from being exposed to a heterogeneity of perspectives. Hence, the quest for greater intellectual diversity is not some theoretically abstract ideal; diversity of thought on campus helps train future leaders to weigh different outlooks and opinions and facts in making a sound judgment. Intellectual diversity is the engine that allows for the Darwinian process of competition to select the best ideas (what we call evolutionary epistemology). In this sense, universities today have become anti-Darwinian cesspools of barren ideological conformity.

It is important to note that the lack of intellectual and political diversity is not restricted to academia. Ideological conformity is rampant across every key industry that deals in information. An analysis of political campaign donations across a broad range of industries uncovered that the four most liberal professions, in decreasing order, were the entertainment industry, academia, online computer services, and newspapers and print media.[45] These professions were *much* more liberal than conservative professions were conservative. In other words, political bias is asymmetric. These general findings were confirmed in another study of political leanings (based on political contributions) across professions. For example, the film and stage production industry had a 93 to 7 Democrat-to-Republican ratio; editors (in the book and magazine publishing industry) had a 92 to 8 Democrat-to-Republican ratio; academia had a 90 to 10 Democrat-to-Republican ratio.[46] An examination of midterm political contributions of $200 or more by employees who work in the technology industry uncovered an astronomical liberal bias. The percentage of contributions that went to Democratic candidates from Netflix was 99.6 percent; from Twitter, 98.7 percent; from Apple, 97.5 percent; from Google/Alphabet, 96 percent; from Facebook, 94.5 percent; from PayPal, 92.2 percent; and from Microsoft, 91.7 percent.[47] Bias? What bias? We often hear the mainstream media scoffing at the idea that they are in any way politically biased. Well, a 2013 study from Indiana University's School of Journalism revealed that American journalists were nearly four times more likely to be Democrats than Republicans.[48] While many proclaimed to be independents, one can safely presume that this was a form of impression management (even if to fool oneself about being ideologically impartial). Of note, beyond industries that deal with information (academia, journalism, social media), there are many professions wherein a political tilt has tangible repercussions. For example, physicians are likely to offer different treatments as a function of their political leanings.[49] To further complicate matters, different medical specialties yield varying patterns of political affiliations, the most conservative of which are surgery, anesthesiology, and urology, and the most liberal being infectious disease, psychiatry, and pediatrics.[50] Choose your psychiatrist carefully lest your schizophrenia be blamed on climate change, an overbearing mother, or Donald Trump.

I end this chapter with a very poignant quote from Ronald Reagan, uttered nearly two decades before he became president of the United States:

> But freedom is never more than one generation away from extinction. We didn't pass it on to our children in the bloodstream. The only way they can inherit the freedom we have known is if we fight for it, protect it, defend it, and then hand it to them with the well-taught lessons of how they in their

lifetime must do the same. And if you and I don't do this, then you and I may well spend our sunset years telling our children and our children's children what it was once like in America where men were free.[51]

Let us heed President Reagan's immeasurably wise words. We must renew our commitment to freedom of speech, and fight against the left's idea pathogens that seek to reduce us to irrationality and ideological conformity.

CHAPTER FOUR

Anti-Science, Anti-Reason, and Illiberal Movements

"Those who can make you believe absurdities can make you commit atrocities."
—*Voltaire*

The idea pathogens on university campuses fall into several large categories. *Postmodernism* posits that all knowledge is relative (no objective truths) while generating obscure and impenetrable prose that is tantamount to random gibberish. This anti-science buffoonery generates positions such as the "Science Must Fall" movement that demands that people "decolonize" their minds from "racist" Western science. *Social constructivism* proposes that the great majority of human behaviors, desires, and preferences are formed not by human nature or our biological heritage but by society, which means, among other things, that there are no biologically determined sex differences, but only culturally imposed "gender roles." *Radical feminism* asserts that these gender roles are due to the nebulous and nefarious forces of the patriarchy. *Transgender activism* purports that biological sex and "gender" are non-binary fluid constructs. Scientifically speaking, postmodernism, social constructivism, radical feminism, and transgender activism are all based on demonstrable falsehoods. But when one's ideological commitments are paramount, the rejection of scientific facts becomes the necessary collateral damage.

Freedom from Reality

Many idea pathogens share one common thread, a deep desire to liberate people from the shackles of reality. Take for example, the blank slate premise of the human mind.[1] It posits that humans are born void of any evolved biological blueprints and innate individual differences. Our eventual life trajectories are thought to be fully shaped by the distinct environments to which we've been exposed. This is a hopeful but delusional belief. John Watson, one of the founders of behaviorism, famously stated:

> Give me a dozen healthy infants, well-formed, and my own specified world to bring them up in, and I'll guarantee to take any one at random and train him to become any type of specialist I might select—doctor, lawyer, artist, merchant-chief and, yes, even beggar-man and thief, regardless of his talents, penchants, tendencies, abilities, vocations, and race of his ancestors. I am going beyond my facts and I admit it, but so have the advocates of the contrary and they have been doing it for many thousands of years.[2]

This is a truly extraordinary statement. It falsely posits that your parents (or Dr. John Watson) could have nurtured you into becoming the next NBA superstar. Move aside Michael Jordan, there is a new kid in town, and he is a chubby and clumsy 5'4" teenager named Mordechai Goldberg who has been expertly trained by John Watson. Watson rejected the notion of heredity and innate talent:

> Our conclusion, then, is that we have no real evidence of the inheritance of traits.[3]

> Everything we have been in the habit of calling "instinct" today is a result largely of training—belongs to man's *learned* behavior. As a corollary from this I wish to draw the conclusion that

> there is no such thing as an inheritance of *capacity*, *talent*,
> *temperament*, *mental constitution*, and *characteristics*. These
> things again depend on training that goes on mainly in the
> cradle.[4] [Italics in original.]

Dear parents, please rest assured that your children might become the next Lionel Messi (arguably the greatest soccer player of all time) or the next Albert Einstein, as long as you provide them with the right environments. It's a truly hopeful message rooted in a rejection of biological science (and common sense).

Similarly, radical feminists refuse to concede that men and women might possess evolutionarily-based distinct abilities, interests, and talents. While the average three-year-old is aware of these self-evident truths and can tell the difference between an NFL linebacker and the diminutive pop star Ariana Grande, social constructivists reject the "patriarchal" notion that men and women are different. But perhaps the greatest tool for liberating oneself from the shackles of reality is the *trans* prefix, which magically makes your biological sex or race (as per Rachel Dolezal, a white woman who self-identifies as black) whatever you want it to be. Do not misunderstand me. There are people, fortunately very few, who truly suffer from gender dysphoria. But their existence should not lead us to reject the biological facts that irrevocably shape who we are. To elevate one's "self-identity" above reality is hardly liberating. It is a rejection of truth. It is perhaps not surprising then that postmodernism is so rampant amongst radical feminists, social constructivists, and trans activists. It is the ultimate epistemological liberator: it frees us from objective truth by celebrating "*my* truth."

Men Get Pregnant and Women Have Penises

In 2002, I had a Kafkaesque chat that served as a prophetic warning sign of the lunacy that would eventually fully engulf not just university campuses but our legislative chambers as well. One of my doctoral students had recently defended his dissertation, so we set up a celebratory dinner to mark the moment. Four people attended the infamous dinner: my wife and I along with my doctoral student and his date.[5] My student had warned me that his date was a graduate student committed to postmodernism, radical feminism, and cultural anthropology, the perfect tsunami of anti-science "thinking." When in mixed company, the norm is to avoid a discussion of politics and religion, and this person's beliefs were akin to a political ideology or a quasi-religious cult, so I reluctantly agreed to be on my best behavior. Surely my student knew me well enough to know that this was a tenuous promise at best. In the immortal words of Bette Davis in the classic film *All About Eve*, "Fasten your seat belts, it's going to be a bumpy night."

Postmodernism proclaims that there are no objective truths. Evolutionary psychologists like myself recognize that human universals exist precisely because they constitute elements of a shared biological heritage. Inevitably, my student's companion and I ended up in a debate. She scoffed at my first principles, and I scoffed at hers, so I laid out a challenge to my interlocutor: I would offer what I considered to be a human universal, and she would tell me why I was wrong. I began with what I was sure was an incontestable example: when it comes to *Homo sapiens*, only women bear children. She rolled her eyes at my gargantuan "stupidity" and told me of a Japanese tribe where men somehow "spiritually" bear children. She scolded me for focusing on the material and biological realm because this was what kept women barefoot, pregnant, and in the kitchen. Apparently, my first example was too toxic and triggering, so I made a second less "controversial" attempt. I proposed to her that sailors have always relied on the fact that the sun rises in the East and sets in the West, and this was an objective universal truth. How do you think she "dismantled" my second example? She went into her toolbox of postmodernist bullshit and deployed a deconstructionist retort: she questioned my use of the "arbitrary labels" *East*, *West*, and *sun*. She then added that what I refer to as the sun, she might call *dancing hyena* (I'm not kidding). Our conversation soon sputtered out. Over the next dozen years, conversations like this started to stack up, especially regarding "gender." (For example, subsequent to a lecture that I delivered at Wellesley College in 2014, one student suggested to me that professors should poll students at the start of class regarding their gender identities.) If language creates reality, as postulated by deconstructionists, then to misgender someone becomes an affront to that person's "reality."

In late September 2016, Jordan Peterson, a professor of psychology at the University of Toronto, produced a YouTube video wherein he criticized legislation in Canada (Bill C-16) that added gender identity and gender expression as protected categories under the rubric of hate crime laws. Peterson defiantly stated that he would not let the government dictate his speech when it came to "gender" pronouns. Needless to say, the progressive academic mob demanded that he be fired from his tenured position. After he reached out to me, I invited him on my YouTube show *THE SAAD TRUTH* to discuss the matter.[6] In May 2017, Peterson and I both testified in front of the Canadian senate regarding Bill C-16. In my testimony, I cited the Office of BGLTQ Student Life at Harvard University, which argued: 1) that an individual's gender identity and gender expression were subject to daily changes (Monday I'm male, Tuesday I'm female, Wednesday I'm non-binary, Thursday I'm gender-neutral, and so on.), and 2) that the promulgation of "fixed binaries" (the idea of male and female) and "biological essentialism" (acknowledging evolved biological realities) was "transphobic misinformation" that amounted to "systemic violence."

In my testimony, I argued that my areas of teaching and research expertise, namely the application of evolutionary psychology to the behavioral sciences could easily be construed as violating Bill C-16. Some of the "progressive" senators scoffed and laughed at such a possibility, while another accused me of being pro-genocide.[7] Hence, in the twenty-first century, a chaired professor who is an evolutionary behavioral scientist has to testify in front of the Canadian senate that humans are a sexually reproducing and sexually dimorphic species composed of males and females. Lest the reader think that this is a uniquely Canadian form of lunacy, at Rocklin Academy in California, a first-grader was investigated and sent to the principal's office for innocently misgendering a classmate.[8] California lawmakers are considering passing a law that would criminalize the "knowing and repeated" misgendering of individuals who are receiving long-term care services. A similar law already exists in New York City and is not restricted to health care settings. I can assure you that the trash talking that took place on the pitch during my competitive soccer career would have resulted in 90 percent of the players being sent to San Quentin for "hurtful language crimes." Of note, my explicit warning to the Canadian senators regarding the proverbial slippery slope has been vindicated, as we have moved from compelled speech (person A should not misgender person B) to the imposition of having to state one's own preferred gender pronouns in email signatures and on name tags.

Do not think for a moment that this tsunami of lunacy has spent itself. If anything, it is gathering force. It is now being argued that men can menstruate (J. K. Rowling, the author and progressive icon, recently fell afoul of the Cancel Culture Brigade for questioning this "fact"), and this "truth" is being taught to children as part of their sex education.[9] In the first Democratic debate for the party's 2020 presidential nomination, Julian Castro stated that biological males who are now transgender women should be guaranteed abortion rights. In a subsequent tweet, Castro issued a correction: "Last night I misspoke—it's trans men, trans masculine, and non-binary folks who need full access to abortion and repro healthcare. And I'm grateful to ALL trans and non-binary folks for their labor in guiding me on this issue."[10] Delusional departures from reality can indeed be confusing. In any case, I tweeted: "Dear @JulianCastro, I'm a trans woman looking to conduct a cervical exam. Do you know of a good gynecologist that you might be willing to recommend?"[11] My satire proved prophetic after the Canadian Cancer Society released an ad campaign with the photo of a trans woman (biological male) to represent a demographic group at risk for cervical cancer.[12] Finally, Senator Elizabeth Warren proclaimed, during her attempt to win the Democratic

Party nomination for president, that if she were elected president, her nominee for secretary of education would have to be cleared by a nine-year-old transgender child.[13] To indulge such fantasies is not harmless; it is a war against reason itself.

Postmodernism: Intellectual Terrorism Masquerading as Faux-Profundity

Sometimes people overestimate their understanding of complicated phenomena, which is what some scholars call the illusion of explanatory depth.[14] A good example is how people will give greater authority to a scientific explanation that includes pictures of multicolored neuronal brain imaging patterns, even when these patterns offer little explanatory power.[15] Postmodernism thrives in academic circles for similar reasons. Postmodernist bullshitters like Jacques Derrida, Jacques Lacan, and Michel Foucault succeeded in academia with their charlatanism because of the assumption that if something is nearly impossible to understand, it must be profound (note that there are individual differences in the extent to which people are swayed by bullshit.[16]) In a conversation with the American philosopher John Searle, Foucault confessed to this faux-profundity: "In France, you gotta have ten percent incomprehensible, otherwise people won't think it's deep—they won't think you're a profound thinker." That admission notwithstanding, Foucault thought that Derrida pushed this strategy too far by engaging in *obscurantisme terroriste*.[17] I, too, independently, have referred to postmodernism as intellectual terrorism. Beware of those trying to impress you with confusing word salads.

The art world is particularly susceptible to postmodernist gibberish because it is a domain where objective metrics of excellence are difficult to establish. Once you use the magic wand of subjectivity, you are able to find the supposed beauty of *invisible art*. Back in 1996, I visited the Carnegie Museum in Pittsburgh. As I strolled through the exhibits, I came across a blank canvas displayed as "art." Notwithstanding the fact that I understood the postmodern twist to this "art work," I asked a museum representative to justify the existence of a blank "painting." She explained that our discussion of the piece was testimony to its value.

London's Hayward Gallery hosted an exhibition in 2012 titled *Invisible: Art about the Unseen 1957–2012*, which featured—well, you guessed it—invisible art![18] Ralph Rugoff, the director of the Hayward Gallery reiterated the importance of using one's imagination when viewing invisible pieces. With that in mind, perhaps I'll try to write an invisible manuscript for my next book project. I'll provide a front and back cover with 300 empty pages. I'll leave it to the reader's rich imagination to fill in the contents. (Actually, a clever American podcaster and commentator named Michael J. Knowles beat me to it with a book titled *Reasons to Vote for Democrats*.)

The Grievance Studies Project

In 1996, Alan Sokal, a physics professor at New York University, published a gibberish article titled "Transgressing the Boundaries: Toward a Transformative Hermeneutics of Quantum Gravity" in *Social Text*, a leading academic journal of postmodernism.[19] The paper was a hoax meant to demonstrate how obscurantist gibberish prose could be published as long as it seemed to be supportive of postmodernist "thinking." The editors of the journal were undoubtedly keen to publish a postmodern analysis of gravity authored by a physicist. This would grant a scientific imprimatur to their edifices of nonsense. If you thought that the parody had a devastating effect on the discipline, you'd be wrong. Since postmodernism purports that reality is subjective, one person's parody is another's gold mine of meaning. With this epistemological sleight of hand, postmodernists are able to extract meaning from the most meaningless of texts. Voilà, postmodernism is akin to the Hydra in Greek mythology. Cut off one of its heads, and several new ones will grow. On a personal note, I contacted Sokal in 2010 to alert him about an article that I had published in my *Psychology Today* column referencing his brilliant hoax.[20] He politely pointed out that my characterization of his prose as "containing pseudo–randomly generated passages" was incorrect. He had assiduously toiled over the choice of every word of his hoax article. There was indeed a method to the madness!

In 2017, James Lindsay and Peter Boghossian (who happens to be a good friend of mine) published a hoax paper (using pseudonyms) wherein they argued that the human penis was a conceptual construct that was a driving force behind climate change. I challenge the readers to go through the paper in question without bursting into uncontrollable laughter. I tried to do so on camera but failed.[21] Once the hoax was publicized, an associate editorial director put out a statement that explained: "Two reviewers agreed to review the paper and it was accepted with no changes by one reviewer, and with minor amends by the other. On investigation, although the two reviewers had relevant research interests, their expertise did not fully align with this subject matter and we do not believe that they were the right choice to review this paper."[22] Apparently, had the proper experts been used to review an utterly non-sensical paper that linked human penises to climate change, the outcome might have been different. I am unaware of any experts in phallic-based climatology but perhaps I did not look hard enough.

Detractors of the penis–climate change hoax paper argued that this was hardly convincing given that the journal that accepted the paper (*Cogent Social Sciences*) was a pay-to-publish predatory outlet possessing little if any academic prestige. Fair enough. But the perpetrators of the hoax had a nuclear option as a rebuttal. They joined forces with Helen Pluckrose (an editor with Areo Magazine) and proceeded to pull off arguably the grandest of Sokal-type projects. They wrote twenty non-sensical papers and submitted them to various leading academic journals to gauge what would happen. In Table 1 below, I list the titles of papers that were accepted before the trio decided to pull the plug on the project and come clean (as they were about to be found out). The articles were a hysterically funny mish-mash of gibberish, but leading journals of feminist philosophy, gender studies, and associated nonsense thought these worthy of publication. I tried to cover this brilliant grand ruse on my channel while keeping a straight face.[23] I failed. To give the reader a sense of how nonsensical these papers were, the first listed paper in Table 1 examines rape culture in dog parks via the use of black feminist criminology while the third one involves a rewriting of Adolf Hitler's *Mein Kampf* using feminist buzzwords. It is difficult to overestimate the extent of the nonsensical lunacy. Peter Boghossian, the only one of the three collaborators working at a university, was investigated by his institution for "ethical breaches."[24] Rather than lauding his intellectual courage for serving as a whistleblower to fraudulent disciplines, his university was looking for ways to punish him.

Life is about navigating a maze of opportunity costs. If you are going to spend years studying in university, spending your parents' hard-earned money on exorbitant tuition fees, perhaps you should refrain from studying critical race theory, intersectional feminism, queer theory, and postmodernism. Avoid topics that are firmly rooted in a desire to liberate students from the shackles of reality.

TABLE 1

The Seven Accepted Grievance Studies Papers	
Titles of Papers	**Journals**
Human Reactions to Rape Culture and Queer Performativity in Urban Dog Parks in Portland, Oregon	*Gender, Place, and Culture*
Going in Through the Back Door: Challenging Straight Male Homohysteria and Transphobia through Receptive Penetrative Sex Toy Use	*Sexuality & Culture*
Our Struggle Is My Struggle: Solidarity Feminism as an Intersectional Reply to Neoliberal and Choice Feminism	*Affilia: Journal of Women and Social Work*

Who Are They to Judge?: Overcoming Anthropometry and a Framework for Fat Bodybuilding	*Fat Studies*
When the Joke Is on You: A Feminist Perspective on How Positionality Influences Satire	*Hypatia*
An Ethnography of Breastaurant Masculinity: Themes of Objectification, Sexual Conquest, Male Control, and Masculine Toughness in a Sexually Objectifying Restaurant	*Sex Roles*
Moon Meetings and the Meaning of Sisterhood: A Poetic Portrayal of Lived Feminist Spirituality	*The Journal of Poetry Therapy*

Trans Activism—The Tyranny of the Minority

Rachel McKinnon, a biological male who self-identifies as a woman, won the 2018 UCI Masters Track Cycling World Championships (35–44 age category).[25] Subsequent to *her* victory, I invited Dr. McKinnon via Twitter to appear on my show: "Dear Dr. @rachelvmckinnon: I appreciate your desire to fight for fairness when it comes to transgender rights. Do you think though that the biological women who lost against you have a right to feel aggrieved when a biological male beats them in a women's competition? Or do you think that the behavioral, anatomical, physiological, morphological, and hormonal advantages that men possess over women in such competitions are mere social constructions imposed by the transphobic patriarchy? I'd be happy to chat with you on my show THE SAAD TRUTH."[26] Care to guess what the response was? Did Dr. McKinnon take the opportunity to use my large platform to defend her positions? After all, as a professor of philosophy she should have jumped at the opportunity to debate me on the matter. Instead she blocked me and started name-calling everyone who questioned her victory. Apparently, Dr. McKinnon could not contemplate how outlandishly unfair her victory was to the actual women who lost to a biological male. This is precisely what I referred to as the *tyranny of the minority* in my Canadian Senate address in 2017. The victimology narrative means that transgender rights supersede women's rights.

As a response to McKinnon's "heroic" victory, I released a clip on my YouTube channel satirizing this sheer insanity.[27] Using the concepts of TransAgeism and TransGravity (I made these up, but they are "my truth," so you cannot critique me), I announced that I would be entering a Judo contest in the U8 category since I self-identify as a child who is under eight years old. Then, using the logic from the Office of BGLTQ Student Life at Harvard University that one's gender identity is subject to daily fluctuations, I declared that I would also be entering the octogenarian Judo competition as my age self-identity changes on a daily basis. Finally, since biological sex, gender, race, and age are mere social constructs, I argued that one's weight is also a social construct subject to the liberating powers of the "trans" prefix. Hence, while I might technically be over 200 pounds, I self-identify as being less than 120 pounds, but particularly so on the days that I self-identify as an octogenarian, and as such I'd be competing against skinny elderly people. As has happened on numerous occasions, my satire proved to be prophetic when less than three weeks later the news broke that Emile Ratelband, a sixty-nine-year-old Dutchman, was seeking to legally change his age to forty-nine (as this would grant him greater advantages on the labor and mating markets, among other things).[28] As I have often remarked on social media, my sarcasm and satire are sharper than a surgeon's scalpel in slicing through entrenched deposits of nonsensical bullshit. However, it is often missed even by otherwise sophisticated individuals. During a recent medical checkup, my physician pulled up a few of my tweets where I lamented my status as a "differently-weighted" individual.

He was apparently concerned about my mental and emotional stability, as he had utterly missed the sarcasm. Here is one of the tweets: "What gives the right of my physician to use antiquated notions of weight to determine that I need to lose weight. Real scientists now know that a given weight scale reading is not fixed but rather fluid. Plus what about those who wish to be weightless? Don't they have rights?"[29]

The gods of victimhood recently offered a test case of competitive intersectionality. In Windsor, Ontario, a trans woman filed a human rights complaint against a spa that refused to provide "her" with waxing services.[30] The wax artist, a Muslim woman, was understandably reticent to wax a biological male. It was a fascinating case of Victimology Poker. Who holds the highest hand, the Muslim woman or the trans woman? Only expert judges in Oppression Olympics could adjudicate such a case. Another trans woman has filed fifteen complaints in British Columbia against spas that refused to perform a Brazilian wax on "her."[31] An even more galling case pitted the Vancouver Rape Relief and Women's Shelter against trans activists. Municipal funding to the shelter was halted because of its refusal to admit trans women.[32] Since 1973, the shelter has granted support to 46,000 women but apparently the wellbeing of innumerable female victims seeking to escape horrifying situations is secondary to granting "inclusion rights" to trans women (who constitute an astonishingly small percentage of the Canadian population). All Canadians are equal, but some are more equal than others.

Cyd Zeigler is an LGBTQ activist and founder of the National Gay Flag Football League. In February 2019, he appeared on Fox News and said there was no scientific evidence that trans athletes might possess any competitive advantages. I asked him the following question in a tweet: "Dear @CydZeigler: I'm currently watching you on @foxnews. Do you not think that transwomen (biological males) exhibit physiological, anatomical, morphological, and hormonal differences as compared to biological females? As an evolutionary behavioral scientist who has researched evolutionary-based sex differences, I was under the impression that sex differences exist. Perhaps you'd like to come on my show and

educate me?"[33] While he did accept my invitation, things quickly deterio-
rated. I wanted to gauge whether a conversation would be productive,
and to do so, I sought to establish whether Zeigler was connected to
reality let alone to banal scientific truths, or whether he was merely a
dogged activist. I privately asked him his thoughts on a tweet that
PinkNews had posted that day: "Transwomen are women. So transwomen's bodies are women's bodies. So transwomen's penises are wom-
en's penises."[34] Zeigler was unhappy with my question. Shortly thereafter,
I publicly tagged him on Twitter regarding two trans women (biological
males) who had finished first and second in the Connecticut girls high
school track and field competition.[35] This was specifically relating to his
original claim on Fox News that trans athletes did not possess any competitive advantages. This is when his activist colors came into full view.
He accused me of being a transphobic culture warrior masquerading as
a scientist, and accordingly it was beneath him to interact with me. Not
one to take personal insults lightly, I went after him repeatedly on Twitter
and declared him president of Unicornia. Needless to say, he blocked me
on Twitter. Such is the reality of trying to engage people who reject biological realities that are as obvious as the existence of gravity.

Lisa Littman is a physician and an assistant professor of the practice
of behavioral and social sciences at Brown University. In 2018, she published a paper in *PLOS ONE* wherein she argued that rapid-onset gender
dysphoria spreads in social networks as a form of contagion fueled in
part by peer pressure.[36] Brown University had originally issued a news
release describing the study's conclusions but then, when faced with an
outcry from transgender activists who thought that the article's conclusions were offensive, expunged the story from its website.[37] As an act of
solidarity toward an embattled colleague, I reached out to Littman and
invited her on my show. She was reluctant to accept my invitation as she
was undoubtedly concerned about possible institutional repercussions
that might befall her. This was yet again a case where faux-outrage
trumps academic freedom. If people scream "I'm offended" loudly
enough, they drive the academic discourse.

I recently engaged the Oscar-winning actress Charlize Theron on Twitter. In my view, Theron and many other parents of newly trans children are exhibiting a classic manifestation of Munchausen syndrome by proxy (via contagion). They can reap the "woke" progressive rewards of being a parent of a trans child. Theron has proclaimed that one of her two adopted children (a biological boy) is transgendered, having advised her at the age of three that he is a girl.[38] Accordingly, Theron is raising the child as a girl since apparently it is not up to her (or to biological science) to decide the gender identity of her child. Some of my relevant tweets included: "So brave, so stunning, so progressive. Well done @CharlizeAfrica. I raised my children as non-arboreal multicellular carbon-based agents. I did not impose a species on them. It's for them to decide whether they wish to be part of Homo sapiens or not." I continued with: "I'm following the lead of the parental heroism of @CharlizeAfrica. I've advised my non-arboreal multicellular carbon-based agents (children) that they do not need to call my wife and I 'mom' and 'dad' respectively. We are gender-neutral non-binary caregivers 1 and 2." And I finished off with the introduction of a new concept, periodic table fluidity: "I don't want my children to be restricted to viewing themselves as carbon-based. This is why I am now immersing them in the fluidity of the Periodic Table. I've asked them to look at all elements and decide which ones they self-identify with (in terms of their building blocks)."[39] My satire is not meant to denigrate the very real, and very rare, condition of gender dysphoria. However, I do recognize the statistical improbability of the number of parents who are now "coming out" as parents of trans children. Children are meant to be protected and cherished in the privacy of a family. They are not meant to be virtue-signaling social-justice pawns for impressing progressive friends.

Progressivism itself is a cognitively inconsistent and axiomatically irrational belief system. Let us examine how age becomes a fluid marker of one's cognitive abilities as a function of ideological expediency. If an individual commits a premeditated heinous murder at the age of seventeen years and three hundred sixty-four days, the progressives would be the first to proclaim that he should be tried in juvenile court. After all, he is a "child" who cannot fully comprehend the consequences of his actions. He is apparently too impulsive to make sound judgments given that his prefrontal cortex is yet to be fully developed. The brains of adolescents continue to develop well into their twenties, and as such, to punish an adolescent murderer is "cruel" and hardly progressive.[40] On the other hand, when it comes to the age at which individuals should be allowed to vote in national elections, many progressive Democrats, including House Speaker Nancy Pelosi, support the idea of reducing the age to sixteen.[41] When it comes to enlisting in the United States military and being shipped off to foreign lands to kill bad guys, one's prefrontal cortex apparently becomes sufficiently developed at the age of seventeen. However, according to many progressive parents including Charlize Theron, a three-year-old has the necessary cognitive and emotional maturity to make a definitive pronouncement about gender identity. Jean Piaget, a historic figure in developmental psychology, is undoubtedly rolling in his grave. Unlike Piaget, whose pioneering work delineated clear stages of cognitive development that apply across children, progressives are very fluid about how age affects our ability to think, feel, and act—which is why we are forbidden to criticize the arrogantly sanctimonious, if not pathologically hysteric, seventeen-year-old Swedish environmental activist Greta Thunberg, who is trying to save us from our evil ways. In the land of progressive Unicornia, science is only valuable if it is consistent with ideological dogma. Otherwise it is nothing more than bigoted hate facts.

In a recent case in Florida, a biologically female middle-school student who self-identifies as male was allowed entry to the boys' locker room without the male students' or their parents' having a say in the matter. One male teacher refused to monitor the locker room in the presence of the trans individual as he did not feel it appropriate to view a naked young biologically female student.[42] Is the teacher being transphobic? Do the boys have a right to refuse to undress in front of a biological girl or would that be an example of transphobia? Is it not illiberal to trample the rights of everyone in order to accommodate the trans student? This is yet another manifestation of the tyranny of the minority. Celebrate and accommodate my self-identity which conflicts with biological reality, or else risk the wrath of the progressive police, and possibly institutional if not legal repercussions.

The Wacky World of Academic Feminism

Feminism, throughout its history, has ameliorated the lives of innumerable women around the world, but, like any ideology or institution, it seeks to perpetuate itself, and that now requires maintaining a manufactured victimhood narrative. How to achieve this perpetual victimhood nirvana? The Ambivalent Sexism Inventory (ASI) offers the solution. It is a psychometric scale consisting of twenty-two items that measures hostile sexism (eleven items) and benevolent sexism (eleven items). The former refers to such unacceptable forms of sexism as sexual harassment or paying women lesser wages than men for the same job, but it might surprise you to learn that if men idolize women, place them on a pedestal, proclaim that their lives are incomplete without them, and seek to protect them, they are vile *benevolent* sexists! The eleven statements used to measure benevolent sexism are reproduced below.[43] Respondents are asked to rate each statement using a six-point *disagree strongly* to *agree strongly* scale. Items 3, 6, and 13 are reverse-coded to ensure that respondents are paying attention to the task and are accordingly being consistent in their answers.

1. No matter how accomplished he is, a man is not truly complete as a person unless he has the love of a woman
3. In a disaster, women ought not necessarily to be rescued before men*
6. People are often truly happy in life without being romantically involved with a member of the other sex*
8. Many women have a quality of purity that few men possess

9. Women should be cherished and protected by men

12. Every man ought to have a woman whom he adores

13. Men are complete without women*

17. A good woman should be set on a pedestal by her man

19. Women, compared to men, tend to have a superior moral sensibility

20. Men should be willing to sacrifice their own well-being in order to provide financially for the women in their lives

22. Women, as compared to men, tend to have a more refined sense of culture and good taste

Humans are a sexually reproducing species, and one of the most fundamental human drives is to find a mate and form a meaningful union with a member of the opposite sex. But according to the ASI, a man who admits to such a drive is succumbing to benevolent sexism. It does not take a sophisticated evolutionary psychologist to understand the utter lunacy of such a stance.[44] Note also that any man who seeks to protect and cherish women is a vile sexist. It is perhaps not surprising then that a recent study found that people are less likely to perform life-saving CPR on women.[45] Apparently, four decades of feminist brainwashing and witch hunts have taught men too well. It is better to be a "non-sexist" cowardly bystander than a "sexist" hero. Someone should advise women to stop fantasizing about courageous firefighters and heroic uniformed soldiers. There is a new sheriff in town who epitomizes a progressive definition of masculinity: Apathetic Cowardly Bystander Man. Incidentally, there is an extraordinary cognitive inconsistency inherent here. Men are repeatedly lectured about stepping up to serve as allies to women in the workplace, but if they do so, they are engaging in benevolent sexism. All roads lead to sexism.

Of the many dreadful anti-science idea pathogens to spring from the delusional world of gender studies, few are as corrosive as the nonsensical concept of toxic masculinity.[46] Nearly twenty years ago, Christina Hoff Sommers authored an important book on the unrelenting attack on boys.[47] The problem has only worsened since. It is perhaps not a good idea to pathologize half of humanity when dealing with a sexually repro-ducing species. Countless prestigious universities now offer talks, semi-nars, if not full courses on how to unlearn, combat, and overcome toxic masculinity.[48] My alma mater Cornell University hosted a talk on the use of fashion to combat toxic masculinity whereas Lehigh University created a Men's Therapeutic Cuddle Group to combat the scourge of this dreadful "pathology."[49] A professor of education has recently suggested that children as young as kindergarten students should be taught how to combat toxic masculinity.[50] Ideologues are always keen on infecting young children with their idea pathogens, as this is the most opportune time for the brainwashing process to begin. Radical feminism is indeed a spreading virus.[51]

What is toxic masculinity? Well, it is apparently the undesirable ele-ments of being male. This might include being hyper-competitive in sports, exhibiting social or physical dominance, or refraining from being too emotional in public. Toxic masculinity is ascribed as the culprit of innumerable social ills including violence, war, and sexual assault. If only we could detoxify men to retain the good components of their masculin-ity—as the Gillette company recently implored all toxic men to do via a breathtakingly condescending and insulting ad—then the world would be a better place. It is important to note, though, that toxic masculinity is not restricted to the stereotypically brawny hyper-masculine types. One should also be wary of toxic geek masculinity as exemplified by the male characters on the television show *The Big Bang Theory*.[52] Note that both hyper-masculine Navy SEALs and beta geeks who belong to the Logarithms Are Cool Club are manifestations of toxic masculinity. All roads lead to toxic masculinity including your preferred diet. Veganism promotes white masculinity, but meat-eating is an instantiation of poten-tially toxic, hegemonic masculinity.[53] To be on the safe side, I recommend that men restrict their diets to eating eggs and cheese. The only prospec-tive problem though is that most eggshells and cheeses are white so this diet might be a subtle manifestation of internalized white supremacy. I truly see only one solution here: men must engage in collective fasting until death visits them, which would directly help reduce toxic masculinity. Dear men, if you truly wish to serve as allies to women, collective suicide or perhaps collective castration should be seriously considered.

Many academic feminists are unhappy with the delineation of toxic masculinity from masculinity in general. Their position, a rather common one in women's studies programs, is that masculinity is inherently "problematic." No need for the toxic qualifier. Lisa Wade, a feminist and sociology professor at Occidental College, explained:

> Trump's masculinity is what we call a toxic masculinity. In the pre-Trump era, the modifier was used to differentiate bad masculine ideals from good ones. Toxic masculinities, some claimed, were behind sexual assault, mass shootings, and the weird thing where men refuse to wear sunscreen, but they didn't reflect masculinity *generally*, so one had to leave that idea alone. But we can only give masculinity so many modifiers for so long before we have to confront the possibility that it is masculinity itself that has become the problem.[54] [Italics in original.]

Since being male is inherently bad, it is perhaps not surprising that Suzanna Danuta Walters, a professor of sociology, director of the Women's, Gender, and Sexuality Studies Program at Northeastern University, and editor of the gender studies journal *Signs* penned an article in the *Washington Post* titled "Why Can't We Hate Men?" It concluded:

> So men, if you really are #WithUs and would like us to not hate you for all the millennia of woe you have produced and benefited from, start with this: Lean out so we can actually just stand up without being beaten down. Pledge to vote for feminist women only. Don't run for office. Don't be in charge of anything. Step away from the power. We got this. And

please know that your crocodile tears won't be wiped away by us anymore. We have every right to hate you. You have done us wrong. #BecausePatriarchy. It is long past time to play hard for Team Feminism. And win.[55]

In 1998, Hillary Clinton said at a conference on domestic violence in El Salvador that "Women have always been the primary victims of war. Women lose their husbands, their fathers, their sons in combat."[56] One might think that since, historically, men are the ones who have died in the millions, often for such noble causes as defending their countries, their homes, and their families, that they might be the *primary* victims of war, but no, women are always the victims. Gender studies programs are founded on the "I am a victim therefore I am" ethos. All roads lead to victimhood. As many feminist academics and female politicians have proclaimed, the future is female indeed.

In case you thought that academic feminism is restricted to the delusional and conspiratorial world of gender studies, let me disabuse you of that notion. Science itself can apparently be illuminated by the unique lens of feminist epistemology. Fields that you might have thought were immune from this nonsense have all been slowly infected with this idea pathogen. We now have feminist architecture, feminist biology, feminist physics, feminist chemistry, feminist geography, feminist mathematics, and feminist glaciology.[57] This next sentence comes from the abstract of the paper on feminist glaciology: "Merging feminist postcolonial science studies and feminist political ecology, the feminist glaciology framework generates robust analysis of gender, power, and epistemologies in dynamic social-ecological systems, thereby leading to more just and equitable science and human–ice interactions." Who knew that ice could be so sexist and patriarchal?

Nearly 125 years ago, the feminist Charlotte Perkins Gilman infamously proclaimed, "There is no female mind. The brain is not an organ of sex. As well speak of a female liver."[58] One would have thought that the thousands of scientific studies documenting the biological, anatomical, physiological, morphological, hormonal, cognitive, emotional, and behavioral differences between the two sexes might have put a dent in those obstinate refusals to accept the existence of biologically-based sex differences. To use an old aphorism, the more things change, the more they remain the same. The latest instantiation of this lunacy is packaged as *neurosexism*. It is apparently sexist to demonstrate that men and women exhibit neuroanatomical differences. Instead, flat-earthers of the human mind and other deniers of reality point to some neuroscientific studies that have yielded similarities across the two sexes on some brain metric such as the thickness of a specific cortical area, and voilà, male and female brains become indistinguishable.[59] This is logically equivalent to arguing that since men and women each have ten fingers, ten toes, two eyes, and two kidneys, they are indistinguishable beings. Along the same lines, since the Great Dane (largest dog breed) and the Chihuahua (smallest dog breed) both have two eyes, one tail, four legs, and two ears, they are indistinguishable. I recently announced on my YouTube channel that my family would be adopting a giraffe since we are unable to distinguish it from a dog (as both have a tail, two eyes, and teeth among many other morphological similarities, they must be the same species).[60] The reality is that there are innumerable neuroanatomical sex differences that have been documented in the literature.[61] That said, even when a specific anatomical trait is the same across the two sexes, this does not imply that its functionality is the same because brain structures interact with hormones in sex-specific ways. What is particularly galling is that neurosexism was positively covered in *Nature*, one of the most prestigious scientific journals.[62] No platform is safe from idea pathogens especially when they are being propagated by individuals willing to sacrifice truth in the service of their pet ideologies.

Radical feminists are staunch supporters of the Diversity, Inclusion, and Equity cult when it suits them, but they are silent on the bewildering lack of gender parity in women's studies departments.[63] I suppose that one would not want to damage the "important" scholarly work conducted in such departments with an infusion of toxic masculinity. Radical feminists do not complain that men constitute the overwhelming majority when it comes to occupational deaths. Nor do they bat an eye at the fact that men are much more likely to commit suicide, be the victim of a murder, be incarcerated, be homeless, and have a much lower life expectancy. These global realities are undoubtedly due to their toxic masculinity. But the radical feminists are very keen to promulgate the illusory gender gap in salaries even though this canard has been refuted on innumerable occasions.[64] The Women's World Cup in soccer recently took place in France. The U.S. women's national team, who won the tournament, trashed lowly Thailand 13–0 in the group stage. The success of the team triggered the ire of a broad range of social justice warriors, all of whom demanded equal pay for female soccer players. Senator Kirsten Gillibrand remarked that since thirteen goals was a record in a World Cup game, women should be paid as much as men.[65] Vox pointed out that the women's team had scored more goals in one game than the U.S. men's team had scored in all of its World Cup games since 2006.[66] And finally, the United Nations pointed to the fact that one male player (Lionel Messi) makes nearly double the income of all female players in the top seven women's leagues.[67] It is truly difficult to imagine that people could offer such unimaginably fallacious "arguments." Leading women's national teams (including the United States team) have played matches against local boys club teams (with boys fifteen years old or younger) and were clobbered.[68] It's the differential talent between the two sexes that drives viewership of the matches. It's called Economics 101. That the U.S. women's team scored thirteen goals in a game is as relevant to the gender pay gap issue as the fact that some youth league team in Denver just defeated another team 15 to 0. Lionel Messi is arguably the greatest soccer player in history. He is probably the most famous person in the world. Most people cannot name five female players, let alone know that seven women's soccer leagues exist. This is not due to the patriarchy but a mere recognition of the fact that economic realities drive many instantiations of the salary gap. It is the same reason that Lady Gaga makes unimaginably more money than I do. Her grotesquely larger salary is not due to endemic anti-Semitism against war refugees (me) but a reflection of how market forces work. Perhaps we could get Alexandria Ocasio-Cortez to use her economics degree to explain this point to Gillibrand.

Given that they are so wrong, how do the ideologues defend their idea pathogens? Under totalitarian regimes, the solution is direct. You criminalize if not violently suppress (or kill) any dissenting voices. In the West, the ideological indoctrination is subtler. It is achieved by an ethos of *political correctness* and best enforced by creating university campuses that lack *intellectual diversity*. Political correctness is like the sting of the spider wasp. Recall that the afflicted spider is dragged to the wasp's burrow in a zombie-like state and is subsequently eaten in vivo by the wasp's offspring. Political correctness achieves the same macabre objective—it allows nefarious ideas to slowly consume us while we sit quietly in a zombie-like state, too afraid to speak out. Political correctness echoes the words that Mohamed Atta, the leader of the 9/11 plot, gave to the doomed passengers of the plane he hijacked: "Nobody move. Everything will be OK. If you try to make any moves, you'll endanger yourself and the airplane. Just stay quiet.... Nobody move, please. We are going back to the airport. Don't try to make any stupid moves."[69] Similarly, intellectual terrorists instruct generations of gullible students to remain quiet in their classroom seats while they inculcate them with anti-science nonsense. Please refrain from asking questions. Please do not engage your faculties of critical thinking. Intellectual resistance is futile. Memorize the content of my indoctrination and be quiet. Universities serve as the training ground of the politically correct thought police and their social justice warriors.

CHAPTER FIVE

Campus Lunacy: The Rise of the Social Justice Warrior

"I'm a liberal professor and my liberal students terrify me. I have intentionally adjusted my teaching as the political winds have shifted.... Hurting a student's feelings, even in the course of instruction that is absolutely appropriate and respectful, can now get a teacher into serious trouble."
—*Edward Schlosser*[1]

"The tyranny of the minority is infinitely more odious and intolerable and more to be feared than that of the majority."[2]
—*President William McKinley*

Student-activist social justice warriors (SJWs) might be outnumbered on campuses, yet they rule via the tyranny of the minority, backed by "progressive" professors and campus administrators. Together, they enforce a stifling climate of political correctness that we associate with things like "trigger warnings," "safe spaces," "microaggressions," and campus speech codes, all of which empower the perpetually indignant and outraged.[3] To progressives, feelings trump truth; empirical statements are no longer judged by their veracity but by whether they are potentially "bigoted"—in which case they must be suppressed in the name of inclusiveness. Given that feelings are the engine by which one's existence is validated, a *culture of offence* has taken shape where it pays to be a member of the perpetually aggrieved. This creates the competitive urge to be positioned advantageously in a *victimhood hierarchy*. The Oppression Olympics (also known as Victimology Poker) is the arena wherein this competition of victimhood takes place, using identity politics and intersectionality ("I am a Queer Fat Muslim Disabled Transgendered Black Feminist") to establish the "winners" of this grotesque theatre of the absurd. I propose that SJWs exhibit a form of Collective Munchausen Syndrome (a psychiatric disorder where an individual feigns a medical condition to garner sympathy). Ultimately, the ethos is *I am a victim therefore I am*. This fetishizing of victimhood was alluded to long ago by the eminent British philosopher Bertrand Russell in his essay aptly titled "The Superior Virtue of the Oppressed."[4]

Even if you hold a strong hand in Victimology Poker, do not presume that the progressive mob of SJWs won't come after you. The bestselling author Ayaan Hirsi Ali is a Somali woman born into the Islamic faith who faced personal hardships at the hands of a deeply patriarchal and misogynist society. The political host Dave Rubin is a gay Jew who used to be a proud member of the left. The journalist Andy Ngo is a gay Asian man. Once they violated central tenets of progressivism (criticizing Islam or the radical left), they lost their protective identity shields. They became fair game to the tornado of progressive rage. Ngo was violently attacked by Antifa agitators, leading to his hospitalization. This was apparently acceptable to many progressives because Ngo held "incorrect" views.[5] Many liberal professors have had to learn this lesson the hard way, including Laura Kipnis (Northwestern University), Rebecca Tuvel (Rhodes College), Bret Weinstein (Evergreen State College), and Michael Rectenwald (New York University). They had the gall to raise, respectively, questions about rape culture on campus, transgenderism, race-based leftist activism on campus, and the radical left on campus. This triggered the ire of the progressive priesthood. When there are no longer scary MAGA hat–wearing Trump supporters to tar and feather on campus, the progressive mob will turn against its less pure members. The radical snake always ends up eating its tail. ISIS kills all Muslims who are not Muslim enough. Progressives denounce all those who are not progressive enough.

Safe Spaces and Echo Chambers Are Maladaptive

SJWs push the victim narrative by saying that opposing viewpoints constitute a form of "violence" from which they need protection, which is why they believe it is perfectly acceptable to force university administrators to disinvite speakers with whom they disagree. With the combination of SJW student activists and the lopsided political leanings of the professoriate, one has the perfect recipe for the creation of the sterile ideological echo chambers that universities have become. Neuropsychiatrist Steve Stankevicius has pointed out the dangers inherent in the intellectual sterility of academia by comparing it to the dangers children face if they grow up in allergen-poor (sterile) environments.[6] Such children are more likely to develop respiratory ailments because the human body requires exposure to allergens in order to jump-start its immunological defenses. An analogical process is taking place among the current generation of university students as they receive their education within intellectually sterile settings. They do not develop the critical thinking skills, let alone the emotional maturity, to navigate through disagreements.

Evolution has endowed us with mechanisms of behavioral adaptation. Evolutionary scientists, for example, explain that people in warmer climates tend to have spicier cuisines, because spices offer antimicrobial protection against foodborne pathogens, which are more likely to be present in warmer climates.[7] This demonstrates how cultural forms (national cuisine) serve as adaptive responses to biological challenges (exposure to microbes). Behavioral ecologists examine such cross-cultural differences as adaptive responses to local contingencies. The capacity to be adaptable, though, does not solely take place at the cultural level. It also occurs within an individual's body. Take our immune system, for example. It has evolved to be adaptable precisely because it needs to combat rapidly mutating pathogens. If our immunological defenses had been selected to solely destroy a fixed set of pathogens, humans would have all died out a long time ago. Instead, the immune system is extraordinarily flexible in its capacity to find "on the fly" solutions when defending against mutated versions of different pathogens. Similarly, our behavioral immune system consists of adaptive responses to distinct conditions.[8] For example, an increase in the extent to which one's immune system has been compromised by illness over a given time period, the more likely one is to prefer spicy foods.[9] Hence, evolution has endowed us with adaptability within an individual (immune system), across individuals (behavioral immune system), and across cultures (antimicrobial use of spices). Our bodies and minds expect exposure to novel and unfolding situations, but when it comes to our critical thinking faculties, we are shutting them down. So many university graduates today are unable to debate because they have never been exposed to opposing viewpoints, and they consider opposing viewpoints simply as heresies to be met with protest and hysterical fits. To function optimally, our evolved faculty for critical thinking expects to be challenged by contrary positions.

Creating sterile safe spaces is not restricted to the university campus. I recently hosted the founder of Twitter, Jack Dorsey, on my YouTube channel.[10] During our conversation, I made the point that it was suboptimal for Twitter to be monitoring people's language on the platform. Healthy human beings are anti-fragile. In other words, people have to be exposed to the ugliness of social interactions. They cannot be protected in a sanitized bubble expecting that all interactions will be polite, uplifting, and enriching. Just as immunotherapy against food allergies exposes young children to minute traces of the allergens so that, with an incremental increase in the exposure dosage, the body will build immunity against that particular allergen, so too do people need to be exposed to the full repertoire of human interactions so that they can develop as intellectually and emotionally healthy individuals.[11] And yet today, we are creating a generation of young people who are too brittle to handle opposing opinions, and who fold into a fetal position of feigned victimhood when confronted by so-called "microaggressions," a concept that lacks scientific validity.[12]

The fostering of emotional fragility is further assured by the use of trigger warnings, which are meant to protect university students from potentially upsetting stimuli. Recall my personal history in Lebanon.

Few people have experienced the horrors that I have lived through, and yet I learned to overcome my past without needing trigger warnings to navigate through life. Needless to say, such distressing experiences of inhumanness have left an indelible mark on my psyche. I may have left Lebanon long ago, but it has never left me. One of the recurring nightmares that has haunted my sleep comes in two forms: 1) I am barricaded in our house and am about to engage (or am engaging) the incoming "bad guys" with my weapon when I realize that I am out of ammunition; 2) The same dream but my weapon jams, and I'm unable to fire it. Notwithstanding this childhood trauma, I have not wallowed in my past. I do not require trigger warnings prior to seeing a war movie. Rather, as any therapist would surely advise, one must overcome negative experiences and move forward. Trigger warnings infantilize human resilience by coddling young adults into thinking that they do not possess the psychological strength to face life. Of course, there are unique situations that require humane and gentle care, and in such instances, a caring and kind professor should consider the matter with due sensitivity. But the wholesale codifying of trigger warnings as a default policy is a grotesque overreach. In a 2015 HuffPost article, I highlighted the extraordinary range of topics that are potentially "triggering" and hence that might necessitate trigger warnings.[13] These include:

- Abuse (physical, mental, emotional, verbal, sexual), child abuse, rape, kidnapping
- Addiction, alcohol, drug use, needles
- Blood, vomit, insects, snakes, spiders, slimy things, corpses, skulls, skeletons
- Bullying, homophobia, transphobia
- Death, dying, suicide, injuries, descriptions, and/or images of medical procedures
- Descriptions and/or images of violence or warfare, Nazi paraphernalia
- Pregnancy, childbirth

- Racism, classism, sexism, sizeism, ableism, other "isms"
- Sex (even if consensual)
- Swearing, slurs (including words such as "stupid" or "dumb")
- Anything that might elicit intrusive thoughts in Obsessive-Compulsive Disorder sufferers

Really, the list is endless, which is why I have suggested the following Universal Trigger Warning: "Using your brain to navigate the real world should not entail a trigger warning. This course will assume that you possess the cognitive and emotional acuity of an adult. Life is your trigger warning."

Trigger warnings are antithetical to a fundamental principle of exposure therapy, a well-researched therapeutic approach for combatting generalized anxiety disorder, social anxiety disorder, phobias (like arachnophobia), panic disorder, obsessive-compulsive disorder, and post-traumatic stress disorder.[14] Under this approach, patients are exposed to their triggering stimulus with the hope that they will learn strategies for coping with their phobias and fears. The few studies that have empirically tested the efficacy of trigger warnings indicate that they make students more likely to avoid "triggers,"[15] hinder emotional resilience,[16] and were ineffective even for people with prior trauma.[17] Even though trigger warnings might offer a temporary reduction in painful emotions, they do not promote a healthy mindset for traversing the stochasticity of life.

What Are Universities For?

Leonhard Euler, the great eighteenth-century mathematician proclaimed: "For since the fabric of the universe is most perfect and the work of a most wise Creator, nothing at all takes place in the universe in which some rule of maximum or minimum does not appear."[18] Many times we need to identify some optimal real-world course of action (such as whether to *maximize* profit or *minimize* wait time). Operations research (or management science) is the academic discipline that uses analytical techniques to find these optimal courses of action. In some instances, natural selection has programmed optimal behavior into an organism's brain. This is the idea behind optimal foraging theory, which examines how animals optimize their foraging behaviors to maximize their caloric intake while minimizing the caloric expenditure.[19]

During my undergraduate studies in mathematics and computer science, and subsequently as an M.B.A. student, I worked as a research assistant at GERAD (*Groupe d'études et de recherche en analyse des décisions*, which in English translates to Group for Research in Decision Analysis). The center is composed of applied mathematicians and computer scientists from across several Montreal universities dedicated to solving optimization problems using a slew of algorithmic approaches. At GERAD, I worked on the *Two-Dimensional Cutting Stock Problem*, a classic optimization challenge. Suppose that a wood, glass, or metal company receives an order to cut specific numbers of rectangles and squares of varying sizes using standard sheets of the raw material in question. How should the guillotine cuts be made so that the order is filled while minimizing the amount of waste in the original sheets? Another minimization problem is the *Travelling Salesman Problem*. Suppose that a salesman is tasked with visiting a given number of cities only once each and return to the starting point. What is the shortest path that would allow the salesman to complete this objective? These are minimization problems, but there are also maximization problems. For instance, consider a firm that produces four different products with four different selling prices, raw materials used, and machine time. The challenge is to identify the optimal product manufacturing mix that will maximize the firm's profits.

The optimal solution to any such problem hinges on which variable one chooses to optimize. An architect might choose to minimize the total cost of erecting a building and/or its time of completion. This might yield drab architectural designs akin to the housing projects found in many large American cities where the objective is to offer a maximal number of dwellings as cheaply and as quickly as possible. Alternatively, an architect might seek to optimize a building's biophilic imprint (maximizing the number of design features that cater to our innate love of nature). The choice of which variable to optimize will yield radically different architectural designs. To further complicate matters, many complex, real-world problems require the concurrent optimization of several discordant variables (such as pursuing an investment strategy that maximizes returns while minimizing risk, which results in a diversified investment portfolio). The challenge then becomes to identify the optimal trade-off between the conflicting variables.

If companies seek to maximize profits while travelling salesmen seek to minimize total distance travelled, which variables should a university be trying to optimize? Surely, universities exist to create and disseminate new knowledge. But this is no longer true. Today the minimization of hurt feelings among preferred groups is fundamentally more important (at least in some disciplines) than the pursuit of truth. The creation of safe spaces supersedes free speech and intellectual enrichment. Social justice activism trumps the quest for truth. To put it in the language of operations research, historically a university's objective function was to maximize the intellectual growth of students and professors subject only to the constraints of university budgets. Today, many universities are driven by a multi-objective optimization problem: maximize intellectual growth while minimizing hurt feelings, or maximize intellectual growth and social justice activism while minimizing hurt feelings.

A case in point is Palo Alto University, a small regional institution that came into national prominence during Brett Kavanaugh's Senate confirmation hearings. This is the university where Christine Blasey Ford, who accused Kavanaugh of a sexual assault that supposedly had taken place thirty-six years earlier, held an appointment as a professor of psychology. I decided to visit the institution's website to gauge its core mission, thinking that it would be a hotbed of social justice warrior activists. I was not disappointed. Here are the first three of its eight listed core values:[20]

1. Social justice, cultural competency, and diversity
2. A student-centered and culturally responsive environment
3. High quality scientific research and scholarship that advances the state of knowledge and practice

If you want to know what's wrong with higher education, this reversal of traditional university priorities—with social justice now at the top and scholarship lower on the totem pole—is a good place to start.

The Homeostasis of Victimology

Bear with me as I provide a little background on the ubiquity of homeostasis, how we study it, and its implications, because it will help illustrate an important point about victimology. Many biological and man-made systems are governed by processes that seek to maintain a set or optimal equilibrium level. For example, a room thermostat regulates the flow of cold or hot air such that a set temperature is maintained. The human body contains several such homeostatic systems including processes that control one's body temperature, glucose levels, and arterial pressure. Homeostatic systems are not restricted to physiological processes. Several influential psychological theories are based on the idea of homeostasis.[21] The psychologist John M. Fletcher drew a parallel between physiological and psychological homeostasis: "The rise of temper against an insult is not essentially different from the rise of temperature against infection. Both represent the attempts of an organism to maintain status; in the one case it is a body status, in the other it is a social status that is to be maintained."[22] Drive-reduction theory posits that humans are compelled to reduce the discrepancy between a current state and a desired state in order to meet a physiological or psychological need. For example, when hungry or thirsty, an individual will to act to slake their hunger or thirst. Drive reduction theory can explain a very broad range of human phenomena. Homeostatic comparisons are also the key element in what is known as multiple discrepancies theory, which focuses on how people measure satisfaction with elements of their lives.[23] For example, I might gauge the discrepancy (if any) between my current income and what I expected to have at this stage in my career. Or I could contrast my current income to that of my relevant peers. The bottom line is that there are multiple ways by which one might establish a discrepancy between a current and desired state, and accordingly be motivated to close that gap.

Homeostatic processes are operative in many applied contexts including in my own field of consumer psychology. According to optimal stimulation level theory, individuals' behaviors are driven in part by a desire to achieve a set threshold of stimulation in their daily lives, with the threshold determined by personality type. For example, consumers who are high sensation seekers are more likely to explore a wider variety of products.[24] Homeostatic processes can help explain cultural differences in consumption patterns. For example, aggregate consumer choices (like a taste for coffee or alcohol) can be linked to a country's climate (temperature and sunlight) and be seen as adaptive homeostatic responses to local environments.[25]

Homeostatic processes can yield unwelcome consequences. Risk homeostasis theory holds that people will alter their behaviors to maintain a desired level of risk in their lives, which is why mandatory safety features on cars—like seat belts, antilock brakes, and airbags—cause some individuals to drive more recklessly.[26] More than twenty years ago, I was approached by two researchers to investigate links between running shoes and various injuries. Specifically, they had found that more expensive running shoes (with ostensibly superior injury-prevention features) yielded greater injuries because of altered gaits.[27] This was likely a manifestation of a gait homeostatic process, where runners subconsciously increased the force with which their feet were hitting the pavement because their shoes had thicker protective padding.

Homeostasis also plays a part in what researchers call the prevalence-induced concept change effect.[28] Suppose that you are asked to identify whether a dot is blue. This should not depend on how many blue dots you've previously been exposed to—but it does. When there are fewer blue dots, people will code purple dots as blue. Researchers replicated this finding using pictures of threatening faces. When participants were shown fewer threatening faces, they judged neutral faces as threatening. In short, I posit that this is a form of homeostasis, namely people are driven to maintain the frequency of a stimulus at a set level, even if they have to engage in perceptual distortions to do so. This is precisely what has led to the spike in the number of exaggerated victimhood narratives, if not outright hate and harassment hoaxes. The narrative that we live in a hate-filled society, where marginalized groups fear for their lives, must be protected at all costs.

Psychologist Nick Haslam's idea of "concept creep" is very relevant to my homeostatic argument.[29] He argues that what constitutes harm and pathology has been massively expanded, and he uses six examples to demonstrate this (abuse, bullying, trauma, mental disorder, addiction, and prejudice).[30] In the abstract to his excellent article, Haslam warns: "Although conceptual change is inevitable and often well motivated, concept creep runs the risk of pathologizing everyday experience and encouraging a sense of virtuous but impotent victimhood." While he offers some speculative explanations for this trend, I would argue that my homeostasis of victimology is the simplest. A set level of victimhood must be achieved. If an insufficient number of victimhood cases exist, alter the definition of victimhood and turn banal daily interactions into "exciting" data supporting faux-victimhood.

The homeostasis of victimology, concept creep, and political correctness can at times lead to truly baffling moral hypocrisy. The Canadian prime minister Justin Trudeau was unwilling to concede that ISIS had committed genocide but was willing to accept the word "genocide" in a report documenting that indigenous women were murdered at a higher rate than the Canadian national average.[31] The great majority of these murdered indigenous women were murdered by indigenous men, but the self-flagellant-in-chief laid the blame on "genocidal" Canadians. The government of Turkey has steadfastly refused to accept the existence of the Armenian genocide while the Canadian government confesses to a fictitious genocide. Both engage in a grotesque murder of the truth, albeit for different reasons.

The homeostasis of victimology can result in truly bewildering cases of feigned outrage and manufactured victimhood. In 2017, Lorne Grabher had his vanity plate "GRABHER" revoked by the Nova Scotia Registrar of Motor Vehicles because of its "inappropriate" nature.[32] The case was heard by the Supreme Court of Nova Scotia and that judgment is now in the hands of the Nova Scotia Court of Appeal.[33] The Nova Scotia government (the defendant) issued an expert report produced by Carrie Rentschler, an associate professor of feminist media studies at McGill University (one of my alma maters), declaring that the license plate condones violence against women and perpetuates rape culture. Rentschler even found a way to link the issue to Donald Trump (as per his leaked interview with Billy Bush wherein he uttered the now infamous phrase "grab them by the pussy"). This is not satire. A man's actual surname is now considered to be a form of violence against women. In 2016, Humanities dean Jodi Kelly of Seattle University was removed from her administrative post when she uttered the word "nigger" in a conversation with a student.[34] This sounds awfully bigoted and inappropriate until one finds out that she was recommending a book of that title written by black civil rights activist Dick Gregory. She was responding to a request for a greater diversity of authors in assigned readings! It is truly soul crushing to see that our society has reached this level of political correctness and faux-outrage. In the immortal words of Voltaire, "Common sense is not so common." The list of faux-outrage is truly endless and includes the temporary removal of weighing scales at a Carleton University gym (as these might be triggering to those with body image issues)[35] and the renaming of an otherwise "sexist" sandwich (Gentleman's Smoke Chicken Caesar Roll by Waitrose).[36] My theory on the homeostasis of victimology is perhaps best captured by a quote from feminist Anita Sarkeesian, "Cause, like, when you start learning about systems, everything is sexist, everything is racist, everything is homophobic, and you have to point it all out to everyone all the time."[37]

Case in point, there is a growing trend on university campuses to identify white supremacy everywhere. If there aren't enough rabid racists around, just make them up to maintain the homeostasis of victimology. The Campus Reform website maintains an excellent repository of campus lunacy. In searching their site using the term "white supremacy," I found that pumpkins, white marble in artwork, milk, university mascots, Halloween costumes, Disney, MAGA hats, statues of Thomas Jefferson, the GOP, Donald Trump, voting for Donald Trump, taking exams, saying "all lives matter" instead of "black lives matter," having white children, calling for civility, refusing to partake in identity politics, promoting diversity of thought, meritocracy, capitalism, the United States Constitution, freedom of speech, Western literature, Medieval studies, scientific objectivity, science, and mathematics are among the many things that have often been "linked" to white supremacy by progressive professors.[38] Incidentally, if you are a non-racist white person who does not appreciate being accused of supporting white supremacy, you undoubtedly suffer from white fragility (according to author Robin DiAngelo, that is).

The Weaponizing of Collective Munchausen

In 2010, I authored a paper in a medical journal offering a possible Darwinian explanation for Munchausen Syndrome by Proxy (MSbP).[39] Unlike Munchausen Syndrome, where a person feigns illness in order to get sympathetic attention, MSbP is when a caretaker harms a child (or sometimes an elderly person or even a pet) to make the victim appear sick and thus gain sympathetic attention for the caretaker. Whereas the majority of sufferers of Munchausen syndrome are women (66.2 percent), nearly all perpetrators of MSbP are women (97.6 percent).[40] Given my familiarity with these two forms of Munchausen disorder, I coined a new condition that captures the faux-victimhood mentality that has taken root in our societies: *Collective Munchausen*.[41] Rather than feigning a medical condition or inflicting an injury, sufferers of Collective Munchausen seek attention, sympathy, and empathy by advertising their supposed victimhood status (or piggybacking on the victimhood of others, *Collective Munchausen by Proxy*). When Donald Trump won the United States presidential election in 2016, I began noticing a hysterical form of Collective Munchausen wherein faux-victims were feverishly vying for top spot on the prospective victimhood hierarchy. A hypothetical but illustrative Facebook post might look as follows: "Hi Gang, I am a bisexual woman of color, and now that Trump is going to be president, I don't feel safe attending my college campus in rural Maine." This might be followed by a cacophony of fake hysteria wherein members of various identity groups would testify as to how deathly afraid they too were of their eventual demise at the hands of Trump's death squads.

Many progressives have as one of their highest aspirations, to sit on top of the victimology pyramid. Forget about becoming a surgeon, a professor, a lawyer, a professional athlete, an artist, or a diplomat. Those pursuits are laden with the dreadful possibility of personal responsibility and hard work. Let the cries of faux-victimhood open the doors for you. Jussie Smollett, the otherwise minimally known actor of the series *Empire*, was unhappy with his "meagre" salary (more than $1 million per year). He was also undoubtedly displeased with his lack of fame. Only one solution remained to address this grave personal injustice: to orchestrate a fake hate crime attack on himself and ascend the victimhood hierarchy. Unfortunately for Smollett, he paid off the two Nigerian-Americans he had hired to "attack" him by check. If he had been smarter and paid in cash, he might be reaping all the societal rewards that befall Noble Victims. The political scientist Wilfred Reilly has documented several hundred "hate crime" hoaxes and analyzed the perpetrators.[42] Unsurprisingly, the hoaxers invariably hold a strong hand in Victimology Poker.

Let us contrast Smollett's chosen path to glory via feigned victimhood to a poignant personal story. When I completed my M.B.A. in

1990, I was trying to decide which doctoral program to enroll in. One of the universities that had accepted me was UC-Irvine, which happened to be close to my brother's office. In the 1980s, he had built a very successful software recruiting company, and he suggested that I explore the possibility of working with him for a few years prior to embarking on my Ph.D. I visited the UC-Irvine campus, met some of the professors, and spent time at my brother's office. I quickly realized that academia was the only path for me and decided against my brother's kind invitation. Upon returning to Montreal, my mother, who had heard of my brother's offer but was unaware that I had rejected it, took me aside for a quick chat. She was very concerned that I might decide against pursuing my Ph.D. and reminded me of the "shame" that might befall me if people were to find out that I had dropped out of school! I had a B.Sc. in Mathematics and Computer Science and an M.B.A. (both from McGill University, one of the world's leading universities) and yet this might be construed as a "drop out." That I pursued a Ph.D. had nothing to do with any parental influences, but the moral of the story is the expected threshold of success that my mother had set for me. The goal was to *achieve* through personal responsibility, hard work, and merit, not to wallow in "victimhood" (which we theoretically could have done as Jewish refugees from Lebanon). Instead, we welcomed the opportunities offered by liberal, democratic countries like Canada and the United States.

All Roads Lead to Bigotry—I Am a Victim Therefore I Am

Fat acceptance activists and transgender activists are two groups questing for victimhood status via claims that offend reason and common sense. The fat acceptance movement has adeptly created a narrative of faux-victimhood by blatant lies on two fronts. First, the activists push a mantra of "healthy at any size" and deny that obesity is linked to a wide variety of serious diseases. Second, they propose that many overweight people (especially women) get ignored in the mating market because of "fatist" attitudes that stigmatize obesity. Some trans activists are just as creative in their rejection of reality. Two popular YouTube trans activists (Riley J. Dennis and Zinnia Jones) have proclaimed that it is "cissexist" for people to restrict their mating preferences to "cisnormative" individuals; or in other words, heterosexuality is bigoted.[43] It would seem that my marriage is transphobic because I never considered a transgendered individual as a prospective wife.[44]

Of course, all roads lead to bigotry. If you are a white man *not* sexually attracted to black women, you are guilty of sexual racism (yes, the term exists). If you are a white man who *is* attracted to black women, you are a racist bigot who stereotypes black women as sexually voracious and objectifies their bodies. Plug any victim group into this equation and it works out the same. We all know that institutional racial segregation constitutes bigotry, but now so too does seeking to immerse yourself in the cultural practices of others—that makes you guilty of the bigotry of "cultural appropriation." The homeostasis of victimology ensures that all roads lead to bigotry, thus violating the philosopher of science Karl Popper's falsification principle (no data could falsify the victimhood narrative).

The list of faux-outrage stemming from cultural appropriation is a long one. The actress Lena Dunham was concerned that her alma mater Oberlin College served sushi in the cafeteria, a clear case of cultural appropriation.[45] A self-described queer woman of color, chef Mithalee Rawat was aghast that white people had violated her Indian heritage by using bone broth, which she deemed colonialist theft.[46] In the immortal words of the Soup Nazi on *Seinfeld*, "No soup for you!" Gastronomic appropriation is hardly the only road to bigotry. Sartorial bigotry can rear its ugly head at any moment, as evidenced by the singer Katy Perry, who had to apologize for having dressed as a geisha in her performance at the 2013 American Music Awards.[47] Keziah Daum, a white high school student, wore a Chinese dress known as a qipao to her prom, and this triggered the faux-outrage brigade.[48] Beware of how you wear your hair, especially if you are white, for this too could be a signal that you are a bigoted Nazi. Katy Perry made that mistake by wearing cornrows and later apologized for it.[49] Kendall Jenner stirred controversy by sporting an Afro during a *Vogue* shoot.[50] And a white male student at San Francisco State University was angrily accosted by a black woman who was outraged that he had dreadlocks.[51] Other examples of faux-outrage over cultural appropriation stemming from the land of the insane (university campuses) include the University of Ottawa cancelling a yoga class,[52] a resident assistant at Pitzer College angered by white people wearing hoop earrings,[53] and Lynne Bunch, a student at Louisiana State University who wrote an op-ed in *The Daily Reveille* (LSU's student newspaper) proclaiming that the thickening of one's eyebrows is a form of cultural appropriation.[54]

Halloween is an event replete with dangerous traps of cultural appropriation and sartorial bigotry. Many universities have taken it upon themselves to warn their adult students to be culturally sensitive when choosing their Halloween costumes—this is best exemplified by what transpired in 2015 at Yale University. Erika Christakis, a lecturer in developmental psychology, wrote an extraordinarily meek and polite email to the Yale community questioning whether institutional warnings regarding Halloween costumes were a good idea, which led to a tsunami of outrage for not recognizing how bigoted Halloween costumes could be, ending ultimately in her resignation. The destructive appetite of the Halloween SJWs was not satiated. More blood had to be spilled so they next turned on her husband, Nicholas Christakis, a physician and professor of sociology, and intercepted him in one of the quads. When it became clear that he was in disagreement with their position (but was willing to engage in a conversation), they swore at him and tried to intimidate him. At one point, an indignant student proclaimed: "Then why the fuck did you accept the position [master of residential life at Silliman College]? Who the fuck hired you? You should step down! If that is what you think about being a master you should step down! It is not about creating an intellectual space! It is not! Do you understand that? It's about creating a home here. You are not doing that!"[55] Apparently, the primary objective of an education at Yale University is not to expand one's intellect and knowledge but to create "safe spaces." In 1944, young men stormed the beaches of Normandy to their near-certain deaths in a quest to combat true evil. Today, social justice warriors brave the evils of Halloween costumes and the diabolical professors who allow such sartorial bigotry to go unchecked.

Never one to miss an opportunity to satirize the naturally lobotomized, I produced a clip on my YouTube channel wherein I offered temporary clearance to those wishing to culturally appropriate classic Lebanese dishes.[56] I also implored my followers to send me their culture-specific clearances and to include a photo of their passports so I could be sure they truly belonged to the cultures they claimed. The responses were astoundingly funny and heartening in that they confirmed that there still remain innumerable sane people who can see through this mass hysteria of faux-outrage.[57] Having cultural appropriation hanging over one's head makes it harder to experience the full richness afforded by a multicultural and pluralistic society.

If there ever were a genuine case of cultural appropriation, Senator Elizabeth Warren is guilty of it. She literally appropriated Native American culture as her own by constructing a false narrative about her ancestry. A subsequent genealogical test revealed that she was somewhere between 1/64 to 1/1024 Native American, making her less of that ancestry than the average white American. And yet, she benefitted for several decades from this false narrative both in her academic and political career. Warren's stunt was a manifestation of Collective Munchausen by Proxy. Piggyback on the tragic history of Native Americans to garner sympathy and gain all of the advantages of being a "victim." Rachel Dolezal constitutes another case of genuine cultural (racial) appropriation. Recall that Dolezal is a white woman who for years presented herself as African American. When her ruse was discovered, she argued that she was transracial (she self-identifies as a black woman even though she is white). I look forward to explaining to my physician that I'm TransGravity, namely I self-identify as a thin person even though I'm overweight. I hope he can stop nagging me about needing to lose weight. Continuing with the trans theme, we now have the term *transabled* to refer to individuals who are born able-bodied but who experience a desire to be disabled; so desperate are they to be victims that they will actually disable themselves through self-harm, an emerging condition known as Body Integrity Identity Disorder.[58] Whether individuals manufacture a faux-narrative of victimhood or literally engage in actions that render them disabled, these are not manifestations of healthy and well-adjusted minds.

Several years ago, Tal Nitzan, then a doctoral student at Hebrew University, authored an award-winning paper that examined the incidence of rape as perpetrated by Israeli Defense Forces on Palestinian women. Undoubtedly, the goal was to uncover an epidemic of rape to demonstrate how diabolical those evil Jews truly were. When no such empirical reality was found, it was concluded (you might need to sit down for this) that this was proof of the extent to which the Israelis *dehumanized* the Palestinians.[59] They were so hateful that they did not even consider the Palestinian women worthy of rape! If rapes are uncovered or if none are discovered, the same conclusion is reached: the Israelis are diabolical. All roads lead to self-flagellation and self-loathing. It's the hallmark of a true "progressive."

Merchants of faux-outrage can not only ascribe victimhood status to Palestinian women for *not* being raped, but they can also construe kindness as a form of Islamophobia. Anisa Rawhani conducted an experiment at Queen's University: she wore a hijab for eighteen days to examine people's reactions to her.[60] Undoubtedly, the working hypothesis was that bigotry and prejudice would be ubiquitous. She was taken aback by the fact that people were very kind and polite to her. In an extraordinary attempt to salvage the victimology narrative, she concluded that this manifest tolerance and kindness was a means by which people overcompensated for their concealed bigotry. If you are unkind to a Muslim woman, you are an Islamophobe. If you are kind to a Muslim woman, you are an Islamophobe. All roads lead to

Islamophobia. Being kind and tolerant is a form of racism in the eco-system of the university campus.

Male Social Justice Warriors as Sneaky Fuckers

In their infinite desire to appear empathetic, compassionate, and sensitive, many male SJWs are pursuing a duplicitous mating strategy that has been documented in the zoological literature as the sneaky fucker strategy. Among *Homo sapiens*, especially on university cam-puses, this is the guy who is the most ostentatiously kind and progressive because he thinks it might give him a better shot with a pretty girl. This is supported by some rigorous and compelling science.

Deception manifests itself in many distinct ways in the animal king-dom. Let us begin with the evolution of deceptive warning signals. Unlike the evolution of camouflaging (to avoid predators), aposematic coloring is an adaptation that makes an animal very visible to prospective preda-tors. The Amazon is a dangerous neighborhood where it pays to be invisible, and yet several frog species have evolved extraordinarily bright colors that serve the exact opposite function. These colors serve as the following warning to looming predators: "If you can see me, it's probably because you don't want to mess with me. I'm poisonous. Stay away." In some instances, completely harmless species will evolve a mimicry of the aposematic coloring. This is known as Batesian mimicry. For example, the coral snake and king snake both have very similar tri-color mark-ings (yellow, red, and black). However, one is very venomous (the coral snake) while the other is harmless. Mnemonics have been used to remember the differences in markings between the two species ("Red on yellow, kills a fellow. Red on black, venom lack.").[61] I have argued somewhat facetiously that the colored hair of many social justice warriors (often bright red or pink or blue) is akin to a form of Batesian mimicry.[62] It communicates ideological fierceness.

There are many other forms of animal deception including brood parasitism. This is when one species deceives another into raising its kids, as occurs with the cuckoo bird. But perhaps not surprisingly, the arena where deception is most rampant is within the domain of mating. The grand struggle of life for all sexually reproducing species involves having to survive (natural selection) and to reproduce (sexual selection). In order to reproduce, organisms have evolved a bewildering number of morpho-logical and behavioral traits as a means of gaining sexual access to prospective mates. Let us take human males as an example. Women hold a universal preference for men who exhibit cues associated with high social status, including intelligence, confidence, ambition, the ability to procure and defend resources, and social dominance. Few women throughout our evolutionary history were driven to sexual frenzy at the prospect of mating with an apathetically lazy, pear-shaped, nasal-voiced, submissive, cowardly, whiny man. Not surprisingly, across all known cultures and eras, men have sought to gain status as a means of being attractive on the mating market, but they've done so via a broad range of trajectories as a function of their unique talents and life circumstances. Some will become successful businessmen, diplomats, professional ath-letes, surgeons, professors, or artists. The definition of status might vary across cultures and time periods (a Harvard degree, for instance, matters little to the Hadza tribe in Africa), but what is universally clear is that status matters to women in choosing men. In instances when men do not possess the desired characteristics, they might "fake it until they make it." Of course, women engage in countless forms of deceptive signaling as well. They are much more likely to lie about their age, weight, and sexual history, as a means of appearing more attractive in the mating market. Several products exist to deceive the male gaze including push-up bras and high heels, both of which create more youthful-looking shapes by lifting women's breasts and buttocks and combating the downward pull of gravity. The harsh reality is that deception is one of several avail-able strategies when seeking to gain an advantage in the struggle for life.

Of all forms of deception in the mating market, perhaps none is as deviously ingenious as kleptogamy (the theft of mating opportunities under false pretense). In the 1970s, a more colloquially vivid term was introduced in the animal behavior literature to explain this phenomenon, the *sneaky fucker* strategy. Female mimicry is one manifestation of this behavior. This occurs when some males of a species either look or act like females of that species to avoid being attacked by dominant guarding males, and in doing so they can sneak mating opportunities.[63] In many instances, the phenotypes of the two types of males is somewhat fixed (some are large and dominant while others are smaller and meeker). This is precisely what makes the giant cuttlefish extraordinary in its implementation of the sneaky fucker strategy, since males are able to alter their physical characteristics on the spot to mimic a female's morphological features.[64] Even more incredibly, the male mourning cuttlefish alters its body shape and coloring to look at the same time like that of a female and a male. Specifically, the part of its body visible to a rival male mimics that of a female while the other part visible to a female emits male courtship cues.[65] Talk about sophisticated duplicity!

My familiarity with this form of mating duplicity led me to apply the sneaky fucker stratagem to a specific human context. I posit that many male social justice warriors are akin to the giant cuttlefish. They don the accoutrements of a sensitive and non-threatening male via their ideological commitment oozing with progressive empathy. In a sense, this is akin to the sensitive guy who befriends women and offers them endless emotional support with the hope that it eventually pays off romantically. Back in the 1980s, John Hughes was responsible for many of the iconic teenage-themed movies of that era, including *Sixteen Candles, The Breakfast Club, Ferris Bueller's Day Off*, and *Pretty in Pink*. In the latter classic movie, Andie Walsh (played by Molly Ringwald), is a working-class teenager with a romantic interest in Blane McDonough (played by Andrew McCarthy), a rich kid from the proverbial better side of the tracks. Andie's best friend, Duckie (played by Jon Cryer, who later gained renewed fame in the TV series *Two and a Half Men*), is the epitome of the sneaky fucker friend. Always there offering his endless sensitive support, hoping that he will eventually be given his due chance at romance. Returning to the male social justice warriors, it is clear that most do not look anything like Navy SEALs. In other words, they do not exhibit the morphological features associated with physical formidability and social dominance. There is growing scientific evidence that men's economic and political outlooks (what they think about economic redistribution, military intervention, and other topics) are associated with their physical strength. Those who are stronger and more physically formidable are less likely to support egalitarianism and more likely to support military intervention.[66] Irrespective of whether male social justice warriors truly believe their stated ideological positions or are merely faking it as a sneaker fucker mating strategy, it is clear that men's morphological features do indeed serve as signature of their sociopolitical outlooks.

Self-Flagellating at the Altar of Progressivism

There is another motive or two behind progressivism. Many of the progressive positions espoused by SJWs are a form of self-flagellation meant to atone for some assumed "Original Sin" (most likely being a white Westerner) and to highlight one's virtuous ideological progressive purity. In this sense, SJW progressivism can almost be seen as an alternative religion to Christianity.

The Name of the Rose remains to this day one of my all-time favorite movies. It features Sean Connery and a very young Christian Slater surrounded by a powerful cast of medieval characters. The story takes places in the fourteenth century at an Italian Benedictine monastery where several individuals have recently died under mysterious circumstances. It is a classic whodunnit set against the backdrop of the religious zealotry of the Middle Ages under the ever-watchful eyes of the all-powerful Inquisition authorities. More than thirty years have elapsed since I first saw this brilliant film, and yet many of its iconic scenes remain etched in my memory, perhaps none more so than the assistant librarian Berengar of Arundel self-flagellating as penance for his homosexuality and for the guilt at having caused the suicide of Adelmo of Otranto (with whom he traded sex for access to a desired book). The theological tenet that one's guilt could be expunged via various form of self-mortification (including self-flagellation) exists in numerous religious traditions. The Catholic flagellants of the Middle Ages engaged in public self-flagellation both to atone for their sins but also as a conspicuous act of extreme piety (and in some cases to ward off great calamities such as the Black Death). Signaling one's religious purity and commitment in this way is costly and handicapping, but done in public it surely makes a more conspicuous case for one's virtue than saying three Hail Marys in a church.[67]

Social justice warriors and various assorted progressive brethren are typically privileged white Westerners. In their warped sense of the world, this is akin to being born with original sin as postulated in Christian doctrine. They must atone for the sin of not having been born poor persons of color in the third world; thus, they might seek penance in a form of ideological self-flagellation. Rather than using a whip or chain to self-harm, they adopt a progressive mindset that is ultimately harmful to them and their society. Take for example the ethos of infinite tolerance. The great philosopher Karl Popper offered perhaps the greatest take on such a mindset.

> Less well known is the *paradox of tolerance*: Unlimited tolerance must lead to the disappearance of tolerance. If we extend unlimited tolerance even to those who are intolerant, if we are not prepared to defend a tolerant society against the onslaught of the intolerant, then the tolerant will be destroyed, and tolerance with them. In this formulation, I do not imply, for instance, that we should always suppress the utterance of intolerant philosophies; as long as we can counter them by rational argument and keep them in check by public opinion, suppression would certainly be unwise. But we should claim the *right* to suppress them if necessary even by force; for it may easily turn out that they are not prepared to meet us on the level of rational argument, but begin by denouncing all

argument; they may forbid their followers to listen to rational argument, because it is deceptive, and teach them to answer arguments by the use of their fists or pistols. We should therefore claim, in the name of tolerance, the right not to tolerate the intolerant.[68] [Italics in the original.]

Infinite tolerance causes Western governments to exhibit reticence to prosecute and ultimately punish returning ISIS fighters. Rather, they seek to reintegrate these brutal individuals into our societies by providing them with job opportunities and enrolling them in "deradicalization" programs. In the words of Ayaan Hirsi Ali, who has fought Islamist intolerance: "Tolerance of intolerance is cowardice."

Beto O'Rourke was among a very large contingent of candidates running for the Democratic nomination in the 2020 United States presidential election. O'Rourke exemplifies the mindset of a male social justice warrior. His campaign consisted largely of a grotesque apology tour of self-flagellation. He apologized for being male, for being white, and for being privileged. He announced that some of his ancestors owned slaves, an admission of guilt by intergenerational association. While watching one of his blubbering admissions of "guilt" on the insufferable television show *The View*, my wife turned to me and remarked that she could not understand why anyone would vote for "Beto the Beta." Therein lies the incongruity between progressive self-flagellants and the rest of us. What they consider introspectively virtuous and pious, we view as weak and self-loathing. No leader should exhibit such cowardly traits—and certainly not one who hopes to hold the most powerful post in the world.

Self-loathing is an affliction that plagues many people. It is a recurring theme in psychotherapy where the goal is to alter an individual's mindset such that they develop a healthy sense of self-worth. Innumerable self-help books exist to address this malady in various ways. *Saturday Night Live* satirized the plague of self-loathing via its recurring sketch *Daily Affirmations with Stuart Smalley* played by Al Franken (the Minnesota senator who resigned in 2018 amidst the hysteria of the #MeToo movement). Perhaps the best-known catchphrase from this series was "I'm good enough, I'm smart enough, and doggone it, people like me." While the segment was comical, no clinical psychologist worth her salt would posit that self-loathing is a desirable state. And that lies at the heart of the extraordinary contradiction facing the West: while liberals know it is a virtue to overcome self-loathing at the individual level, they believe it is also a virtue to wallow in self-loathing at the group level ("I hate my white identity"; "I hate my Western culture"; "I hate my Christian roots"). Angela Merkel's astounding open border policy granting close to a million Muslim immigrants entry into Germany could be seen as self-flagellation for Germany's historical transgressions. Laced with typical progressive lunacy, what better way to make up for the Holocaust than by admitting "refugees" who frequently exhibit genocidal hatred of Jews?[69] A similar form of self-flagellation is taking place among American progressives when it comes to the current illegal immigration crisis at the U.S. border. Why are Central Americans coming to the United States? According to social justice warriors and their ilk, it's because the United States caused their societies to collapse via imperialistic meddling. So, in self-flagellating recompense, we owe the noble *undocumented immigrants* free entry into the United States.[70] Beto O'Rourke went one better than that and suggested that Central Americans were fleeing the ravages of climate change—and the United States is supposedly a key culprit. All roads lead to self-flagellation. It is the only progressive path to redemption.

The reflex to collective self-flagellation is causing several candidates for the 2020 Democrat presidential nomination to proclaim their support for reparations for African Americans, prostrating themselves before such great moral arbiters as Al Sharpton. Senator Elizabeth Warren expanded the discussion of reparations to gay couples. Some entrepreneurial merchants of victimhood have seized on this opportunity. Cameron Whitten has organized a Reparations Happy Hour in (where else?) Portland, Oregon, where white people pay for drinks for black, brown, and indigenous people but don't attend the event because their white presence might be too triggering.[71] If paying for drinks does not redress your white guilt, you can enroll in the Race to Dinner program. You get to invite two women of color, Regina Jackson and Saira Rao, to dinner to bear witness to their pain.[72] If drinks and dinners prove insufficient in curbing your white guilt, you can enroll in a yoga seminar in Seattle to detoxify from your whiteness.[73] My family escaped execution in Lebanon, and we escaped from slavery in ancient Egypt. How much am I owed in reparations?

In order to espouse their endless irrational positions while maintaining a straight face, social justice warriors must ignore, deny, or reject reality. Progressivism has become an enemy of reason.

CHAPTER SIX

Departures from Reason: Ostrich Parasitic Syndrome

"Most men would rather deny a hard truth than face it."
—George R. R. Martin[1]

"The easiest way to solve a problem is to deny it exists."
—Isaac Asimov[2]

*"The human brain can protect us from seeing and feeling
what it believes may be too uncomfortable for us to
tolerate. It can lead us to deny, defend, minimize, or
rationalize away something that doesn't fit our worldview."*
—Bandy X. Lee[3]

Science should be about the pursuit of truth, and not about the defense of one's preferred political ideology or personal beliefs. Richard Lowentin and the late Stephen Jay Gould, two eminent Harvard scientists, were staunch critics of sociobiology, a precursor to evolutionary psychology, in part because it did not adhere to their Marxist worldviews. Their animus toward their Harvard colleague E. O. Wilson, a leading figure of sociobiology, became part of the greater culture war that raged on university campuses in the 1970s.[4] But perhaps the greatest clash between Marxism and science was orchestrated in the Soviet Union by the agronomist Trofim Lysenko.[5] He rejected the established mechanisms of heredity (Mendelian inheritance), and instead proposed his pseudoscientific theories that were perceived as consistent with Marxist collectivism. Under the leadership of Josef Stalin, this allowed him to gain great political and scientific influence, including the capacity to severely punish contrarian Soviet scientists who dared to critique his quackery. His rejection of established theories in genetics went beyond the murder of truth. It led to agricultural practices in the Soviet Union and in China that arguably led to the starvation of millions of people.

Anti-vaccine activism is a modern-day version of Lysenkoism. In 1998, Andrew Wakefield published a paper in the leading medical journal *The Lancet* (the article has since been retracted) that supposedly demonstrated a link between the Measles, Mumps, and Rubella (MMR) vaccine and autism. It served as a powerful catalyst for the ensuing anti-vax movement led by several Hollywood celebrities, perhaps most notably by the actress Jenny McCarthy whose son suffers from autism. Few parents want to accept that their child might have been born with a predisposition to autism. It is psychologically much more comforting to blame an environmental agent. This is particularly tempting in the case of autism, which is commonly diagnosed around the same time that children receive the MMR vaccine, prompting some parents to draw an illusory link between the two events, and even to conclude, hopefully, that if the MMR vaccine "caused" autism, there might be an easy fix to reverse the condition.

The pediatrician and virologist Paul A. Offit has been at the forefront of combatting the anti-vaxxers, writing several books about the dangers of denying vaccine science and relying on celebrities and politicians for health recommendations.[6] Researchers have found that almost half of the advice offered on shows like *The Dr. Oz Show* and *The Doctors* either had no scientific basis or was contrary to existing scientific evidence.[7] One of my most popular *Psychology Today* articles dealt with the problem of celebrities talking about scientific issues.[8] If a large segment of the population decides to refrain from vaccinating their kids because Jenny McCarthy has shared "her truth," we have a problem. We have personal anecdotes versus science, with potentially deadly consequences, as children are needlessly exposed to dangerous viruses. By emphasizing the scientific consensus against the anti-vax quackery, one can reverse this dangerous instantiation of science denialism.[9]

Ostrich Parasitic Syndrome

Of course, the desire to deny reality extends far beyond science. The human capacity for deception (and self-deception) is enormous; in fact, some scientists suspect one reason our intelligence evolved as it has is so we can successfully manipulate others.[10] In the service of such manipulative intent, we have evolved a parallel proclivity to self-deceive, which protects us from betraying our duplicity.[11] The first step in being a good liar is believing the lie.

While these evolutionarily-based reasons for deception yield adaptive benefits, there is one form of self-deception that seems rather peculiar. At times, we deny facts that are as evident as the existence of the moon. The father of psychoanalysis, Sigmund Freud, noted the human capacity to suppress unpleasant information and referred to it as "this ostrich policy."[12] This human ostrich effect—based on the comic image of an ostrich burying its head in the sand to avoid unwelcome realities (a behavior the ostrich doesn't actually exhibit in nature)—has been documented in many contexts, including financial investments.[13] Several years ago, when I realized that idea pathogens were causing more and more people to reject reality, I coined the term Ostrich Parasitic Syndrome (OPS). Here's how I defined this dreadful attack on reason:

> This disorder causes a person to reject realities that are otherwise as clear as the existence of gravity. Sufferers of OPS do not believe their lying eyes. They construct an alternate reality known as Unicornia. In such a world, science, reason, rules of causality, evidentiary thresholds, a near-infinite amount of data, data analytic procedures, inferential statistics, the epistemological rules inherent to the scientific method, rules of logic, historical patterns, daily patterns, and common sense

are all rejected. Instead, the delusional ramblings of an OPS sufferer are rooted in illusory correlations, non-existent causal links, and feel-good progressive platitudes. Ostrich Logic is always delivered via an air of haughty moral superiority.[14]

I once visited a physician because I was suffering recurring bouts of bronchitis. As I sat in his office, he was chain smoking. I asked him if that was a good idea while treating an asthmatic patient suffering from bronchitis. He laughed it off. I share this story to remind people that experts are not immune from poor judgment and faulty reasoning. Notwithstanding the fact that I coined OPS, I have myself succumbed to Ostrich Logic, by thinking that if I ignore my weight gain it will go away (instead of leaving me thirty pounds heavier).

Six Degrees of Faux-Causality

Those infected with OPS succumb to a broad range of cognitive biases as a means of protecting them from reality. One of them involves ascribing an illusory network of connectedness between variables. Many important phenomena in our daily lives are organized as networks,[15] be it the small world phenomenon (human connectedness),[16] the neurons in our brains (connected to one another via synapses), the World Wide Web, electric power grids, social networks (like Facebook), or biological systems.[17] That our world consists of an endless number of interconnected elements has led to the so-called butterfly effect, the idea that a small perturbation in the starting conditions of a system could yield substantial downstream effects.[18] While it is indeed true that our world is composed of countless networks of interconnected parts, the problem arises when people construct networks of faux-causality to explain a given phenomenon.

For example, in 2015, Bill Nye (a self-described "science guy") found a way to connect an Islamist terror attack in Paris to climate change, saying:

It's very reasonable [to conclude] that the recent trouble in
Paris is a result of climate change. There is a water shortage
in Syria, this is fact based—small and medium farmers have
abandoned their farms because there's not enough water,
not enough rainfall. And especially the young people who
have not grown up there, have not had their whole lives
invested in living off the land, the young people have gone
to the big cities looking for work. There's not enough work
for everybody, so the disaffected youths, as we say—the
young people who don't believe in the system, believe the
system has failed, don't believe in the economy—are more
easily engaged and more easily recruited by terrorist organizations, and then they end up part way around the world
in Paris shooting people. You can make a very reasonable
argument that climate change is not that indirectly related
to terrorism. It's related to terrorism. So this is just the start
of things. The more we let this go on, the more trouble
there's going to be. You can say, "We'll stamp out the terrorists," but everybody's leaving their farms because of
water shortages, that's a little, bigger problem.[19]

One wonders why Chile has not produced a greater number of terrorists given that one of the most arid places on earth is its Atacama
Desert. But through the magic of assumed connectedness you can link
anything to anything if you are not bound by logic and fact-based rules
of causality.

Why do individuals succumb to such shoddy thinking? In his book
The Conduct of Inquiry, the philosopher Abraham Kaplan wrote: "In
addition to the social pressures from the scientific community, there is
also at work a very human trait of individual scientists. I call it the *law
of instrument*, and it may be formulated as follows: Give a small boy a
hammer, and he will find that everything he encounters needs pounding.
It comes as no particular surprise to discover that a scientist formulates

problems in a way which requires for their solution just those techniques in which he himself is especially skilled."[20] [Italics in original.] The humanist psychologist Abraham Maslow in *The Psychology of Science* added: "I suppose it is tempting, if the only tool you have is a hammer, to treat everything as if it were a nail."[21] This is very much related to the notion of methodological fixation, which occurs when researchers become single-minded about the use of specific data collection or data analytic procedures irrespective of their suitability for a given research problem.[22] If you are a climate activist, all calamities are due to man-made climate change. If you are a radical feminist, the patriarchy along with toxic masculinity are to blame. (Perhaps not surprisingly climate change has been blamed on toxic masculinity.[23]) If you are a member of the Diversity, Inclusion, and Equity cult, then naturally all ills stem from a lack of diversity, inclusion, and equity. If you are a member of the Democratic Party, all problems originate with Donald Trump.

In the philosophy of science, the principle of "Ockham's razor" means that all things being equal, simple explanations should be preferred to convoluted ones (a useful guard against the faulty epistemology of faux-causality). In his *Philosophiæ Naturalis Principia Mathematica*, Sir Isaac Newton proclaimed: "We are to admit no more causes of natural things than such as are both true and sufficient to explain their appearances. To this purpose the philosophers say that Nature does nothing in vain, and more is in vain when less will serve; for Nature is pleased with simplicity and affects not the pomp of superfluous causes." The problem with those who succumb to the Six Degrees of Faux-Causality trap is that they generate long sequences of illusory causal pathways. This can be necessary if you spout progressive platitudes that are manifestly untrue.

Open Borders—Diversity Is Our Strength

Of all the platitudinous slogans uttered by Canadian Prime Minister Justin Trudeau, he is undoubtedly best known for repeatedly invoking the mantra "Diversity Is Our Strength." He appears to believe that any problem is solved by simply repeating his slogan enough times that the problem disappears. Increasing diversity is the solution to all challenges—be they economic, social, political, environmental, or related to security. Simply double down on the cultural, ethnic, and religious diversity of the massive influx of immigrants into Canada and watch as we all eventually hold hands in brotherly unison while singing John Lennon's "Imagine." This is the type of Ostrich Logic that is destroying the future of the West. There are many forms of cultural enrichment, including restaurants of varied cuisines, that come from living in a heterogeneous and pluralistic society, but the cultural and religious values that some immigrants bring with them to the West manifestly do not add to our strength. They only sow hatred, intolerance, and divisiveness. My good friend Professor Salim Mansur testified eloquently on this in front of the Standing Committee on Citizenship and Immigration in the Canadian House of Commons on October 1, 2012:

> The flow of immigration into Canada from around the world, and in particular the flow from Muslim countries, means a pouring in of numbers into a liberal society of people from cultures at best non-liberal. But we know through our studies and observation that the illiberal mix of cultures poses one of the greatest dilemmas and an unprecedented challenge to liberal societies such as ours, when there is no demand placed on immigrants any longer to assimilate into the founding liberal values of the country to which they have immigrated. Instead, a misguided and thoroughly wrong-headed policy of multiculturalism encourages the opposite....
>
> We may want to continue with a level of immigration into Canada annually that is about the same as it is at present. We cannot, however, continue with such an inflow of immigrants under the present arrangement of the official policy of multiculturalism based on the premise that all cultures are equal

when this is untrue. This policy is a severe, perhaps even a lethal, test for a liberal democracy such as ours....

We should not allow bureaucratic inertia to determine not only the policy but the existing level of immigrant numbers and source origin that Canada brings in annually. We have the precedent of how we selectively closed immigration from the Soviet bloc countries during the Cold War years, and we need to consider doing the same in terms of immigration from Muslim countries for a period of time given how disruptive is the cultural baggage of illiberal values that is brought in as a result.

We are, in other words, stoking the fuel of much unrest in our country, as we have witnessed of late in Europe.

Lest any member wants to instruct me that my views are in any way politically incorrect, or worse, I would like members to note that I come before you as a practising Muslim who knows out of experience, from the inside, how volatile, how disruptive, how violent, how misogynistic is the culture of Islam today and has been during my lifetime, and how it greatly threatens our liberal democracy that I cherish, since I know what is its opposite.[24]

It is difficult to argue that Mansur is a bigoted white supremacist Islamophobe given that he is a brown man of Indian descent and a practicing Muslim. He is an honest man who recognizes that all cultures are not equally liberal.

The idea that unrestrained diversity is a magical elixir when it comes to creating stable and peaceful societies is a profoundly imbecilic notion. Science tells us that, generally speaking, homophily (being attracted to those who are similar) has been documented in a very broad range of social contexts.[25] For instance, if marital success is your ultimate objective then the research is very clear: choose someone who is similar to you. We also choose our friends partly based on genetic homophily,[26] our dogs based on morphological homophily,[27] and our global trade partners based on cultural homophily.[28] It follows that when it comes to immigration, people who share foundational values are more likely to get along than those who don't. If you are a classically liberal, modern, pluralistic, and secular society, opening your door to innumerable immigrants whose cultural and religious heritage is rooted in religious supremacy, homophobia, misogyny, intolerance toward religious minorities with a special hatred for Jews, rejection of freedom of speech, and freedom of conscience, will not yield good outcomes. To state this is not "bigoted"; it is recognizing a reality as clear as the existence of the sun.

Reciprocal altruism is an evolved mechanism (the West grants entry to a manageable number of refugees fully expecting that they will reciprocate our generosity by adopting our secular, liberal, and modern values); suicidal empathy is not. We should never compromise the fabric of our modern societies in order to engage in a pious exercise of civilizational self-flagellation. I say this as a proud Canadian immigrant. Those who repeatedly hurl "racist" at anyone who seeks to discuss rational immigration policies suffer from an insidious form of Ostrich Parasitic Syndrome.

Nothing to Do with Islam

Since the September 11, 2001, Islamist terrorist attacks on the United States, Islamic terrorists have perpetrated more than 35,000 attacks across the globe.[29] The attacks have occurred in nations that vary on every conceivable metric, including race, ethnicity, culture, religion, language, economic vitality, and political system. No other religion has come even remotely close to Islam in inspiring, justifying, or supporting terrorism. And yet, the progressive intelligentsia insist that none of these documented attacks have anything to do with Islam. Instead, a bewildering number of other "causes" have been offered.[30] Before I delve into some of these supposed causes, it is worth noting that the obfuscation starts with the use of fantastical euphemisms and misdirection in referring to the terror attacks.

Apparently, the terror attacks are senseless acts of random violence; they are unprovoked, non-ideological mass murder; they are a manifestation of homegrown extremism; they are instantiations of criminality or workplace violence; and as Barack Obama's administration reminded us all, they are man-made disasters.

The perpetrators of these "man-made disasters" are supposedly pushed to commit these heinous attacks because they are disenfranchised, marginalized, alienated, isolated, desperate, or humiliated. Furthermore, they lack hope, purpose, or meaningful relationships. They are social losers or family rejects. Many are "lone wolves." Many are also young (who amongst us did not head off to Raqqa in his youth to join ISIS and throw gays off rooftops; it's youthful indiscretion). Other "root causes" range from climate change, to toxic masculinity, to violent video games, to Western colonialism, to the Crusades (apparently revenge is a dish best served *really* cold). In fact, to progressives, anything—except for the obvious thing, Islamic doctrines—can be a root cause of Islamist terrorism. The Noble Faith must be protected at all costs.

How Ostrich Parasitic Syndrome Sufferers Protect Islam

There are innumerable cognitive biases to which OPS sufferers succumb in their desperate attempts to reject any honest criticism of Islam. Humans have evolved a preference for trusting the veracity of personal anecdotes over "cold" aggregate data. We are a storytelling animal, and as such our personal experiences carry great weight in shaping our views of the world. Now imagine that I am a Muslim individual who was raised by parents who are loving, kind, and tolerant. They have never harbored a single Jew-hating sentiment in their lives. They are well-respected members of their mosque. It becomes very easy for such an individual to argue that his parents exemplify True Islam. This yields two forms of Ostrich Logic, namely the #NotAllMuslims canard ("My father/brother/uncle/friend Ahmed is Muslim, and he is a very kind, peaceful, tolerant, and liberal individual") and the *Unicorn Islam* fallacy ("but True Islam is a feminist religion that loves Jews and gays, and it supports freedom of conscience"). Islam is a system of beliefs. Many Muslims pick and choose the parts that they wish to adhere to and reject those parts that they find objectionable. That your friend Ahmed eats pork and drinks whiskey says nothing about whether Islam permits these behaviors or not. Similarly, the imposition of your personal morality onto your religion does not alter its contents. That your Muslim parents taught you to love and respect Jews says nothing about whether Islam cherishes or despises Jews.

In 2010, a Canadian Jewish friend contacted me by email to help her better understand Islam (and specifically whether it contained doctrines of hate). At the time, she had a friend who was an apparently lovely Muslim woman who was pursuing a Ph.D. at a leading Canadian university. As commonly occurs with folks infected with OPS, my friend was having a difficult time reconciling her personal interaction with a liberal and peaceful Muslim with the growing evidence of never-ending global mayhem inflicted in the name of Islam. Among much else, I sent her a montage of clips demonstrating the profound Jew-hatred found in Islamic societies, with children, politicians, imams, clerics, and television personalities spewing nearly unimaginable genocidal hate. Alas, she, along with her friend, responded with a tsunami of clichés—all religions have violent extremists, the Bible contains violent passages, most Muslims are nice people—that amounted to a nonsensical apologia, and she ended one of our tense email exchanges with: "you're starting to sound fanatical yourself, Gad." Regrettably, she is hardly the only "progressive" Jew to engage in such disordered thinking when it comes to Islam.

The *deflect* strategy which she employed is a very common progressive defense of Islam. By pointing to ugly realities elsewhere, progressives hope to absolve Islam from criticism. The *All Religions Have Extremists* fallacy is immeasurably deceptive. It is true that a minuscule number of Christian individuals have used their faith as a justification for attacking abortion providers in the United States over the past twenty-five years.[31] People with functioning brains, though, recognize that the scale of a phenomenon matters. Even though Islam does not hold a *monopoly* on ideologically-based violence, it is certainly much more conducive to violence than, say, the beliefs of extremist Jains (who would assiduously use a broom to ensure that they do not walk on ants). Boxing and bowling are both labelled as sports, and yet we do not presume that they have an equal likelihood of yielding injuries. All religions are not equal in their capacity to mete out violence and genocidal hate. To say otherwise is to be hopelessly misguided or profoundly duplicitous. Two other popular deflections are *But What about the Crusades?* and *But the Bible Also Has Violent Passages.* The Crusades were a response to hundreds of years of Islamic aggression, and they took place within a very restricted time and place, nearly a millennium ago. As for the Bible, you can count on one hand the number of individuals who have used violent passages from Deuteronomy to justify acts of terrorism in the twenty-first century. On the other hand, innumerable Jihadis around the world use Islamic doctrines to justify their violent actions. Scale matters.

Another classic ploy used by apologists is the *No True Scotsman* fallacy. This argues that entire Islamic countries, Islamic governments, and leading Islamic scholars are "fake" representations of the true faith. If you point to sharia law in Saudi Arabia, the retort is that this does not represent True Islam. Similarly, Iran's mullahs apparently do not represent True Islam. Osama bin Laden was a "fake" Muslim. Other "fake" Muslims include Amin al-Husseini (the Grand Mufti of Jerusalem who was on friendly terms with Adolf Hitler), Sheikh Hassan al-Banna (founder of the Muslim Brotherhood), Grand Ayatollah Khomeini (the leader of the 1979 Iranian revolution), Sheikh Yusuf al-Qaradawi (arguably the leading Sunni theologian today), and Caliph Abu Bakr al-Baghdadi (the late leader of ISIS). Remember your friend Ahmed who is gay, eats prosciutto, and drinks cognac? He is a real Muslim; all these others are "fake." Denial is a very powerful trap.

OPS sufferers also employ the *Infinite Spiral of Delegitimization* strategy meant to delegitimize your right to critique Islam. For most Westerners it takes only one question: Do you speak Arabic? But other questions might include: Did you grow up in the Middle East? Are you a Muslim? Do you understand Qur'anic philology? Are you a hafiz (someone who has memorized the Qur'an in its entirety)? Did you attend Al-Azhar University (the supposed leading institution of Sunni Islam)? Are you an imam? Or, if all else fails: Are you one of the faithful companions of Muhammad? No? Well, shut up then. You don't have the right to criticize the Noble Faith. Given that Arabic is my mother tongue and that I'm from Lebanon, it takes longer to "delegitimize" me. Most Westerners don't stand a chance.

A more subtle delegitimization strategy is to deflect any critical scrutiny of Islam by historical cliché. For instance, "How do you explain the peaceful coexistence of Muslims, Jews, and Christians in Andalusia in the fifteenth century?" One answer—and a perfectly acceptable one—is that: "Well, that was Andalusia in the fifteenth century. Let's talk about today." But most historical clichés trotted out by progressives are also false, and the Andalusian era of alleged peaceful coexistence is a historical myth.[32] People of the Book (Jews and Christians) were at times tolerated as second if not third-class citizens, but they needed to know their place in the grand fabric of Islamic society. They held the status of a *dhimmi*, which required that they adhere to specific laws including the payment of the *jizya* (protection tax). In Muslim societies, non-Muslims are tolerated until they are not—at which point you better run fast. You never know when this is going to happen, but you know that the looming metaphorical heart attack is just around the corner. My family lived in Lebanon under relative safety—until the day that we had to run for our lives.

In a quest to appear nuanced, many academics will posit that a given phenomenon (like global jihad) is due to a broad range of hyphenated and concatenated factors that represent a complex multifactorial problem. I call this the *concatenation strategy*. I have often satirized this form of intellectual duplicity whenever another terror attack takes place with the perpetrators yelling *Allahu Akbar*. I remind people (satirically) that the true motives of the terrorists may never be known but they are likely due to a confluence of paleo-botanic, sociocultural, biopolitical, neurophysiological, psycho-economic, hetero-historical, geo-organic, and ethno-ketogenic factors. The more nonsensical terms that you can strew together, the greater the illusion of explanatory profundity.

The "nuanced" enemies of reason also like to use euphemisms to cover realities that are too politically incorrect to name. Hence, the West is not fighting Islamic terror, rather we are combatting Radicalized Militant Violent Extremist Man-Made Fanaticism (the dreaded RMVEMMF ideology). Those who are a bit more honest will recognize that it is linked to Islam, but they will use the "ism" algorithm to sanitize the reality. Hence, it is not due to Islam, but Islamism. It's not Islam but Jihadism, Wahhabism, or Salafism. Or they will place a qualifier to draw a distinction between Islam and Radical Islam or Extremist Islam. Many people have a strong aversion to directly blaming Islam because it feels gauche or intolerant to do so. They would rather give Islam a pass and place the blame on some supposedly "distorted" version of the faith. The reality though is that there are no codified holy books of Islamism that are distinct from those of Islam. Islamism, the political element of Islam, is an integral element of the religion. Fortunately, a great majority of Muslims ignore the unpalatable parts of their religion. This does not mean that they are practicing some Unicorn Gentle True Islam. If Mordechai Rubinstein chooses to eat pork and shrimps, he is not practicing a more liberal form of Judaism. He is simply ignoring those elements of Kosher laws that he finds too culinarily difficult to adhere to.

When faced with the unsavory nature of many Islamic doctrines, progressives argue that these cannot be taken seriously because the interpretation of texts (hermeneutics) is a subjective exercise, and very clear Islamist edicts of genocidal hate have, we are told, been mistranslated, misinterpreted, and misunderstood (I call this the Holy 3M of Apologia[33]). Using the political philosophy of *multiculturalism*, OPS sufferers refrain from criticizing truly abhorrent cultural and religious practices such as female genital mutilation, child brides, and honor killings under the guise of *moral and cultural relativism*. It is apparently wrong to apply universal moral principles when judging the precepts of a given society. Thus, Western critics are silent if not supportive of cultural and religious practices that otherwise should be universally condemned, as it would be "racist and bigoted" to question the traditions of others. Indeed, before he became Canada's prime minister, Justin Trudeau declared himself angrier that such practices could be declared barbaric than he was at the practices themselves.[34]

Radical Western feminists grant cover to such horrifying abuses of women under a similarly misguided notion of cultural relativism. In such a convoluted worldview, the burqa, the niqab, and the hijab become symbols of female empowerment while the bikini is construed as a symbol of patriarchal oppression. Using the *hierarchy of victimhood*, OPS sufferers refuse to criticize Islam because it would be "gross and racist" (to utilize Ben Affleck's infamous words). Instead, they fetishize all Muslims as inherently noble, peaceful, and kind, a new manifestation of the myth of the Noble Savage (all brown people are lovely while the white man is to blame for all ills).

I once shared a clip on my personal Facebook page of an Iraqi astronomer arguing that according to Islamic scriptures the earth was indeed flat. I received an irate reply from a white Western "progressive" female scientist who chastised me for sharing such a story. In her view, we should be nicer to Muslims. Hence, a fellow scientist was not angered by the nonsense that this Iraqi gentleman was spewing. Instead, she was upset at my having shared his idiocy. In her quest to be politically correct, she was willing to kill the truth.

In his book *That's Offensive!* Stefan Collini addresses the misguided progressive desire to shield some groups from equal scrutiny.

> Similar arguments apply to attempts to exempt the views or tastes of any group from reasoned appraisal and measured judgment. However well intentioned, all such attempts are, in the end, condescending. They assume that, in relation to a given topic, those who are in a disadvantaged "minority" (we

are all in minorities in relation to certain topics) need—in addition to efforts to remedy their disadvantage—the further protection of not having their most cherished convictions critically scrutinized. This in effect posits a two-tier society intellectually with the grown-ups deciding not just what may or may not be said in front of the children but who are to count as children in the first place. This eventually engenders a situation in which it is considered acceptable to criticize, mock or give offence to those deemed to be among the privileged but not to those deemed to be among the less privileged—a moral asymmetry which is ultimately corrosive of genuine respect and equality.[35]

Is Sharia Law Consistent with Western Legal Standards?

If one had to identify the legal system most antithetical to the American one, sharia law fits that bill, and yet many OPS sufferers will argue otherwise. Many Westerners might be repulsed by sharia's extraordinarily harsh corporeal punishments for theft (cutting off the hand) and adultery (stoning). And you might think that the lower status of women when it comes to the validity of their legal testimony or their bequeathing rights (half that of men) might be grotesque to Western sensibilities. Surely most Westerners would find it astoundingly cruel and unjust, if not insane, that under sharia law a female rape victim needs the eyewitness testimony of four men to be believed.

But sharia law is even more fundamentally opposed to Western legal standards because Islam rejects the Western idea of impartial justice applied fairly regardless of an individual's identity. Under sharia, punishments are applied as a function of the identity of the victim and perpetrator. A Jewish man who kills a Muslim man is judged very differently than a Muslim man who kills a Jewish man.[36] Sharia law specifically states that no retaliation can take place when a Muslim kills a non-Muslim and that indemnities depend on the identities of the parties in question.

04.9 (A: For the rulings below, one multiplies the fraction named by the indemnity appropriate to the death or injury's type of intentionality and other relevant circumstances that determine the amount of a male Muslim's indemnity (def: 04.2-6 and 04.13).)

The indemnity for the death or injury of a woman is one-half the indemnity paid for a man.

The indemnity paid for a Jew or Christian is one-third of the indemnity paid for a Muslim.

The indemnity paid for a Zoroastrian is one-fifteenth of that of a Muslim.

This is what identity politics does to a legal system—and this is precisely the standard adhered to by progressives. Men can be sexist, but women can't be. Whites can be racist, but blacks can't be. Permissible speech is governed by identity and political allegiance. A straight white Christian conservative man should shut his mouth and cede the floor to the progressive Muslim indigenous trans woman of color. Know your place, white guy. Don't speak out of turn. Hence, it is true that both sharia law and progressive identity politics adhere to the exact same principle. The repercussions of this fundamental attack on individual rights manifest themselves differently across the two ecosystems, but the mindset is nearly identical. The only difference is that progressives uphold the idea of equality, which sharia law does not. Still, progressive equality is a very special kind of equality. It was best captured in the immortal words of George Orwell in his novel *Animal Farm*: "All animals are equal, but some animals are more equal than others."[37]

Profiling Is Racist!

I spent the summers of 1983 and 1984 in Israel where many members of my extended family live. On one trip, I was detained at the border and eventually called in for questioning because I was a young man born in

Lebanon. I tried to explain that I was a Lebanese Jew with extensive family in Israel. The Israeli agent noted my family members' names (my eldest brother is Moshe or Moses in English, and my name is a biblical Hebrew name), and asked me in Hebrew if I were Jewish, and the matter was quickly resolved. In 1999, I returned to Israel to present a paper at a conference. During that visit, I took a short break in Dahab (Egyptian Sinai). When I reentered Israel, I was once again interrogated. The Israeli agent wanted proof that I was a professor and holder of a Ph.D., to which I responded that I was not in the habit of carrying my doctoral diploma with me, but the matter was quickly resolved.

More recently and closer to home, I was detained at the American border for more than one hour as I tried to make my way to Clarkson University to deliver an invited lecture. I was travelling with my wife and young daughter (who was then two years old). The delay was an inconvenience, but in the big picture, a minor one. I bring these incidents up to ask a question: Are the Israelis and Americans raging racists who are targeting an innocent, olive-skinned Middle Eastern man? Are they vile bigots engaging in a discriminatory form of profiling? The answer is an unequivocal "yes" if you've been infected with OPS. It is a "no" for anyone with a functioning brain.

If a dark alley offered a shortcut on your way home, would you be more or less likely to take it if you noticed four young men or four elderly women loitering there? Using common sense, you realize that young men are more likely to be dangerous than elderly women, and you might go another way if you saw the young men. This does not make you sexist or ageist. Most young men are not violent, but there is a greater possibility that they could be, which warrants trepidation. Back in 1993, a rabid white racist uttered the following infamous words: "There is nothing more painful to me at this stage in my life than to walk down the street and hear footsteps and start thinking about robbery. Then (I) look around and see someone white and feel relieved."[38] Oh no wait, that was no Grand Wizard of the KKK. It was none other than African American activist Jesse Jackson. Does the Reverend Jackson suffer from internalized bigotry against his own race? Or, perhaps he recognizes race-based patterns of criminality based on aggregate data and responds accordingly.

In my first semester as a doctoral student at Cornell University, I read *Homicide*, a book authored by two of the leading figures of evolutionary psychology, which had a profound effect on my eventual scientific career.[39] In it, the authors use the evolutionary lens to analyze a broad range of criminal behavior including child abuse and domestic violence. Two of the breathtaking conclusions arising from their analyses are: 1) The best predictor of whether a child will be abused (by a factor of 100) is whether a child grows up with a stepparent (dubbed the *Cinderella effect*); and 2) The most dangerous person in a woman's life is her male partner. Specifically, men are driven to violent actions when they suspect or become aware of infidelity. These are universal facts that transcend culture and time precisely because they are rooted in an evolutionary calculus that shapes dark elements of our shared human nature. It is not surprising then that when the police investigate a woman's murder, the first person they consider as a suspect is the male partner. They know perfectly well that most men will never commit such acts, but the police also know the odds (by experience if nothing else) that justify their actions. Similarly, the Cinderella effect holds true, notwithstanding the obvious existence of loving and caring stepparents. Personal anecdotes do not invalidate the statistical realities. Our brains have evolved to detect statistical regularities in our environment. To act on this knowledge is not bigoted, racist, or hateful; it is at the root of human cognition. To discriminate, in the sense of making a distinction rooted in a probabilistic reality, is to be human.[40] To profile is to be human.[41]

Those infected with OPS reject this logic. Instead, in the desire to adhere to the "reality is racist" tenets of progressivism, they refuse to profile because to do so would be discriminatory (in the prejudicial sense of the word). They belong to what the political humorist Evan Sayet referred to as the *Cult of Indiscriminateness*.[42] This is precisely why when travelling to Southern California in 2011, my then-two-year-old daughter was randomly chosen for a more thorough security check at the Montreal airport. It is precisely why a posse of elderly nuns would be just as likely to be picked for an enhanced security check as a group of young men from Pakistan, Yemen, and Syria travelling together. In Unicornia, all people are just as likely to be terrorists. To think otherwise is to be a hateful bigot. OPS is a terrible affliction of the human mind.

CHAPTER SEVEN

How to Seek Truth: Nomological Networks of Cumulative Evidence

"One of the most salient features of our culture is that there is so much bullshit. Everyone knows this."
—Harry G. Frankfurt[1]

"Reason, we argue, has two main functions: that of producing reasons for justifying oneself, and that of producing arguments to convince others."
—Hugo Mercier and Dan Sperber[2]

A fundamental feature of an individual's civic duty in a free society is to be an informed citizen on issues of societal import. This is not an easy task to accomplish as most people succumb to several cognitive and emotional traps along the way. First, humans are cerebral misers; namely they are too intellectually lazy to collect the relevant information on a given issue and instead prefer to form opinions while expending as little mental effort as possible. Second, the informational landscape is laden with data of varying levels of veracity. Third, once an individual has committed to a position, it is notoriously difficult to get him to consider opposing evidence. Along with his two coauthors, Leon Festinger, the pioneer of the theory of cognitive dissonance, reminded us more than six decades ago about the difficulty of getting someone to change his mind:

A man with a conviction is a hard man to change. Tell him you disagree, and he turns away. Show him facts or figures, and he questions your sources. Appeal to logic, and he fails to see your point.

We have all experienced the futility of trying to change a strong conviction, especially if the convinced person has some investment in his belief. We are familiar with the variety of ingenious defenses with which people protect their convictions, managing to keep them unscathed through the most devastating attacks.

But man's resourcefulness goes beyond simply protecting a belief. Suppose an individual believes something with his whole heart; suppose further that he has a commitment to this belief, that he has taken irrevocable actions because of it; finally, suppose that he is presented with evidence, unequivocal and undeniable evidence, that his belief is wrong: What will happen? The individual will frequently emerge, not only unshaken, but even more convinced of the truth of his beliefs than ever before. Indeed, he may even show a new fervor about convincing and converting other people to his view.[3]

More recently, Dan Sperber and Hugo Mercier developed their argumentative theory of reasoning, which speaks to the fact that it might be difficult for people to alter their opinions even when faced with contrary evidence. They posit that our reasoning faculties did not necessarily evolve to seek truth but rather to convince ourselves and others in a battle of wits. Given the apparent innate penchant for most people to engage in motivated reasoning (biased information processing to protect one's beliefs, attitudes, or ideological positions), is it feasible to expect people to seek an objective truth? As an optimistic realist, I'd like to think so.

Intellectual courage—or as I prefer to call it, testicular fortitude—is a necessary first step for anyone who wishes to participate in the battle of ideas. But this is insufficient. All of the courage in the world is not going to sway anyone's opinions if you do not possess mastery of the relevant information and the appropriate critical thinking skills to process such information. That is why you need to tap an extraordinarily powerful epistemological tool, nomological networks of cumulative evidence, to help you coherently synthesize information from multiple and disparate sources.[4]

How to Establish Truth

Philosophers have offered many frameworks to define truth. Mathematical proofs, for instance, are *axiomatic truths*. *Empirical truths*, on the other hand, are sought via the scientific method: in simplified form, a researcher proposes a question, develops a hypothesis, collects and analyzes the relevant data, tests the hypothesis, and draws the fitting conclusion. If a given scientific phenomenon is replicated a sufficient number of times, it becomes part of the core knowledge of the field. To take a banal example, it is an empirical truth that men commit more violent crimes than women (this pattern has been documented across time and cultures using disparate data sources).

Scientific truths are always provisional because they should be always potentially falsifiable (open to testing). As such, one might be tempted to think that scientists are impartial processors of information. The reality though is that they are human beings capable of the same penchant for motivated reasoning. Back in 2008, I was invited to deliver two lectures about my work at the intersection of evolutionary psychology and consumer behavior in front of the top-ranked psychology and marketing departments at the University of Michigan. I confirmed with one of my hosts that there would be no overlap between the two audiences; so I prepared to deliver the same lecture to the two groups. The first lecture took place in the psychology department, where my ideas were very well received. The second lecture on the following day was undoubtedly the most hostile academic crowd that I've ever faced. I was unable to finish a line of thinking without being badgered, interrupted, and harassed by numerous faculty members. The deluge of ignorant hostility began prior to my delivering the lecture, in the one-on-one meetings with faculty that preceded my talk. One marketing professor "explained" to me in his office that evolution was unfalsifiable (so it wasn't real science) to which I dismissively replied: "So how long have you been at the University of Michigan?" In other words, I quickly gauged the futility of engaging the individual in question and sidestepped his buffoonish comment. There was a general pattern to the hostility. Many of the doctoral students or junior faculty were open to my ideas, while older, established professors seemed much more resistant. This makes perfect sense in that the latter are entrenched in paradigms that define their professional work. They wrongly construed my evolutionary research as a threat to their scholarship, and accordingly huffed and puffed in indignation. The doctoral students on the other hand did not have any paradigmatic vested interests, and as such were receptive to novel approaches. I have noted a similar pattern of resistance to my scientific work when comparing marketing practitioners to marketing academics. Practitioners only care that my scientific work is applicable and relevant, whereas academics judge my contributions by how well these fit into their established paradigms.

Scientific breakthroughs are precisely those most likely to shake orthodoxy and be resisted, if not outright rejected, by defenders of the status quo.[5] Scientists, like everyone else, have personal biases and agendas. As Nobel Prize–winning physicist Max Planck noted: "A new scientific truth does not triumph by convincing its opponents and making them see the light, but rather because its opponents eventually die, and a new generation grows up that is familiar with it."[6] This general sentiment was shared by the zoologist Frederick R. Schram who proclaimed: "Science is not a superhuman activity immune to the foibles of human nature. Lack of progress in science is never so much due to any sparcity of factual information as it is to the fixed mindsets of scientists themselves."[7] Eventually though, via the auto-corrective process of science, superior ideas do win out. The cardiologist Dean Ornish was of that opinion when he pronounced, "And although scientists can often be as resistant to new ideas as anyone, the process of science ensures that, over time, good ideas and theories prevail."[8] I agree.

How do scientists decide that a given finding is suitably robust to be considered an empirical truth worthy of being added to the pantheon of core knowledge of a given discipline? As a first step, the finding has to be replicated by a sufficient number of independent researchers. This is a cornerstone of the scientific method, and yet the social sciences have an abysmal rate of replicable results.[9] Another integral part of the scientific process is the literature review. A research project is part of a grand scientific story to which other researchers have previously contributed. Accordingly, if you wish to recount the full narrative of your scientific journey, you must recognize the predecessors who have provided important pieces of the larger puzzle. Or in the immortal words of Sir Isaac Newton, "if I have seen further, it is by standing on the shoulders of giants." I always remind my students that the key objective of a literature review is to offer a compelling narrative of the previous works upon which you've built. Let us suppose your project is on the evolutionary roots of gift-giving to romantic partners. You could contrast your approach with those who have utilized an economic or sociological framework. Alternatively, you could compare nuptial gift giving in the human and animal worlds. Whatever narrative you choose, the literature review offers a valuable snapshot of current knowledge in the field.

At times, of course, a literature review will yield no consensus. For instance, in the late 1990s, I investigated the effects of dysphoria (the opposite of euphoria) on decision making.[10] I discovered that in the scientific literature there was no consensus on the topic. So how does one integrate contradictory findings with one's own research? Meta-analysis addresses this conundrum. Meta-analysis is a statistical technique for combining comparable studies into one "mega-study." A key element of a meta-analysis is deciding which studies to include while being mindful of the so-called "file drawer" problem where editorial bias leads to the exclusion of studies in the literature that yielded null results. In my dysphoria research I found no differences between dysphorics and non-dysphorics on fifteen out of sixteen dependent measures. In other words, the null effect dominated across a broad range of variables. When I attempted to publish a paper on my research, the editor rejected it on that exact basis (too many null effects). At times, null effects are extremely important to document within the scientific literature, and certainly so when conducting a meta-analysis.

Replication studies, literature reviews, and meta-analyses are means by which scientists amass cumulative evidence for a given phenomenon typically within rigidly defined methodologies, paradigms, and disciplines. But beyond this, there is a way to generate and organize knowledge so that it becomes difficult even for one's staunchest detractors, wallowing in ideological biases, to deny your conclusions.

Nomological Networks of Cumulative Evidence

Charles Darwin ranks among the leading thinkers of all time for offering an elegant mechanism (natural selection) to explain how species evolve. One reason his 1859 book *On the Origin of Species* is a masterpiece is that it amassed evidence from biogeography, geology, entomology, comparative anatomy, botany, embryology, and paleontology. A judicious district attorney patiently amasses a mountain of evidence prior to bringing his case in front of a jury. Darwin, the ever-so-careful scientist, was more assiduous than any legal prosecutor could ever be. He collected data for several decades before he felt sufficiently confident to present his case before the world. This approach epitomizes the gift of the human intellect. It is akin to building a jigsaw puzzle. No single piece is sufficient to see the full image but once all of the pieces are placed in their rightful positions, the final pattern emerges clearly.

Nomological networks of cumulative evidence constitute a modern manifestation of Darwin's synthetic approach. Suppose that you wish to demonstrate that men's universal preference for the hourglass figure was shaped by evolution. How would you go about achieving such a task? The objective would be to build a network of cumulative evidence stemming from widely different sources, all of which serve to construct the final jigsaw puzzle (undoubtedly of a beautiful woman possessing the hourglass figure). Here are some compelling findings:[11] 1) the hourglass figure has been associated with greater fertility and superior health;[12] 2) across a broad range of cultures, online female escorts advertise the hourglass figure to prospective patrons—whether they are lying about said measurements is immaterial; 3) online escorts who possess the hourglass figure command larger fees; 4) statues and figures spanning varied cultures across several millennia exhibit the desired hourglass figure; 5) *Playboy* centerfolds and Miss America winners throughout the twentieth century possess the preferred hourglass figure; 6) men's preference for the hourglass figure has been documented across diverse cultures and races using many methods including brain imaging and eye tracking; and 7) men who have never had the gift of sight are also drawn to the hourglass figure (using touch to establish the preference). This constitutes an unassailable body of evidence. This is precisely the reason that I'm able to lecture about such evolutionary principles in front of otherwise hostile audiences (such as radical feminists) with my usual swagger. Once the enemies of truth are presented with these nomological networks of cumulative evidence, they typically quietly nod in defeated resignation. Your feelings cannot protect you from the truth. These networks provide key epistemological benefits in explaining scientific phenomena including explanatory coherence,[13] theoretical integration,[14] and consilience (unity of knowledge).[15]

Nomological Network of Cumulative Evidence for Toy Preferences

Social constructivists have long argued that parents inculcate "arbitrarily sexist" gender roles in their children by the toys they give them: the general narrative is that boys are encouraged to play with toy soldiers and trucks while girls are given dolls and playhouses. This early socialization—aggression for boys and nurturing for girls—supposedly results in countless downstream sex differences later in life. If only little Suzie had been encouraged to engage in rough and tumble play, she could have been the world record holder in pow-erlifting (across the sexes). But her sexist parents held her back via the imposi-tion of toy preferences when she was a young child. This imbecilic premise is not restricted to the rarified world of academia. It has seeped down to toy manufacturers, some of whom, in their efforts to appear progressive, have created advertising campaigns that are contrary to the standard pattern of toy preferences (such as showing a boy playing with a doll). If I wanted to convince you that toy preferences are biologically based, how would I go about building such a nomological network?[16]

One of the strategies used by evolutionary psychologists to demon-strate that a preference is hardwired is to document it in infants that have yet to reach the developmental stage that would allow them to be social-ized to that preference. In other words, one can easily refute the social constructivist argument by showing that infants exhibit sex-specific toy preferences. This has indeed been shown in several studies and serves as sufficient evidence to reject the idea that it is "arbitrary sexist" standards that are the root cause of toy preferences. But we are only getting started with the building of the nomological network in question! The relative lengths of the index and ring fingers are known as the digit ratio. It is a sexually dimorphic trait meaning that human males and females exhibit a consistent difference along this trait. Specifically, the ring finger is longer than the index finger for males whereas the two fingers are closer in length to one another in females. The digit ratio captures the extent of androgen exposure to which an individual has been subjected in utero. In other words, more masculinized digit ratios are markers of greater exposure to testosterone. Along with some of my former graduate stu-dents, I have conducted several studies linking the digit ratio to risk-taking proclivities and courtship-related behaviors.[17] Of relevance to the current toy example, researchers have demonstrated that very young boys who possess more masculinized digit ratios exhibit more masculinized play behaviors and toy preferences. The hormonal roots of toy prefer-ences and play patterns have also been shown via the collection of urine samples (to measure testosterone levels) from infants starting from the age of seven days until six months of age. Using clinical data, two separate groups of researchers have documented that little girls suffering from congenital adrenal hyperplasia—a masculinizing endocrinological malady—exhibit more masculinized toy preferences. So, we have proof of the incontestable biological roots of toy preferences using developmental, morphological, and pediatric endocrinological evidence stemming from normal and clinical populations. But we are still only getting started!

Comparative psychology is a sub-branch of the discipline that seeks to understand human cognition by contrasting it with that of other species. Two important principles in that pursuit are homologies and analogies. A homologous trait between species A and B is evidence that the two species have a common evolutionary ancestor whereas an analogous trait highlights the fact that evolution can arrive at the same adaptation (such as the fact both birds and bats have the ability to fly) through independent means. It turns out that vervet monkeys, rhesus monkeys, and chimpanzees exhibit the same sex-specific toy preferences that humans do. This homologous toy preference suggests that there is a clear operative evolutionary/biological signature. Social constructivists might retort that this only proves that the evil sexist patriarchy wields its nefarious influence across several primate species! Never underestimate the delusional and dogmatic lunacy inherent in those afflicted with Ostrich Parasitic Syndrome.

In building an airtight nomological network of cumulative evidence, one should try to anticipate and address all counterarguments that detractors are likely to levy. Recall that social constructivists posit that men and women are socialized into arbitrary gender roles, with toy preferences serving as an early manifestation of such "sexist" learning. How might one wield a death blow to this nonsensical premise? The answer lies with Sweden. The cross-cultural psychologist Geert Hofstede has ranked Sweden as the most feminine country with the greatest gender parity across fifty disparate nations. This Scandinavian oasis of progressive platitudes has been conducting what amounts to a longitudinal social engineering experiment for the past several decades wherein they have sought to create the perfect utopian gender-neutral society. Hence, if there ever was a perfect case study of whether a more gender egalitarian nation yields non-sex-specific toy preferences, Sweden is that country. Well, data have a pesky way of trashing the utopian dreams of delusional ideologues. An expansive study of Swedish children's toy preferences found that children's sex-specific toy preferences are not as malleable as social constructivists would like you to believe: it turns out that boys will be boys, and girls will be girls.[18]

Social constructivists could still raise two possible remaining concerns: that the relevant studies stem from Western cultures, and that they originate in the current era. Well, the anthropologist Jean-Pierre Rossie conducted a detailed analysis of dolls and doll-play among various tribes within Saharan and North African territories. The peoples included the Belbala, the Chaamba, the Chaouia, the Ghrib, the Kabyles, the Moors, the Mozabites, the Reguibat, the Sahrawi, the Teda, the Tuareg, the inhabitants of the Saoura Valley, the populations of the Moroccan countryside, and the town-dwellers of Algeria, Morocco, and Tunisia. Hardly, a repository of Western cultures. Rossie documented two key results of relevance to the current discussion: 1) Girls are much more likely than boys to play with dolls; 2) Female dolls are much more prevalent than male dolls. I uncovered a study that examined illustrations of children on funerary monuments in Ancient Greece. The same pattern emerged: boys are depicted playing with wheels, and girls are depicted playing with dolls. Since I first reported this nomological network in 2017, an exhaustive review and meta-analysis has revealed that the sex-specific toy preferences are indeed operative across ages, eras, and cultural contexts.[19] It is difficult to imagine a greater tsunami of evidence against the premise that children's toy preferences are due to social construction. Nomological networks of cumulative evidence serve as a crucial antidote to those afflicted with OPS.

Nomological Network of Cumulative Evidence for Sex Differences in Human Mating

Humans are a sexually dimorphic species meaning that they exhibit sex differences rooted in evolutionary realities. An obvious manifestation of this fact is the size difference between the two sexes. On average, men are taller and heavier than women. This statement holds true at the population level even though we could all think of innumerable individual exceptions. I call this the "But Katie Holmes is taller than Tom Cruise" cognitive bias exhibited by many OPS sufferers.[20] People presume that a singular example serves as a refutation. It does not. To state that humans are a sexually reproducing species possessing a fundamental and powerful mating drive is not, for instance, invalidated by the existence of celibate people (such as Catholic priests).

Countless robust sex differences have been documented in the scientific literature across an extraordinarily broad range of human domains (physiological, morphological, behavioral, hormonal, and affective, to name a few).[21] While not all sex differences are the result of evolution, those dealing with mating typically are. Recall that sexual selection is the evolutionary mechanism by which sexually reproducing species evolve sex-specific preferences in their mates (such as peahens' preference for the peacock's conspicuous tail). It is not surprising then that men and women have evolved sex-specific preferences for their ideal mates. These mating preferences hold across time periods and cultural settings precisely because they are a reflection of our shared biological heritage. Of all human sexual dimorphisms, the most documented one has been sex differences in the desired attributes sought in prospective mates. In a 1989 classic paper, the evolutionary psychologist David Buss examined the importance that men and women ascribe to several evolutionarily important attributes including *good financial prospect, ambition and industriousness, preferred age of mate* (in relation to self), and *good looks.* The sample size consisted of 10,047 individuals from 37 highly distinct cultures spanning the entire globe, and that otherwise vary greatly in terms of ethnicity, race, religion, political and economic system, and language.[22] Men preferred younger mates in all studied cultures (thirty-seven out of thirty-seven) and cared more about physical attraction in thirty-four of the thirty-seven cultures. Women assigned greater importance to a partner's financial prospect (thirty-six cultures) and ambition/industriousness (twenty-nine cultures). Statistically significant findings that were contrary to evolutionary expectations were exceptionally rare. A recent study has confirmed the greater importance that men and women place on physical attractiveness and good earning potential respectively across thirty-six countries that otherwise vary in terms of their gender inequality scores.[23]

In order to quell the concern that Buss's data only capture Westernized contemporary realities, Jonathan Gottschall and his colleagues conducted a content analysis of mating preferences of male and female characters in 658 folktales arising from 48 highly disparate cultural settings and in 240 classic works of Western literature.[24] A broad coverage of societies (bands, tribes, and preindustrial states) and time periods was included. The greater importance ascribed to physical attractiveness and wealth/status by men and women respectively were strongly confirmed across this breathtakingly exhaustive data set. These universal mating preferences have been confirmed across temporal periods and cultural settings using extraordinarily broad and innovative data sources, including cross-generational surveys, analyses of mail-order brides, speed dating events, online dating behavior, content analyses of personal ads, ethnographies and ethnologies of preindustrial societies,[25] cultural products (song lyrics, movie plotlines, music videos, romance novels),[26] and the lyrics of medieval troubadours.[27]

De Clérambault's syndrome, more colloquially known as erotomania, is a psychiatric disorder wherein sufferers hold the delusional belief that they are loved by a target individual. Margaret Mary Ray's erotomania toward former late-night talk show host David Letterman is perhaps one of the best-known manifestations of this condition. The psychiatrist Martin Brüne analyzed 246 global cases of erotomania and coded key characteristics of the targets of the delusion as a function of the sex of the sufferer.[28] In other words, for women who suffer from erotomania, are the targets of their delusion different from those of men afflicted with this disorder? In line with evolutionary psychology, women erotomaniacs were more likely to be deluded about being loved by a high-status older male whereas male erotomaniacs focused their delusion on beautiful young women. In other words, universal mating preferences in normal populations replicate in the context of a psychiatric condition.

Parental investment theory provides a grand meta-framework for understanding patterns of sex differences across a bewildering number of sexually reproducing species.[29] In most species, females are more invested as parents than males are, and, as a consequence, are more judicious in their sexual behaviors. But in species where males are more invested as parents than females are, typical sex differences are reversed. Such females are larger, more aggressive, and more sexually unrestrained.[30] An example of such a species is the prehistoric-looking Cassowary bird, native to Australia. Among humans, women's parental investment is much higher than men's. Women produce on average 400 fertilizable ova from the onset of their menstrual cycle to menopause while men produce on average 250 million spermatozoa in a single ejaculation. As such, female gametes are precious and rare while those of men are abundant and cheap. Add the physiological costs of gestation and breastfeeding, the risk of childbirth mortality, and other sex-specific costs (women are at increased risk of predation when they are pregnant), and the parental investment scale tilts overwhelmingly toward women. Parental investment theory would predict that women would be much less interested in unrestricted sexuality than men—and this is universally true. The Sociosexual Orientation Inventory (SOI) is a psychometric scale that measures this exact construct.[31] The International Sexuality Description Project, founded by David P. Schmitt, examines human sexuality around the world. As part of that initiative, the SOI was administered to 14,059 participants coming from 48 countries representing many different cultures.[32] In every single country, women exhibited statistically lower SOI scores. It is difficult to imagine universal data that are more compelling. The global sex difference in SOI scores documented for heterosexual participants replicates for their gay counterparts. In other words, this sex difference is rooted in male versus female psychology irrespective of whether the desired target is opposite-sex or same-sex. Behavioral data offers converging support that women are much less interested in having sex with strangers (a measure of unrestricted sexuality). Across two studies, when approached to have sex with a stranger (on an American university campus), not a single woman accepted the offer whereas most men (up to 75 percent) did.[33] Several additional papers have since confirmed this finding in other cultural settings.

Sexual fantasies serve as another source of data for examining sex differences in human mating. This constitutes a unique source of scientific evidence in that it offers a window to people's most private thoughts and latent desires. A study that examined this issue found that men engaged in more daily sexual fantasies than did women; they fantasized about a greater number of individuals than did women; their fantasies involved greater sexual imagery (including genitalia) than those of women; and men were more likely than women to fantasize strictly about having sex with someone.[34] In other words, the sex difference that is captured via the SOI is replicated using this unique data set. Incidentally, the differential desire in sexual variety is one of several reasons that, historically speaking, male rulers stemming from widely distinct cultures have been much more likely to have harems of wives and concubines,[35] and why 85 percent of documented cultures have permitted polygyny (one man marrying multiple wives).[36] Once a man achieves a high social status, he is often very quick to instantiate his evolved penchant for sexual variety whether he is a despotic ruler, a famous athlete (ask Wilt Chamberlain), or a rock star (ask Gene Simmons of the group Kiss or Michael James Hucknall, the lead singer of Simply Red). Female rulers, female athletes, and female rock stars do not seem to exhibit a similar desire for sexual variety.

The differential interest across the two sexes in "no strings" sex is evident in countless other ways. Given men's greater proclivity for short-term mating, one would expect them to have evolved a "rapid fire" physiology including a greater penchant to be more quickly aroused by sexual stimuli. Not surprisingly, men and women do indeed exhibit different physiological and neuronal responses to visual sexual stimuli.[37] These universal realities manifest themselves in countless commercial settings. It is no coincidence that nowhere in the world does the number of strip bars targeting female patrons outnumber those targeting male patrons. It is also the reason that, around the world, romance novels are largely read by women while hard-core pornography is overwhelmingly viewed by men, and why sex services are largely purchased by men. I am unaware of a culture that has ever been documented where women are more likely to purchase short-term sexual services than are men.

With two of my former graduate students, I investigated the question of how much information—ranging over twenty-five attributes—from two prospective suitors do men and women need before rejecting both suitors or choosing one.[38] Women required less information to reject a pair of suitors. Furthermore, women searching for a short-term mate were the most likely to reject a pair of suitors whereas men searching for a short-term mate were the least likely to do so. In a second study, we found that women evaluated a greater number of prospective mates than did men prior to committing to a winning suitor. With one of my other former graduate students, I also looked at how framing alters the manner in which prospective mates are evaluated. For example, suppose that you are asked to judge how desirable a prospective suitor is based on one of two equivalent descriptions: 1) seven out of ten people who know this individual think that he/she is intelligent (positive frame); or 2) three out of ten people who know this individual do not think that he/she is intelligent (negative frame). Women succumbed more to the framing effect because negatively framed information looms larger to women when making mate choices.[39] These two sets of studies demonstrate that men and women have evolved sex-specific cognitive processes when searching for and evaluating prospective mates in line with parental investment theory.

Although humans are a biparental species wherein both males and females invest heavily in their children (albeit not in equal measure), only men face the threat of paternity uncertainty. This sex-specific threat is at the root of many mating-related differences across the two sexes including the triggers of romantic jealousy. For example, recall that men and women do not respond similarly to emotional versus sexual infidelities. A comprehensive meta-analysis revealed that men respond more adversely to sexual infidelity, while women react more harshly to emotional infidelity.[40] Men fear paternity uncertainty, while women fear abandonment of the relationship.

What triggers men to envy other men, and women to envy other women, has also been studied from an evolutionary perspective.[41] For example, men are more likely to envy other men's social status, and women are more likely to envy other women's physical attractiveness. We envy people whose traits compete with our desirability as a mate.

Regret is another emotion that has been explored within the mating domain. Researchers have examined how men and women experience regret at having missed out on short-term mating opportunities (greater regret by men) as well as the regret after having had a short-term dalliance (greater regret by women).[42] In other words, men's greater interest in sexual variety and unrestrained sexuality is captured via the psychology of sexual regret.

This cumulative evidence is only the tip of the relevant data iceberg. That said, in building this nomological network, I have presented confirming evidence across cultures, time periods, dependent variables, and methodological approaches. Is the nomological approach strictly reserved for scientific phenomena? No! It is a rigorous method for marshaling the powers of science, logic, and reason in tackling innumerable issues of great societal importance. I turn to such a concrete and timely example next.

Nomological Network of Cumulative Evidence for Islam

Since 9/11, the West has been exposed to Islam like almost never before (at least since the end of the Middle Ages). A religion that had largely been absent in Canada and the United States has become hyper-present across many facets of our daily lives. Most Westerners are confused about the nature of Islam. Is it a merciful, tolerant, and peaceful religion or is it a religion of violence, intolerance, and domination? Countless Western politicians including George W. Bush, Barack Obama, and Justin Trudeau have repeatedly reassured us that Islam is indeed a religion of peace. Yet daily realities might suggest otherwise. How should we go about answering such a delicate and sensitive question? Identify all relevant data sources that shed light on the matter and systematically build the associated nomological network of cumulative evidence.[43] Whether Islam is profoundly peaceful or immeasurably intolerant can be established with logic, reason, and science, with data drawn from historical, survey-based, and canonical sources to name a few. I begin with an examination of how Islam has spread globally, and how well religious minorities fare under Islamic rule.

Infectious Memeplexes, Historical Data, and the Plight of Religious Minorities

Are you more afraid of the measles or Ebola? The answer to this question is not straightforward since it requires some epidemiological knowledge. One measure of the dreadfulness of an infectious disease is your likelihood of dying if you contract it. All other things equal, a disease with a 100 percent fatality rate is scarier than one with a 25 percent fatality rate. However, this does not tell the full story. The deadlier disease might have a low reproduction number, meaning that it is not very contagious, while a disease with a lesser mortality rate might be much more contagious.[44] Epidemiological models of infectious diseases usually include several components when seeking to capture the contagiousness of a disease including the infectious period, the contact rate, and the transmission mode. The infection period for a cold is in the order of several days while that of HIV is open-ended. The contact rate captures the extent to which uninfected people will come in contact with those who are infected. For example, all other things equal, population density (dense urban centers versus sparsely populated rural areas) will increase the contact rate of a given infectious disease. Finally, the transmission mode captures the manner by which the disease is passed between individuals. HIV requires a more intimate interaction between two individuals (sexual activity or sharing a hypodermic needle) than say an airborne virus that can spread by being exposed to a cough.

The framework for understanding the epidemiology of infectious diseases is relevant to examining the spread of ideas, beliefs, urban legends, and other packets of transmissible information such as religions. Why does one company rumor spread like wildfire on the internet while another fizzles out after a few shares on social media? Why do some ideas propagate across vast social networks while others fail to catch on? Take for example Islam and Judaism. Before reading on, could you estimate the number of worldwide adherents that each faith counts within its ranks? I posed this exact question to Joe Rogan during one of our chats on his podcast. More specifically, I asked him whether he could guess the number of Jews in the world. I did so precisely because most people grossly overestimate the actual figure. He began with a first guess of one billion and then revised it to 500 million. The actual number: 14.5 million Jews in the entire world! Countless people overestimate this number perhaps because of the extraordinary achievements that have been tallied by Jews despite their minuscule numbers. He was so stunned by this figure that he had to get it confirmed by his producer while we were live on air. The number of Muslims on the other hand is around 1.8 billion. In other words, roughly 25 percent of humanity is Muslim. For every Jew, there are roughly one hundred twenty-five Muslims. Judaism is about 2,500 years older than Islam, and yet it has not been able to attract nearly as many followers. If we construe religions as memeplexes (a collection of interconnected memes), to borrow Richard Dawkins's term, the Islamic memeplex has been extraordinarily more successful than its Jewish counterpart (from an epidemiological perspective, that is). Why is that? To answer this important question, we must look at the contents of the two respective memeplexes to examine why one is more "infectious" than the other.

Let us explore the rules for converting into the two religions and apostatizing out of them. In Judaism, the religious process for conversion is onerous, requiring several years of commitment and an absence of ulterior motive. (For example, converting to Judaism because you are marrying a Jewish person is considered an inadmissible ulterior motive.) Not surprisingly, given the barriers to entry, relatively few people convert to Judaism. On the other hand, to convert to Islam simply requires that one proclaim openly one sentence, the shahada (the testimony): "There is no true god but Allah [God], and Muhammad is the Messenger (Prophet) of Allah." It does not require a sophisticated epidemiological model to predict which memeplex will spread more rapidly. Let us now suppose that one wishes to leave the religion. While the Old Testament does mention the death penalty for apostasy, it has seldom been applied throughout Jewish history, whereas to this day apostasy from Islam does lead to the death penalty in several Islamic countries.

But perhaps the most important difference is that Judaism does not promote or encourage proselytizing, whereas it is a central religious obligation in Islam. According to Islam, the world is divided into dar al-harb (the house of war) and dar al-Islam (the house of Islam). Peace will arrive when the entire world is united under the flag of Allah. Hence, it is imperative to Islamize the nations within dar al-harb. There is only one Jewish country in the world, Israel, and it has a sizeable non-Jewish minority. But there are fifty-seven member states of the Organization of Islamic Cooperation (OIC). In many OIC countries, Islam is not only the majority religion, it is practically the only religion. Here is a list of Islamic countries where Muslims currently comprise between 95 and 100 percent of the total population: Afghanistan, Algeria, the Comoros, Iran, Iraq, Jordan, Kosovo, Libya, the Maldives, Mauritania, Morocco, Niger, Pakistan, the Palestinian Territories, Saudi Arabia, Senegal, Somalia, Sudan, Tajikistan, Tunisia, Turkey, Uzbekistan, Western Sahara, and Yemen. The most populous Arab Muslim nation, Egypt, has a small and continually dwindling population of Coptic Christians. In other words, the manner by which the two religions spread and the extent to which they tolerate plurality is well captured by their religious doctrines.

Among the intelligentsia of the West, it is common to self-flagellate by pointing to Western colonialism and American global hegemony. The West, we are told, was built by war and conquest whereas Islam spread via love and peace. The reality is that Islamic history is replete with endless conquests. In the now infamous words of the Harvard political scientist Samuel P. Huntington, "Conflict along the fault line between Western and Islamic civilizations has been going on for 1,300 years." And even more succinctly, "Islam has bloody borders."[45] Since its founding in the seventh century, Islam has subjugated, converted, or killed hundreds of millions of people.

Contemporary FBI Data

The FBI maintains a global list of its most wanted global terrorists.[46] Twenty-six out of the current twenty-eight members that compose this infamous group are connected to Islamic groups. Though Muslims make up roughly 25 percent of the world's population, they comprise 92.9 percent of terrorists on the FBI list. The twenty-six individuals are: Husayn Muhammad Al-Umari (Palestine), Ali Saed Bin Ali El-Hoorie (Saudi Arabia), Sajid Mir (Pakistan), Abd Al Aziz Awda (Gaza Strip), Jaber A. Elbaneh (Yemen), Ibrahim Salih Mohammed Al-Yacoub (Saudi Arabia), Mohammed Ali Hamadei (Lebanon), Raddulan Sahiron (Philippines), Abdullah Ahmed Abdullah (Egypt), Ramadan Abdullah Mohammad Shallah (Gaza Strip), Hasan Izz-Al-Din (Lebanon), Abdelkarim Hussein Mohamed Al-Nasser (Saudi Arabia), Ali Atwa (Lebanon), Ahlam Ahmad Al-Tamimi (Jordan; female), Jehad Serwan Mostafa (United States), Ayman Al-Zawahiri (Egypt), Abdul Rahman Yasin (United States), Saif Al-Adel (Egypt), Muhammad Ahmed Al-Munawar (Kuwait), Muhammad Abdullah Khalil Hussain Ar-Rahayyal (Lebanon), Wadoud Muhammad Hafiz Al-Turki (Iraq), Jamal Saeed Abdul Rahim (Lebanon), Liban Haji Mohamed (Somalia), Ahmad Ibrahim Al-Mughassil (Saudi Arabia), Ahmad Abousamra (France), and Adnan Gulshair El Shukrijumah (Saudi

Arabia). These individuals come from around the world, they are of different races, they speak different languages, and some are born in Western countries. If only there was a way to connect them under a common rubric. Apparently, we may never know their true motives, a position that has often been espoused non-satirically by Western police when Islamic terrorists commit a brutal attack.[47]

Given the demographic realities of terror attacks, it might perhaps be minimally surprising that no-fly and watch lists contain a great number of Muslims, although the actual lists are unavailable for public viewing. But, of course, the general response is the screeching cry of Islamophobia because any other reaction would be bigoted.

Content Analysis of Canonical Texts

Bill Warner, a former professor of physics and founder of the Center for the Study of Political Islam has conducted content analyses on the three canonical sources of Islam: the Qur'an (which represents the inerrant, universal, and eternal word of Allah), the hadith (the amalgamation of the traditions, deeds, and sayings of Muhammad, the prophet of Islam), and the Sira (the biography of Muhammad).[48] Warner has analyzed the percentages of the three texts that are devoted to the Kafir (pejorative term for non-Muslims), to Jew-hatred, to politics, and to Jihad (holy war against non-believers). The conclusions are striking. For example, 51 percent of the trilogy of texts is devoted to uncomplimentary and unloving portrayals of the Kafir, and there is more Jew-hatred in the trilogy (9.3 percent) than in Adolf Hitler's *Mein Kampf* (7 percent).

ISIS Membership, Converts' Proclivity to Commit Terror Acts, and Terror Groups

Discriminant analysis is a very powerful statistical technique for analyzing data, including electoral and consumer choices. Figure 2 below illustrates data that might be gathered for a politician, showing who voted for him (dots) and who did not (parallelograms). Simply by eyeballing the data, it is clear that his supporters are younger and wealthier voters.

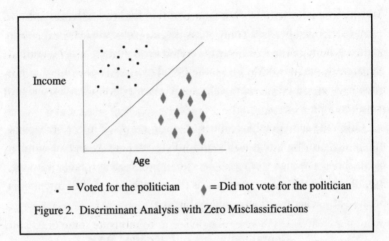

Figure 2. Discriminant Analysis with Zero Misclassifications

Of course, the real-world does not typically consist of such clean data with clear lines of division. Figure 3 depicts a more realistic and slightly "messier" data set. You'll note that four parallelograms and three dots are "misclassified"—that is, they appear on the "wrong" side of a clear line division.

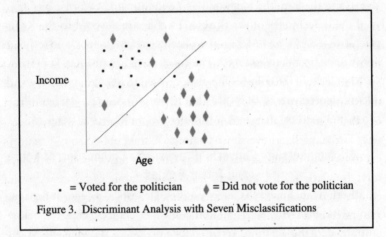

Figure 3. Discriminant Analysis with Seven Misclassifications

Discriminant analysis iteratively tests numerous possible lines of division until it identifies the one that minimizes the number of misclassifications;

and discriminant analysis is not limited to two predictor variables and two categories of membership. I only chose this simple example for expository clarity. Now suppose that one were trying to apply discriminant analysis to determine membership (or not) in ISIS. Individuals from eighty countries have joined ISIS, and they have one thing in common: they are all Muslims.[49] It does not require a fancy multivariate statistical tool such as discriminant analysis to crack this particular mystery. It is difficult to imagine data that are any clearer, and yet Western analysts engage in endless bouts of suicidal Ostrich Parasitic Syndrome to protect the populace from this reality.

Religious conversion is common to innumerable religions, yet it would appear that only one religion seems to motivate some of its converts to commit terrorism around the world. Why don't recent converts to Jainism, orthodox Judaism, or Buddhism ever seem to "misinterpret" their peaceful religions and become terrorists? Somehow only one religion seems to produce converts who repeatedly misinterpret, mistranslate, and misunderstand their otherwise "peaceful" faith.

Numerous countries maintain official lists of terror organizations, and so it is instructive to examine the distribution of ideologies that drive such terror groups. In Table 2 below, I list the sixty-eight current terror groups present on the U.S. Department of State's Foreign Terrorist Organization List. Eighty-one percent of the terror groups (fifty-five of them) are Islamic. Two other terrorist groups (the Kurdistan Workers Party and the Revolutionary People's Liberation Party/Front) are largely composed of Muslim individuals but their founding is not rooted in Islamic theology. The Canadian government maintains the Public Safety Canada's list of terrorist organizations.[50] It lists fifty-five terror groups, of which forty-four are Islamic (80 percent). These Islamic groups vary along ethnic, racial, linguistic, economic, political, and geographical lines but are united by a common religious ideology.

Several databases and websites keep track of documented terror attacks around the world. These include the University of Maryland's Global Terrorism Database, Wikipedia, and the Religion of Peace website. The latter maintains a running counter of the number of Islamic terror attacks since September 11, 2001. As of July 19, 2019, there have been 35,339 Islamist terror attacks in nearly 70 countries.[51] This is astronomically higher than all other religions combined. The National Consortium for the Study of Terrorism and Responses to Terrorism produced a background report of global terrorism (for the year 2017) including the number of victims killed by the twenty most active terror groups.[52] An astonishing 96.6 percent of the victims were murdered by Islamic groups (19,089 out of 19,752).

TABLE 2: U.S. Department of State's Foreign Terrorist Organization List[53]

ISLAMIC GROUPS	NON-ISLAMIC GROUPS
Abu Sayyaf Group (ASG)	Aum Shinrikyo (AUM)
Gama'a al-Islamiyya (Islamic Group–IG)	Basque Fatherland and Liberty (ETA)
HAMAS	Kahane Chai (Kach)
Harakat ul-Mujahidin (HUM)	Kurdistan Workers Party (PKK, aka Kongra-Gel)
Hizballah	Liberation Tigers of Tamil Eelam (LTTE)
Palestine Liberation Front (PLF)	National Liberation Army (ELN)
Palestine Islamic Jihad (PIJ)	Revolutionary Armed Forces of Colombia (FARC)
Popular Front for the Liberation of Palestine (PFLP)	Revolutionary People's Liberation Party/Front (DHKP/C)
PFLP-General Command (PFLP-GC)	Shining Path (SL)
al-Qa'ida (AQ)	Real Irish Republican Army (RIRA)
Islamic Movement of Uzbekistan (IMU)	Communist Party of the Philippines/New People's Army (CPP/NPA)

Jaish-e-Mohammed (JEM)	Continuity Irish Republican Army (CIRA)
Lashkar-e Tayyiba (LeT)	Revolutionary Struggle (RS)
Al-Aqsa Martyrs Brigade (AAMB)	
Asbat al-Ansar (AAA)	
al-Qa'ida in the Islamic Maghreb (AQIM)	
Jemaah Islamiya (JI)	
Lashkar i Jhangvi (LJ)	
Ansar al-Islam (AAI)	
Islamic State of Iraq and the Levant (formerly al-Qa'ida in Iraq)	
Islamic Jihad Union (IJU)	
Harakat ul-Jihad-i-Islami/ Bangladesh (HUJI-B)	
al-Shabaab	
Kata'ib Hizballah (KH)	
al-Qa'ida in the Arabian Peninsula (AQAP)	
Harakat ul-Jihad-i-Islami (HUJI)	
Tehrik-e Taliban Pakistan (TTP)	
Jundallah	
Army of Islam (AOI)	
Indian Mujahedeen (IM)	
Jemaah Anshorut Tauhid (JAT)	
Abdallah Azzam Brigades (AAB)	
Haqqani Network (HQN)	
Ansar al-Dine (AAD)	
Boko Haram	
Ansaru	

al-Mulathamun Battalion (AMB)	
Ansar al-Shari'a in Benghazi	
Ansar al-Shari'a in Darnah	
Ansar al-Shari'a in Tunisia	
ISIL Sinai Province (formerly Ansar Bayt al-Maqdis)	
al-Nusrah Front	
Mujahidin Shura Council in the Environs of Jerusalem (MSC)	
Jaysh Rijal al-Tariq al Naqshabandi (JRTN)	
ISIL-Khorasan (ISIL-K)	
Islamic State of Iraq and the Levant's Branch in Libya (ISIL-Libya)	
Al-Qa'ida in the Indian Subcontinent	
Hizbul Mujahideen (HM)	
ISIS-Bangladesh	
ISIS-Philippines	
ISIS-West Africa	
ISIS-Greater Sahara	
al-Ashtar Brigades (AAB)	
Jama'at Nusrat al-Islam wal-Muslimin (JNIM)	
Islamic Revolutionary Guard Corps (IRGC)	

Global Surveys, Global Patterns of Jew-Hatred, Global Indices

There are many global sources of data that track people's attitudes towards the values of modern, enlightened, liberal societies. Take for example the Pew Research Center, a nonpartisan and unbiased organization that conducts exhaustive global surveys on a broad range of issues. In 2010, a Pew survey captured the extent to which people from Islamic countries held unfavorable views of the Jews.[54] Jew-hatred is the proverbial canary in the coal mine when it comes to measuring a society's hateful prejudices. In Lebanon, 98 percent of those surveyed admitted to holding unfavorable views of Jews; in Jordan, the number was 97 percent; in the Palestinian territories, 97 percent; in Egypt, 95 percent; in Pakistan, 78 percent; in Indonesia, 74 percent; in Turkey, 73 percent; in Nigeria, 60 percent of Muslims dislike Jews, while a relatively paltry 28 percent of Christians do; and among Israeli Arabs, 35 percent. The Anti-Defamation League produced a global report of Jew-hatred using interviews with 53,100 individuals carried out between July 2013 and February 2014 in 101 countries and the Palestinian Territories (West Bank and Gaza).[55] Here is the list of the sixteen most anti-Semitic countries, in decreasing order of hate: West Bank and Gaza, Iraq, Yemen, Algeria, Libya, Tunisia, Kuwait, Bahrain, Jordan, Morocco, Qatar, United Arab Emirates, Lebanon, Oman, Egypt, and Saudi Arabia. If only there was a way to uncover a unifying rubric for these bastions of love, peace, and tolerance.

Examining a society's attitudes towards gay people serves as another valuable indicator of tolerance. Pew conducted a global survey in 2013 asking respondents whether homosexuality should be rejected by society.[56] Islamic countries led the way in intolerance toward gays. Here are some of the relevant data: Senegal, 98 percent; Jordan, 97 percent; Egypt, 95 percent; Tunisia, 94 percent; the Palestinian territories, 93 percent; Indonesia, 93 percent; Pakistan, 87 percent; Malaysia, 86 percent; Lebanon, 80 percent; Turkey, 78 percent. The Western LGBTQ activists who belong to or support *Queers for Palestine* might be interested to know that Israel (even counting its Muslim population) is more than twice as tolerant of homosexuals as is Palestine. Incidentally, homosexuality can merit a death sentence in ten countries: Yemen, Iran, Mauritania, Nigeria, Qatar, Saudi Arabia, Afghanistan, Somalia, Sudan, and United Arab Emirates.[57]

How well do women fare around the world? In 2018, the World Economic Forum released "The Global Gender Gap Report," wherein countries were ranked in terms of gender gaps in four domains: health, education, economics, and politics.[58] Out of 149 countries, here are the twenty worst for women, in decreasing rank order: Turkey, Ivory Coast, Bahrain, Nigeria, Togo, Egypt, Mauritania, Morocco, Jordan, Oman, Lebanon, Saudi Arabia, Iran, Mali, Democratic Republic of Congo, Chad, Syria, Iraq, Pakistan, and Yemen.

In 2018, the Foundation for the Advancement of Liberty, a Spanish libertarian think tank released its 2018 World Index of Moral Freedom wherein 160 countries were ranked on a composite score composed of five freedom measures.[59] Here are the rankings of the fourteen worst countries, in decreasing order: Libya, Oman, Algeria, Brunei, Pakistan, Iran, Egypt, Afghanistan, Kuwait, Qatar, Iraq, United Arab Emirates, Yemen, and Saudi Arabia. These nations vary along ethnic, racial, linguistic, economic, and sociopolitical metrics, but they have one thing in common.

The West believes in freedom of conscience when it comes to religion. But not every country in the world shares that view. Here are the countries that currently impose a death penalty for atheism: Afghanistan, Iran, Malaysia, Maldives, Mauritania, Nigeria, Pakistan, Qatar, Saudi Arabia, Somalia, Sudan, United Arab Emirates, and Yemen.[60] Moreover, the Pew Research Center examined which countries have the most governmental restrictions on religion.[61] Combining the data from the 2013 and 2014 surveys, the twenty worst countries are China, Indonesia, Uzbekistan, Iran, Egypt, Afghanistan, Saudi Arabia, Malaysia, Burma, Russia, Syria, Turkey, Azerbaijan, Sudan, Brunei, Eritrea, Kazakhstan, Turkmenistan, Laos, and the Maldives. Seventy-five percent of the worst countries are Muslim-majority nations.

The building of this nomological network, composed of heterogeneous confirmatory cumulative evidence, is not, of course, an attack on individual Muslims. It is the application of a dispassionate epistemological approach to scrutinizing an ideology and establishing whether it promotes peace, pluralism, and liberty. The conclusion of this analysis is veridical even though the great majority of Muslims are undoubtedly kind and decent people. In a free society, people should be able to analyze such data without accusations of bigotry. That is how we come to the truth.

The application of nomological networks of cumulative evidence is relevant to countless other contemporary "hot button" issues. Take for example the ongoing debates regarding man-made climate change. The discussion is laden with hysterical emotional appeals as exemplified by Greta Thunberg, the seventeen-year-old Swedish activist who, in a disturbingly angry, sanctimonious, and eschatological United Nations speech, proclaimed that the failure of Western adults to act against climate change had robbed her and future generations of childhood innocence. Nomological networks of cumulative evidence might be deployed to examine the extent to which climate change is man-made, and subsequently to explore the types of intervention strategies that are feasible, practical, and rational. To request that such an analysis be carried out does not make one a "climate denier" or a "science denier."

Nomological networks of cumulative evidence inoculate us against the quicksand of feel-good platitudes and emotional appeals. Let your intellect—not misplaced emotions or tribal ideologies—inform your positions. To be a truly wise person requires that we recognize those domains best served by our intellect versus those best guided by our emotions. Stay loyal to the Tribe of Truth by applying the powerful epistemological tool covered in this chapter in forming your position. Ask yourself: What would be the cumulative evidence that I need to cull in support of my position? Nomological networks of cumulative evidence constitute a powerful means by which we can synthesize complex information in our quest to make rational decisions.

CHAPTER EIGHT

Call to Action

*"First they came for the communists, and I did not speak
out—Because I was not a communist.
Then they came for the trade unionists, and I did not
speak out—Because I was not a trade unionist.
Then they came for the Jews, and I did not speak out—
Because I was not a Jew.
Then they came for me—and there was no one left to
speak for me."*
—Martin Niemöller, German theologian[1]

"A time comes when silence is betrayal."
—As quoted by Martin Luther King Jr.[2]

All things being equal, whether you are talking about a military conflict or the battle of ideas, it is generally better to have a large army
than a small one. The more people we have defending our core values,
the more likely we are to triumph against the enemies of reason. And yet,
countless persons who share our values fail to speak out. The reasons
are manifold.

Most people are too busy to notice the dangers of idea pathogens or
wrongly assume that they are unimportant. The intrusion of anti-science,
anti-reason, and illiberal movements occurs slowly and incrementally
without many people becoming aware of the larger problem. Hence, the
slow and inexorable death of the West by a thousand cuts. Instead of
ignoring the problem, recognize that while it affects others today, it could
reach you tomorrow. You may not have children in college, but if you
work for a firm or are perhaps a business owner, campus lunacy will

affect your business soon—if it does not already—perhaps starting with your human resources department and the enforcement of "progressive" government regulations that demand adherence to the cult of diversity, inclusion, and equity. Parts of Europe already have sharia enclaves that are no-go areas for infidels (and the police). You might not have them in your city yet, but your nation's immigration policies (and Ostrich Parasitic Syndrome) might bring no-go areas sooner rather than later.

Another reason people are reluctant to join the battle of ideas is what we call "diffusion of responsibility" or "the bystander effect." In the late 1960s, psychologists John Darley and Bibb Latané documented what at first glance seems counterintuitive. The greater the number of people present, the less likely an individual is to help someone in need because it is easier to rationalize that someone else will do it. It is easy to diffuse responsibility to others who are willing to stick their necks out: "Thank you, Dr. Saad, for standing up on our behalf. I really support your efforts. You got this." No, I don't. Everybody has a voice. Activate your sense of personal responsibility. You have agency. Participate. Do not be a bystander as truth, reason, and logic call out for your help. Do not subcontract your voice to others. Do not self-censor. You and your children have a stake in the outcome of this battle, so don't be afraid to speak up. Do not succumb to the Tragedy of the Commons (as popularized by the ecologist Garrett Hardin in 1968), in this case a tragedy of collective inaction.

The battle of ideas knows no boundaries, so there is plenty to do. If you are a student and hear your professors spouting postmodern nonsense or spewing anti-science drivel, challenge them politely and constructively. If you are a graduate and your alma mater is violating its commitment to freedom of speech and freedom of thought, withdraw your donations—and let the school know why. If your Facebook friends are posting comments with which you disagree, engage them and offer an alternative viewpoint. Do not fear the possible loss of friendship. Anyone who is willing to end a relationship because of a reasoned difference of opinion is not worthy of your friendship. If you are sitting at your local pub having a conversation about a sensitive topic, do not refrain from speaking your mind. If your politicians are succumbing to suicidal political correctness, vote them out of office. Donald Trump won the United States presidency in 2016 because a silent electoral majority in the middle of America shouted from the ballot box: "We are tired of being patronized. We are tired of politically correct platitudes. We are tired of identity politics and the ethos of victimhood. We are tired of the extraordinarily biased mainstream media." And by expressing their frustration on election day, they won.

Believe in the Power of Your Voice

Social media—despite Big Tech's nefarious actions to silence or punish some voices—has democratized media platforms; and no matter how small your media platform is initially, it can grow exponentially. Mark Dawson self-published his way into becoming a bestselling thriller writer who now garners a very sizeable yearly income. Andy Weir's *The Martian*, which was originally self-published online and then sold on Kindle for ninety-nine cents, was eventually adapted into a blockbuster Hollywood movie directed by Ridley Scott and starring Matt Damon.[3] PewDiePie is a YouTube channel hosted by Swedish gamer Felix Kjellberg. It is one of the most popular channels with more than 100 million subscribers and more than 25 billion total views (as of May 2020). Kjellberg's yearly income is now well over $10 million, which is not too shabby for a university dropout. Joe Rogan, with whom I have developed a warm friendship, has created the most popular podcast in the world. He holds long-format conversations with a very eclectic group of guests including but not limited to scientists, entrepreneurs, athletes, actors, and comedians. His yearly downloads are well into the hundreds of millions. How did he start out? He was a college dropout, with a short career as a martial artist, and a longer career as a stand-up comedian, actor, television host, and Ultimate Fighting Championship commentator. His open-mindedness and willingness to engage a broad range of individuals (the antithesis of an echo chamber) has been handsomely rewarded. Rogan earned $30 million last year from his podcast alone.[4] Dave Rubin also started off as a stand-up comic but today he is the host of a fully independent show, *The Rubin Report,* where he holds meaningful conversations with people from across the political spectrum—and has more than one million subscribers and more than 260 million total views as of June 2020. Granted, most people who self-publish or start a YouTube channel will not find an audience of hundreds of thousands, but in the battle of ideas, every voice counts—even if your circle of influence is limited to your family, friends, and neighbors.

Do Not Be Afraid of Judging Others or Giving Offense

Many people, of course, worry about straining friendships if they broach sensitive topics. But true friendships are precisely those that should withstand the stress of such conversations. A deep friendship should be antifragile (to use the concept of Nassim Taleb). The English historian Henry Thomas Buckle famously remarked: "Men and women range themselves into three classes or orders of intelligence; you can tell the lowest class by their habit of always talking about *persons*; the next by the fact that their habit is always to converse about *things*; the highest, by their preference for the discussion of *ideas*."[5] [Italics in original.] I would argue that a similar taxonomy captures the strength of a friendship: idle chatter is well suited for breaking the ice with strangers and engaging in banter with acquaintances; deep meaningful conversations about important ideas in politics and religion should be a central feature of any valuable friendship. If so-called friends are unable to accept a difference of opinion on a substantive issue, then they are unworthy of your friendship. Two poignant French sayings come to mind: 1) *Mieux vaut être seul que mal accompagné* [Best to be alone than poorly accompanied]; and 2) *Dis-moi qui sont tes amis et je te dirai qui tu es* [Tell me who your friends are, and I'll tell you who you are]. Humans are a social species. We thrive emotionally and cognitively when we forge intense bonds of friendship. In the pursuit of happiness, we should strive to establish friendships with individuals with whom we can experience the full range of cerebral engagement. This can't happen if we are too afraid to disagree with our close friends on consequential issues. Choose your friends wisely.

In a similar way, many well-intentioned individuals are too afraid to judge others.[6] The *Cambridge Dictionary* lists the following synonyms and related words for *non-judgmental*: open-minded, enlightened, freethinking, inclusive, liberal, live and let live (idiom), permissive society, and tolerant.[7] Recall the colloquialisms that speak to this aversion to judge: *Who am I to judge? I am not one to judge; No judgment*. Where does this reticence stem from? The West is founded on a bedrock of Judeo-Christian traditions and many assume, as per Christian theology, that judging others can be a sin. Several gospels contain edicts against judging others.[8] In the Pericope Adulterae (John 7:53–8:11) Jesus says, "Let any one of you who is without sin be the first to throw a stone at her." (in reference to the imminent stoning of a woman who has committed adultery), and in Matthew 7:1–2 one finds, "Do not judge, or you too will be judged. For in the same way you judge others, you will be judged, and with the measure you use, it will be measured to you." In Luke 6:37 we have, "Do not judge, and you will not be judged. Do not condemn, and you will not be condemned. Forgive, and you will be forgiven." Finally, James 4:12 posits, "There is only one Lawgiver and Judge, the one who is able to save and destroy. But you—who are you to judge your neighbor?" Many people interpret these teachings as implying that the act of judging is divinely forbidden, a cosmic command to *live and let live*. But this is incorrect; these edicts are referring to moral hypocrisy. People who spew falsehoods *should* be judged. I do it every day.

Cultural relativism also impedes people from casting judgments, especially against otherwise abhorrent religious and cultural practices. Several generations of university students have been indoctrinated into the false belief that it is gauche if not bigoted to judge people of different ethnic or religious backgrounds, especially if you are a white Westerner. In April 2011 the University of Notre Dame hosted a debate between William Lane Craig (a Christian theologian) and Sam Harris (an atheist neuroscientist) on the natural versus supernatural foundations of morality. During the debate, Harris recounted an anecdote that perfectly summarizes the moral blindness that cultural relativism engenders. It centered around a conversation he had with an appointee to President Obama's Council on Bioethics.[9]

> She said, "How could you ever say that forcing women to wear burqas is wrong from the point of view of science?" I said, "Well, because I think it's pretty clear that right and wrong relate to human well-being, and it's just as clear that forcing half the population to live in cloth bags and beating them, or killing them when they try to get out, is not a way of maximizing human well-being."
>
> And she said, "Well, that's just your opinion." And I said, "Well, okay, let's make it even easier. Let's say we found a culture that was literally removing the eyeballs of every third child, ok, at birth. Would you then agree that we have found a culture that is not perfectly maximizing well-being?"
>
> And she said, "It would depend on why they were doing it." So after my eyebrows returned from the back of my head, I said, "Okay, well say they were doing it for religious reasons. Let's say they have a scripture which says, 'Every third should walk in darkness' or some such nonsense." And then she said, "Well, then you could never say that they were wrong."

Harris pointed out that this same individual had deep moral reservations about using brain imaging as a lie-detecting technology on apprehended terrorists. Pause for a moment to marvel at how broken this individual's moral compass is. She was callously unconcerned about the removal of children's eyes, should such barbarism be done in the service of a grotesque religious belief, and she was not the least bit disturbed by women's being forced to wear the burqa because this was done in the service of Islamic religious belief. But don't you dare infringe on a terrorist's neuronal freedom. This immoral and confused individual had succumbed to two biases, namely a devastating case of cultural relativism mixed with the ethos of cultural self-flagellation. She was perfectly happy to hold her own culture to astonishingly punishing moral standards in the handling of a captured terrorist, but she was unable to judge the barbaric behaviors of people from other cultures or religions. This is the epitome of moral cowardice.

To judge is to be human. It is perfectly natural to judge others. It is an integral part of being a well-functioning adult. A central feature of human decision making is the process of judging several competing alternatives. This is precisely why the Society for Judgment and Decision Making and its flagship journal *Judgment and Decision Making* exist. We judge whom to include within our close circle of friends. We judge various prospective suitors prior to marrying our eventual spouse. We judge the performance of our students and employees. Life is laden with endless judgments. If I were to ask you to think about the people whom you consider to be most interesting, they would likely have one thing in common: they judge; they opine; they take positions. Fence-sitters who equivocate about the pros and cons of every conceivable issue without ever pronouncing a judgment are profoundly boring people. To never judge is to be an intellectual coward for it serves as an insurance policy against the possibility of being a polarizing figure. The most charismatic public intellectuals are typically those who share their judgments on a broad range of issues. Thomas Sowell and the late Christopher Hitchens are two of the leading public intellectuals of the past four decades precisely because they never shied away from sharing their opinions on contentious issues. Of course, not all judgments are created equal. The difference between a judgmental ideologue and a judgmental intellectual is the process by which each arrives at his position. As long as one uses well-articulated arguments in support of one's judgments, it is perfectly acceptable to judge.

Do Not Virtue-Signal

Each time that a terrorist attack takes place in some Western city, nauseating hordes of cowards do one of two things: 1) Change their social media handles to the flag of the country that was attacked; 2) Share a hashtag on Twitter to signal their solidarity with a given cause (#JeSuisCharlie following the terror killings at the *Charlie Hebdo* offices in Paris; #BringBackOurGirls, made famous by Michelle Obama, in support of the Nigerian girls kidnapped by Boko Haram). Politicians seek to outdo one another in offering vacuous "heartfelt" condolences while in many cases continuing to enact policies that are directly responsible for the terror attacks in question. In the great majority of instances, these are utterly useless endeavors meant to do nothing but advertise one's supposed virtue to the world (hence the term virtue-signaling). It is a form of cheap and costless self-aggrandizing that feeds one's ego. I must be a good person who truly cares, as evidenced by my progressive hashtag. Nothing could be further from the truth. Those who engage in such platitudinous signaling are cowardly and meek. I'll use some fundamental principles from evolutionary biology to explain why this is so.

Recall that the struggle for life involves two fundamental challenges: survival and reproduction. In a sexually reproducing species, individual organisms must ensure that they will survive until reproductive age, at which time they must possess desirable attributes to attract a suitable mate. Adaptations evolve either because they bestow a survival advantage to an organism or because they yield a reproductive advantage. When it comes to survival, the two fundamental challenges can be boiled down to: get food and avoid becoming someone else's food. The beaks of Darwin's finches evolved to be of different forms as a result of selection pressures in various local niches (due to the specific availability of foods in those environments). A thinner beak might result in a survival advantage on one of the Galapagos islands whereas a thicker one would be ideal on another island. A morphological trait (type of beak) evolved as a means of procuring food sources. Unless an organism is the apex predator within a given ecosystem, it is under constant threat of predation.

The evolution of camouflaging serves as an example of how an organism avoids becoming a predator's next meal. Leaf insects have evolved exoskeletons that allow them to blend seamlessly into their environments with both coloring and textural camouflage. Recall though that survival is only half the battle. An organism must reproduce in order to ensure its reproductive fitness. There are two types of adaptations that bestow a mating benefit, those that evolve for intersexual wooing (the peacock's tail; the "moonwalk" dance of the red-capped manakin) or for intrasexual competition (moose antlers; the cranial structure of rams for butting heads). In other words, behavioral or morphological features evolve to either impress members of the opposite sex or to directly compete with members of one's sex for mating rights.

The astute reader might ask at this point, what does all of this have to do with virtue-signaling? For this, we turn to the peacock's tail. This morphological feature evolved via female mate choice despite the fact that it disadvantages the survivability of the peacock (by increasing the likelihood of its predation). Why would peahens find a very large tail comprised of beautifully patterned plumage with dazzling colors so alluring? Choosing the right mate is a profoundly important decision to the genetic interests of any organism. With such high stakes at play, it is necessary that an organism find a way to differentiate prospective suitors into one of two broad categories: unworthy fakers and worthy candidates. Evolution has solved this conundrum in an extraordinarily elegant and efficient manner. Trustworthy signals must be costly in order to serve as honest depictions of an organism's quality. In other words, they must be handicapping in a way that they exclude the pretenders and fakers from being able to pull off the same signal.[10] The peacock is effectively communicating the following: "The beauty of my plumage tells you that I'm free of parasites. My elaborate tail makes me more prone to predation, and yet here I am. I must be the real deal. The fakers can't pull this off. Pick me."

I have used this principle in explaining many human phenomena including conspicuous consumption (purchasing a Ferrari), philanthropy (non-anonymous donations to signal one's status), art collecting (spending outlandish prices on infantile art that a monkey could have created), and rappers shown throwing away huge wads of money in music videos (only those sufficiently wealthy could be so cavalier in their pecuniary waste). Costly signaling is also relevant in explaining rites of passage across various cultures meant to serve as an honest signal of one's courage, bravery, and toughness. The Sateré-Mawé, an indigenous Amazonian tribe, have a very powerful way of differentiating prospective warriors from their fake counterparts. They sedate bullet ants, whose sting is akin to being shot, and then weave them into leaf gloves. Initiates wear the gloves for several minutes and must withstand the stings of hundreds of these ants as they come out of their sedated torpor. One sting causes unimaginable pain, and yet the inductees must withstand the suffering with restrained dignity (they cannot holler). One such ordeal would be sufficient to test anyone's toughness, and yet the young men must endure this tribulation twenty separate times. If all it took to become a warrior was the completion of ten push-ups, nearly everyone could complete the task. It would leave the tribe in the unenviable position of not knowing who the truly tough individuals were. However, create a rite of passage that serves as an honest signal of toughness and courage, and you've solved the problem of identifying the fakers.[11]

During a highly publicized 2017 event held in Toronto, Oren Amitay, Jordan Peterson, and I were asked to identify our respective freedom of speech heroes. I responded that the ultimate heroes are those who risk their lives to defend such freedoms. I pointed to individuals from the Middle East (some of whom have been guests on my show) who are willing to defend these ideals knowing full well that they may pay the ultimate price. This is what having skin in the game looks like. This is costly virtue, not virtue-signaling. Over the past year or so, I have become good friends with Ensaf Haidar, the wife of jailed Saudi blogger Raif Badawi, and I had the pleasure of meeting her three lovely children at a dinner organized by the actor Mark Pellegrino and his wife. Raif is serving a ten-year prison sentence and was scheduled to receive one thousand lashes ("only" fifty of which have thus far been administered) for having the temerity to question, in a rather tepid manner, various religious and cultural realities in the region. Retweeting #JeSuisCharlie is impotent virtue-signaling; critiquing the Saudi regime from within Saudi Arabia is courage in action.

Many people living in the West tell me they want to defend our liberties but cannot do so publicly because they could suffer professional or social consequences. Therein lies the problem. Did the young Allied soldiers landing on the shores of Normandy in World War II ask for (or expect) a guarantee of their safety before charging German machine guns and mortars? We recently commemorated the centenary of the end of World War I where nearly 67,000 Canadians lost their lives.[12] Their selfless heroism granted me the freedom to type what you are currently reading. Millions of individuals have sacrificed their lives so that your children and mine could live in free societies. And yet, most people today are unwilling to speak their minds lest they be unfriended by an acquaintance on Facebook. Cowardice should be added to the list of seven deadly sins. There is no way to participate in the grand battle of ideas for the soul of the West without facing any threats.

Most people recognize the gargantuan courage that is required to speak my mind in the manner that I do (especially so as an academic and public figure). There isn't a sacred belief that I'm unwilling to critique, and yet whenever I implore people to get engaged, I am at times flippantly told: "But professor, you are protected by tenure." Tenure is not an all-encompassing magical shield that repels all the threats and harmful consequences that can come from being an outspoken defender of reason. Tenure did not protect me from having to take security measures in Fall 2017 whenever I went to teach classes at my university. Tenure did not protect me from the innumerable death threats that I've received, which led to my having to file a report with the Montreal police while accompanied by a human resources representative from my university. Tenure did not protect me from the numerous professorships that I would have received from other institutions were it not for my public engagement (including a very lucrative professorship at my dream location). Tenure did not protect me from being ostracized from many of the academic circles that serve as gatekeepers for the advancement of my career. My purity of spirit (as I recall my mother's words) does not permit me to place any careerist considerations ahead of my defense of truth. I would not be able to sleep at night knowing that I had sacrificed a millimeter of truth or an ounce of freedom for selfish reasons. My best advice is if you are going to fight these idea pathogens, go all in. Make your engagement count.

In the *Nicomachean Ethics*, Aristotle argues that a successful and happy life requires that one find moderation in the pursuit of a given virtue (think of the adage "All good things in moderation"). Aristotle proposed that courage (a virtue) lies between excessive fearlessness and cowardice (the two extremes that ought to be avoided). Aristotle discusses the courage of a soldier in physical battle, but in the current context it applies to intellectual courage as needed for the battle of ideas. An individual who decides to wear a "Draw Mohammad" t-shirt in Yemen (to protest Islamic blasphemy laws) is undoubtedly exhibiting excessive fearlessness. On the other hand, the media's reluctance to challenge an imam's statement that "Islam is peace" is a manifestation of cowardice. Between these two endpoints lies the sweet spot of tempered and reasoned engagement.

Be the Penalty Kicker

Soccer, better known as football to the rest of the world outside North America, is a low-scoring sport. Of all possible game situations, the penalty kick yields the highest probability of scoring a goal. A penalty kick is awarded when a foul (like tripping an opposing player) is committed inside the eighteen-yard box. The ball is placed in the center of the field, twelve yards away from the net, and a designated penalty kicker takes a shot solely against the goalkeeper. The success rate is around 70 percent, so the pressure is largely on the kicker.[13] In addition to penalty kicks awarded during a game, penalty shoot-outs are used to break ties in tournament games. It takes testicular fortitude to make a kick under such crushing pressure, but it is a fortitude that we all have to cultivate because now we are all playing in the World Cup of Ideas. All of us need to step up and take metaphorical penalty kicks when we have a chance to score a goal for Team Reason. There are two types of people: those who see a woman being accosted in an alley and intervene, and those who furtively walk by pretending that they never heard her screams for help. Be the former and not the latter.

Activate Your Inner Honey Badger

Honey badgers are fearlessly ferocious when attacked. A single honey badger (the size of a small dog) is so extraordinarily aggressive that it can fend off a group of lions. If you attack it, prepare to fight. Given the ubiquity of e-mob bullying (which is really a form of thought policing), let the honey badger serve as your source of inspiration. Never back down from those seeking to intimidate you into silence. Shortly after Serena Williams's loss to Naomi Osaka at the 2018 final of the U.S. Open tennis championships, I commented on social media about Williams's execrable behavior during the match. She was penalized for receiving illegal coaching, for smashing her racket in anger, and for verbally abusing the umpire (calling him a "thief" and later effectively accusing him of sexism). As you might expect, in today's zeitgeist, it is seldom a good idea to criticize a black woman because you set yourself up for false charges of sexism and racism. I was hardly surprised when I began receiving many angry responses to my criticisms of Williams. But one diabolically unhinged woman decided I had committed an unforgivable sin and wanted to terminate my academic career. She tagged my university on Twitter, hoping it would respond by firing me. Refusing to bow to such cretinous pressure, I went on the offensive. I highlighted what this woman was doing, and many supporters of mine weighed in against this would-be social justice warrior, who realized she was unable to defend her position.

She deleted some of her own tweets, eventually shut down her Twitter account, and then tagged me from a new Twitter account demanding that I remove her earlier tweets and my responses. I refused, she ludicrously threatened to sue me for "defamation," and she eventually disappeared into her black hole of faux-outrage.

There are two important lessons to take away from this story. First, never ever cede an inch to those who wish to silence you. Today it's an inch, tomorrow it will be a yard. Second, learn the strategies that these enemies of freedom utilize to bully others, and try to turn these against them. In my case, I hold a winning hand in Victimology Poker. I am a Lebanese Jew and hence a "person of color" (to use the obnoxious parlance of the social justice warriors). I am a war refugee who escaped religious persecution, and I am a "person of size" (I am overweight). It is difficult to beat me in the Oppression Olympics, and accordingly I utilize my royal flush of victimhood against those who typically seek to accuse me of faux-racism, faux-sexism, and faux-bigotry. In my tormentor's case, she was a white American woman, and so I accused her of coming after me perhaps because she harbored hatred against my identity via her "privileged position of Whiteness."[14] This is the proverbial kryptonite against these charlatans of faux-justice, and so unsurprisingly she went away. I have been targeted for occupational harassment on a few other occasions perhaps most notably in Fall 2017. As a general rule, I try to reduce my interactions with detractors to a minimum on social media because it seldom yields satisfactory outcomes. However, once in a while, I get suckered into a spicy exchange. An obnoxious and insulting individual had denigrated me on Twitter in a truly bewildering way at which point I joined the thread and went after him full throttle. This included my referring to him as a "retarded schmuck" and a "degenerate" but always within the strict confines of semi-friendly banter. It would seem that he did not possess the emotional fortitude to handle such retorts. He first tried to muster a charge of bigotry against me because, using his lobotomized logic, my use of the word "degenerate" was somehow code language for homophobia (I had no inkling of the biological sex of the individual in question let alone his/her sexual orientation).[15] When this tactic did not stick, he began to repeatedly tag my university seeking to get me in trouble with my employer.[16] When this did not work, he contacted my university and filed a complaint against me. I know this because I received an ominous email from a representative from my university's human resources department asking to speak to me urgently (without telling me what the issue was about). We agreed to have a phone chat that evening to discuss the matter. When she confirmed to me that the complaint stemmed from the Twitter person in question, I went on the offensive. I reminded her that I was communicating via my personal Twitter account to a person who was not in any way associated with my professorial duties at my institution. I offered her a hypothetical example to ponder: If she were with her daughter at a pharmacy, and I saw her there and thought she spoke to her daughter offensively, would it be acceptable for me to call the university and report her? The conversation ended shortly thereafter, and the case was closed.

When dealing with miscreants, appeasement is seldom a winning strategy. British Prime Minister Neville Chamberlain's policy of appeasing Adolf Hitler was a notorious failure, and many governments today refuse to negotiate with terrorists because they know it only brings more demands for appeasement. Israel does not appease its enemies because it knows that in the Near East, might is right. In the West, however, blubbering apologies when none are needed has become de rigueur. On October 7, 2018, astronaut Scott Kelly tweeted: "One of the greatest leaders of modern times, Sir Winston Churchill said, 'in victory, magnanimity.' I guess those days are over."[17] The usual online mob of faux-outrage jumped into action saying that Kelly had cited a genocidal racist (apparently, Churchill is just as bad as Hitler). Kelly issued a Twitter apology the following day: "Did not mean to offend by quoting Churchill. My apologies. I will go and educate myself further on his atrocities, racist views which I do not support. My point was we need to come together as one nation. We are all Americans. That should transcend partisan politics."[18] I tweeted several replies to Kelly's cowardly caving including this: "Stop apologizing. Stop compromising your positions for fear that you might offend the perpetually offended. Grow a pair. Stand tall. Be confident in your personhood. Know which side of the track truth is to be found. Stop the cowardice. Stop it @StationCDRKelly."[19] If quoting a key historical figure who helped defeat the Nazis necessitates an apology, the abyss of infinite darkness looms. If you support the foundational principles of Western civilization, if you stand for freedom of speech and thought (as Churchill did), then don't retreat. Let your animal spirit be that of the honey badger; be ferociously uncompromising in defending your integrity and in protecting truth. Follow the lead of Gibson's Bakery whose owners sued Oberlin College (a hotbed of leftist lunacy) for its role in promulgating the false narrative that the bakery was guilty of racism.[20] Three black students had been caught shoplifting and when they were confronted by an employee (the owner's son), they assaulted him. The students admitted their guilt and confirmed that no racism had taken place, and yet Oberlin was instrumental in stirring the faux-outrage. The bakery was awarded a $44 million judgment,[21] (though this has since been reduced).[22] The bakery did not cave to the protests, boycotts, and false accusations. It did not issue an abject apology saying the owners had learned a valuable lesson from "people of color." No, they fought this grotesque injustice and won. Be a honey badger. Never back down when attacked by ideological bullies.

To criticize Islam does not make you an Islamophobe (a nonsensical term) nor a hater of individual Muslims. To scrutinize radical feminism does not make you a misogynist. To question open borders does not make you a racist. You can have an open heart filled with empathy and compassion and yet reject open borders. To assert that trans women (biological males) should not be competing in athletic competitions with biological females does not make you a transphobe. Many situations in life involve a calculus of competing rights. With that in mind, the right of your eight-year-old daughter to feel comfortable and safe in a public bathroom supersedes that of a 230-pound, six foot two trans woman. To reject the idea that so-called "other forms of knowing" (whether the indigenous way of knowing or postmodernism) are as valid as the scientific method does not make you a close-minded bigot. To reject the hysterical demonization of white men as exemplars of toxic masculinity and white supremacy does not make you Adolf Hitler. The name-calling accusations are locked and loaded threats, ready to be deployed against you should you dare to question the relevant progressive tenets. Most people are too afraid to be accused of being racist or misogynist, and so they cower in silence. Keep your mouth shut and nod in agreement or else prepare to be tarred and feathered. Don't fall prey to this silencing strategy. Be assured in your principles and stand ready to defend them with the ferocity of a honey badger.

How to Fix Our Universities

While civil and aeronautical engineers are constrained by physical laws when designing bridges and planes, the humanities professors spreading anti-science, anti-logic idea pathogens are impervious to downstream ill effects. These professors have created a university culture where insanity is rewarded. This must stop. And the first step might be to fight back against unconstitutional speech codes and delimited free speech zones. Under the Constitution, the entire United States is a free speech zone. Say no to the thought police, expose your mind to a heterogeneity of thoughts and perspectives, and engage with people who might question your positions. Ideological intolerance is not restricted to conservatives or liberals.[23] Every one of us prefers talking with people who share our opinions. That is an indelible part of human nature. But our minds are elevated when we discuss opposing points of view respectfully. This should be a major focus of our universities.

Similarly, our universities should recommit themselves to the pursuit of academic excellence and kick identity politics (and its cult of "diversity, inclusion, and equity") into the dustbin of history. No one should have to apologize for being white, male, Christian, or heterosexual—or feel "pride" in their sexual orientation. Immutable characteristics should not be the subject of either pride or shame, and we should neither inculcate or placate an ethos of perpetual victimhood and indignant offence. We should stop coddling students and provide no allowances for trigger warnings or safe spaces, no indulgence for the foolishness of "cultural appropriation" or "microaggressions." These are nonsensical concepts that embolden weakness and fragility. Instead, foster an environment that promotes intellectual and emotional strength. In the words of John Ellison, dean of students in the College at the University of Chicago, in his welcoming letter to the class of 2020:

> Members of our community are encouraged to speak, write, listen, challenge, and learn, without fear of censorship. Civility and mutual respect are vital to all of us, and freedom of expression does not mean the freedom to harass or threaten others. You will find that we expect members of our community to be engaged in rigorous debate, discussion, and even disagreement. At times this may challenge you and even cause discomfort.
>
> Our commitment to academic freedom means that we do not support so-called "trigger warnings," we do not cancel invited speakers because their topics might prove controversial, and we do not condone the creation of intellectual "safe spaces" where individuals can retreat from ideas and perspectives at odds with their own.
>
> Fostering the free exchange of ideas reinforces a related University priority—building a campus that welcomes people of all backgrounds. Diversity of opinion and background is a fundamental strength of our community. The members of our community must have the freedom to espouse and explore a wide range of ideas.[24]

It is tragic that such a position has to be enunciated to incoming students at a world-class university in the twenty-first century. And yet, Dean

Ellison is a breath of fresh air in an ecosystem of fevered idea pathogens. They are the same sort of idea pathogens that encourage students to occupy administrators' offices with lists of outlandish "social justice" demands— and that all too often lead administrators to capitulate to them. I encourage readers to flip through *The Plan for Dartmouth's Freedom Budget: Items for Transformative Justice at Dartmouth* to better understand what such demands entail—but you can probably guess.[25]

Universities need to return to the meritocratic ethos they once had and to resist commodifying education and lowering academic standards. In 1990, when I earned my M.B.A. at McGill University, I had to complete two years of full-time studies, that is, four semesters of courses ranging from five to six graduate courses per semester, an extraordinarily heavy load (I was exempted from one additional course by passing an entrance mathematics exam). Since then, the number of credits required to obtain an M.B.A. degree continues to decrease, with many business schools now offering an accelerated one-year M.B.A. At the business school where I teach, the number of credits now required for completing an M.B.A. is substantially lower than it was when I graduated back in 1990. More than a decade ago, I critiqued this outlandish lowering of standards in a *Psychology Today* article titled "I'll Have Large Fries, a Hamburger, a Diet Coke, and an M.B.A. Hold the Pickles: The Student-as-Customer Metaphor Is Poor Educational Policy."[26] M.B.A. requirements are being watered down not because students are much smarter and better prepared than they were thirty years ago, but because of competitive pressures for schools to find new ways to attract students.

This same desire to attract and retain students manifests itself in grade inflation. Stuart Rojstaczer, a former professor of geology/Earth and ocean sciences at Duke University, has conducted extensive longitudinal analyses on the pattern of grade inflation at American universities. He reports some truly bewildering grade facts including that the most common grade during the Vietnam era was C; now it is an A.[27] Yes, you read that correctly. Everyone is a winner. Everyone comes in first place. Everyone gets a trophy. Incredibly, some leading business schools, law schools, and medical schools have done away with standard letter grading and instead focus on versions of the "pass-fail" system. At my alma mater Cornell University, students have enacted a grade non-disclosure policy; recruiters are not supposed to ask Cornell students about their grades, and Cornell students are not supposed to reveal their grades until after they've received a full-time job offer.[28]

Humans are both cooperative and competitive, and any group—from a clique of awkward teenagers to a professional soccer team to a military organization—will establish clear hierarchies. Humans are not indistinguishable and equal worker ants. E. O. Wilson, the Harvard entomologist and evolutionary biologist, is reputed to have said of socialism: "Great idea. Wrong species." Any system that is built on a false understanding of human nature is doomed to fail. Building a society where the primary objective is to protect one's fragile self-esteem from the dangers of competition will only lead to a society of weakness, entitlement, and apathy. Life is necessarily competitive; society is necessarily hierarchical. It does no one any favors to pursue a utopian vision of society where no one's feelings are hurt.

Parting Words

For decades now, a set of idea pathogens, largely stemming from universities, has relentlessly assaulted science, reason, logic, freedom of thought, freedom of speech, individual liberty, and individual dignity. If we want our children and grandchildren to grow up in free societies as we have done, then we have to be assured in our principles and stand ready to defend them.

Having grown up amidst the brutality of the Lebanese Civil War and witnessed the erosion of common sense in our universities, I implore you to get engaged. You have the power to effect necessary change. The cure is before you: it is the pursuit and the defense of truth; it is the recommitment to the virtues of the Western Scientific Revolution and

Age of Enlightenment. March on, soldiers of reason. Together we can win the battle of ideas.

Acknowledgements

I am thankful to all of the institutions and conference venues that invited me to deliver lectures as I was developing the contents reported in this book. These include the Freedom Project (Wellesley College), the Institute for Liberal Studies (the University of Ottawa), the Global Forum on Countering Violent Extremism (the Montreal Institute for Genocide and Human Rights Studies at Concordia University), Logical LA, the Manning Conference, the Canadian Institute for Jewish Research, Parliament Hill (Canadian government), the M103 Conference: Learning Circle on Free Speech, the University of Regina, the event on the Stifling of Free Speech on University Campuses (Toronto), Civitas, and the Society for Academic Freedom and Scholarship. The favorable responses that I kept receiving from audience members gave me a clear indication that the public was desirous to hear my message. This wave of encouragement was amplified by the millions of people who engaged me on my social media platforms, who viewed my numerous media appearances, and who watched my YouTube channel.

Many thanks to Harry Crocker, Tom Spence, and the rest of the team at Regnery Publishing for being such enthusiastic supporters of this book. Additional thanks to Harry for his careful reading of my manuscript including his valuable recommendation that I shorten the length of the book. Thank you to Laura Swain for her copyediting efforts. The challenge of writing such a book is rendered immeasurably easier when an author has the full backing of his publisher.

My wife and children provide me with the solace that permits me to fight in the arena of ideas. Without their love and support, I would not have the peace of mind to fight mind pathogens.

To all those who throughout history have fought for science, reason, individual liberty, and individual dignity, the world owes you.

Notes

Preface

1. Follow the thread for the remaining tweets. Gad Saad (@GadSaad), "Some people are truly irredeemably clueless. They post comments attacking me for criticizing the SJW mindset instead of supposedly tackling 'important' matters. Yes, because having a set of idea pathogens take complete control over the minds and souls of millions of people in," Twitter, April 6, 2019, 12:15 p.m., https://twitter.com/GadSaad/status/11 14562406649421824?s=20.
2. R. A. Fisher, *The Genetical Theory of Natural Selection* (Oxford: Clarendon Press, 1930).

Chapter One
From Civil War to the Battle of Ideas

1. Lucy Pasha-Robinson, "Teaching Maths Perpetuates White Privilege, Says University Professor," The Independent, October 25, 2017, https://www.independent.co.uk/news/world/americas/teaching-maths-white-privilege-illinois-university-professor-rochelle-gutierrez-a8018521.html.
2. Michael Marmot, *The Status Syndrome: How Social Standing Affects Our Health and Longevity* (New York: Henry Holt, 2004).
3. Joanna Kempner, Jon F. Merz, and Charles L. Bosk, "Forbidden Knowledge: Public Controversy and the Production of Nonknowledge," *Sociological Forum* 26, no. 3 (September 2011): 475–99.
4. Stephen J. Gould, "The Self-Manipulation of My Pervasive, Perceived Vital Energy through Product Use: An Introspective-Praxis Perspective," *Journal of Consumer Research* 18 (September 1991): 104.
5. Ibid., 202.

6. Ibid., 203.
7. George Orwell, "Notes on Nationalism," *Polemic* 1 (May 1945): 1.
8. For a discussion of parasitoid wasps, see Frederic Libersat, "Parasitoid Wasps: Neuroethology," in *Encyclopedia of Animal Behavior,* eds. Michael D. Breed and Janice Moore, 2 (Oxford: Academic Press, 2010), 642–50.
9. For an academic treatise on the subject, see Janice Moore, *Parasites and the Behavior of Animals* (New York: Oxford University Press, 2002). For a less technical discussion, see Kathleen McAuliffe, *This is Your Brain on Parasites: How Tiny Creatures Manipulate Our Behavior and Shape Society* (Boston: Houghton Mifflin Harcourt, 2016).
10. Richard Dawkins, *The Selfish Gene* (New York: Oxford University Press, 1976); See also Susan Blackmore, *The Meme Machine* (Oxford: Oxford University Press, 1999).
11. These include Richard Hofstadter, *Anti-Intellectualism in American Life* (New York: Knopf, 1963); Allan Bloom, *The Closing of the American Mind* (New York: Simon & Schuster, 1987); Jonathan Rauch, *Kindly Inquisitors: The New Attacks on Free Thought* (Chicago: University of Chicago Press, 1995); Greg Lukianoff, *Unlearning Liberty: Campus Censorship and the End of the American Debate* (New York: Encounter Books, 2012); Heather Mac Donald, *The Diversity Delusion: How Race and Gender Pandering Corrupt the University and Undermine Our Culture* (New York: St. Martin's Press, 2018); and Greg Lukianoff and Jonathan Haidt, *The Coddling of the American Mind: How Good Intentions and Bad Ideas Are Setting Up a Generation for Failure* (New York: Penguin Press, 2018).
12. These include Paul R. Gross and Norman Levitt, *Higher Superstition: The Academic Left and Its Quarrels with Science* (Baltimore, Maryland: Johns Hopkins University Press, 1994); Alan Charles Kors and Harvey Silverglate, *The Shadow University: The Betrayal of Liberty on America's Campuses* (New York: The Free Press, 1998); Alan Sokal and Jean Bricmont, *Fashionable Nonsense: Postmodern Intellectuals' Abuse of Science* (New York: Picador, 1999); Daphne Patai and Noretta Koertge, *Professing Feminism: Cautionary Tales from the Strange World of Women's Studies* (New York: Basic Books, 1994); Salim Mansur, *Delectable Lie: A Liberal Repudiation of Multiculturalism* (Brantford, Ontario: Mantua Books, 2011); and Bruce Bawer, *The Victims' Revolution: The Rise of Identity Studies and the Closing of the Liberal Mind* (New York: HarperCollins, 2012).

Chapter Two
Thinking versus Feeling, Truth versus Hurt Feelings

1. David Hume, *A Treatise of Human Nature*, 1739 edition (Oxford: Clarendon Press, 1896), 415.
2. Hans J. Eysenck, *Rebel with a Cause* (London: W. H. Allen & Co., 1990), 119.
3. Michael Shermer, *How We Believe: Science, Skepticism, and the Search for God* (New York: Henry Holt, 2000), 90.
4. Gad Saad, "Evolutionary Consumer Psychology," in *Handbook of Evolutionary Psychology*, ed. David M. Buss (New York: Wiley, 2015), 1143–60.
5. Matt Ridley, *Nature Via Nurture: Genes, Experience, & What Makes Us Human* (New York: HarperCollins, 2003), 280.
6. Gad Saad, *The Consuming Instinct: What Juicy Burgers, Ferraris, Pornography, and Gift Giving Reveal about Human Nature* (Amherst, New York: Prometheus Books, 2011).
7. Richard E. Petty and John T. Cacioppo, "The Elaboration Likelihood Model of Persuasion" in *Advances in Experimental Social Psychology*, ed. Leonard Berkowitz, 19 (New York: Academic Press, 1986), 123–205.
8. M. J. Rosenberg, "An Analysis of Affective-Cognitive Consistency," in *Attitude Organization and Change: An Analysis of Consistency Among Attitude Components*, eds. C. I. Hovland and M. J. Rosenberg (New Haven, Connecticut: Yale University Press, 1960), 15–64.
9. Randolph M. Nesse and Phoebe C. Ellsworth, "Evolution, Emotions, and Emotional Disorders," *American Psychologist* 64, no. 2 (2009): 129–39.
10. David M. Buss *et al.*, "Sex Differences in Jealousy: Evolution, Physiology, and Psychology," *Psychological Science* 3, no. 4 (1992): 251–55.
11. Christopher K. Hsee *et al.*, "Lay Rationalism: Individual Differences in Using Reason versus Feelings to Guide Decisions," *Journal of Marketing Research* 52 (February 2015): 134–46.
12. Mark Steyn, "The Absurd Trial of Geert Wilders," *Maclean's*, February 18, 2010, https://www.macleans.ca/general/%20/the-absurd-trial-of-geert-wilders/.
13. "Academics' Mobbing of a Young Scholar Must Be Denounced," Quillette, December 7, 2018, https://quillette.com/2018/12/07/academics-mobbing-of-a-young-scholar-must-be-denounced/.

14. Theodore Dalrymple, "A Foolish, Fond Old Man," *BMJ* 335, no. 7623 (2007): 777.

15. Gad Saad, "Tell My Wife That I Love Her," *THE SAAD TRUTH* 343, January 20, 2017, YouTube video, https://www.youtube.com/watch?v=LquFudV-nLA.

16. Rachel Brown, "Talking Points: Three Cheers for White Men," Fencing Bear at Prayer Blog, June 5, 2015, https://fencingbearatprayer.blogspot.com/2015/06/talking-points-three-cheers-for-white.html.

17. Peter Wood, "Anatomy of a Smear," *Inside Higher Ed*, September 10, 2018, https://www.insidehighered.com/views/2018/09/10/slurring-medieval-scholar-attempt-silence-those-who-disagree-opinion.

18. See my appearance on Sam Harris's *Waking Up* podcast shortly prior to election day.

19. For an exhaustive list of decision rules, see John Payne, James Bettman, and Eric Johnson, *The Adaptive Decision Maker* (New York: Cambridge University Press, 1993).

20. Elizabeth F. Loftus, "Eyewitness Science and the Legal System," *Annual Review of Law and Social Science*, 14 (2018): 1–10.

21. Lawrence H. Summers, "Remarks at NBER Conference on Diversifying the Science & Engineering Workforce," January 14, 2015, Cambridge, Massachusetts. See also Sam Dillon, "Harvard Chief Defends His Talk on Women," *New York Times*, January 18, 2015, https://nyti.ms/2xm2tMM.

22. "Psychoanalysis Q-and-A: Steven Pinker," *Harvard Crimson*, January 19, 2005, https://bit.ly/2OX2PiL.

23. Wendy M. Williams and Stephen J. Ceci, "National Hiring Experiments Reveal 2:1 Faculty Preference for Women on STEM Tenure Track," *Proceedings of the National Academy of Sciences of the United States of America* 112, no. 17 (2015): 5360–65.

24. Gad Saad, "The Consuming Instinct," *Talks at Google*, July 21, 2017, YouTube video, https://www.youtube.com/watch?v=_qHYmx7qPes&t=3s.

25. Gad Saad, "My Chat with Ex-Google Employee James Damore," *THE SAAD TRUTH* 540, November 6, 2017, YouTube video, https://youtu.be/aTfk4DkijVs.

26. Daisuke Wakabayashi, "Google Fires Engineer Who Wrote Memo Questioning Women in Tech," *New York Times*, August 7, 2017, https://nyti.ms/2ukvZD8.

27. "Cern Scientist Alessandro Strumia Suspended after Comments," BBC, October 1, 2018, https://bbc.in/2AbeVj7.

28. "Statement on a Recent Talk at CERN," High Energy Physics Community Statement, https://www.particlesforjustice.org.

29. "Gender Controversy Comes to Physics: A Response to the Statement against Alessandro Strumia," Areo Magazine, October 31, 2018, https://bit.ly/2yKI4lo.

30. Roland Bainton, *Here I Stand: A Life of Martin Luther* (New York: Abingdon Press, 1950).

31. Gad Saad, "My Chat with Physicist Alessandro Strumia," *THE SAAD TRUTH* 809, December 10, 2018, YouTube video, https://youtu.be/4hAqLr-InT8.

32. Martin Rosenbaum, "Pseudonyms to Protect Authors of Controversial Articles," BBC, November 12, 2018, https://www.bbc.com/news/education-46146766.

33. Robin McKie, "Tim Hunt: 'I've Been Hung Out to Dry. They Haven't Even Bothered to Ask for My Side of Affairs,'" *The Guardian*, June 13, 2015, https://bit.ly/2rQAZvY.

34. Robin McKie, "Sir Tim Hunt: My Gratitude to Female Scientists for Their Support," *The Guardian*, June 20, 2015, https://bit.ly/3fviSTC.

35. Gordon G. Gallup Jr., Rebecca L. Burch, and Steven M. Platek, "Does Semen Have Antidepressant Properties?" *Archives of Sexual Behavior* 31, no. 3 (2002): 289–93.

36. Gardiner Harris, "Head of Surgeons Group Resigns over Article Viewed as Offensive to Women," *New York Times*, April 17, 2011, https://nyti.ms/2OXSoeN.

37. Michael Smerconish, "Lazar Greenfield's 'Semengate' Stuns Scientific Community," HuffPost, April 25, 2011, https://www.huffpost.com/entry/semengate-stuns-scientifi_b_853164.

38. Boris Johnson, "Dr. Matt Taylor's Shirt Made Me Cry, Too—with Rage at His Abusers," *The Telegraph*, November 16, 2014, https://bit.ly/2GxBkIm.

39. Taylor Wofford, "An Interview with the Woman behind the #Shirtgate Shirt," *Newsweek*, November 20, 2014, https://bit.ly/2THs3FC.

40. Gad Saad, "Niqab Is 'Freely Chosen' while Bikini Is Oppressive?" *THE SAAD TRUTH* 47, June 22, 2015, YouTube video, https://youtu.be/2Kjrww0hKSY.

Chapter Three
Non-Negotiable Elements of a Free and Modern Society

1. John Stuart Mill, *On Liberty*, rev. ed. (Boston: Ticknor and Fields, 1863) 35–36.

2. Niall Ferguson, *Civilization: The West and the Rest* (New York: Penguin Books, 2011).

3. U.S. Senator Josh Hawley has proposed such legislation: https://www. hawley.senate.gov/sites/default/files/2019-06/Ending-Support-Internet-Censorship-Act-Bill-Text.pdf.

4. "Disinvitation Report 2014: A Disturbing 15-Year Trend," Foundation for Individual Rights in Education, May 28, 2014, https://www.thefire. org/disinvitation-season-report-2014/.

5. "Best and Worst Student Unions Regarding Practices," Campus Freedom Index, 2019, http://campusfreedomindex.ca/summary/#ranking-chart.

6. Salman Rushdie, "Democracy Is No Polite Tea Party," *Los Angeles Times*, February 7, 2005, https://www.latimes.com/archives/la-xpm-2005-feb-07-oe-rushdie7-story.html.

7. Patricia Cohen, "Yale Press Bans Images of Muhammad in New Book," *New York Times*, August 12, 2009, https://www.nytimes. com/2009/08/13/books/13book.html.

8. Gad Saad, "Blasphemy Laws Belong in the Dark Ages," *Psychology Today*, December 14, 2011, https://www.psychologytoday.com/ca/blog/ homo-consumericus/201112/blasphemy-laws-belong-in-the-dark-ages.

9. Gad Saad, "Masturbating with a Crucifix in a Film...No Riots?" *Psychology Today*, September 20, 2012, https://www.psychologytoday. com/ca/blog/homo-consumericus/201209/ masturbating-crucifix-in-film-no-riots.

10. Stephen J. Ceci and Wendy M. Williams, "Who Decides What Is Acceptable Speech on Campus? Why Restricting Free Speech Is Not the Answer," *Perspectives on Psychological Science* 13, no. 3 (2018): 299–323.

11. Wyndham Lewis, *Rude Assignment* (London: Hutchinson, 1950), 48.

12. Peter Sloterdijk, *Critique of Cynical Reason* (Minneapolis, Minnesota: The University of Minnesota Press, 1987), 288.

13. Thomas Jefferson, "Thomas Jefferson to Francis Adrian Van der Kemp," Founders Online, National Archives, July 30, 1816, https://founders. archives.gov/documents/Jefferson/03-10-02-0167.

14. Sarah Crown, "Poem of the Week," July 2, 2007, *The Guardian*, https:// www.theguardian.com/books/booksblog/2007/jul/02/poemoftheweek6.

15. Richard Dawkins (@RichardDawkins), "Listening to the lovely bells of Winchester, one of our great mediaeval cathedrals. So much nicer than the aggressive-sounding 'Allahu Akhbar.' Or is that just my cultural upbringing?" Twitter, July 16, 2018, 3:00 p.m., https://twitter.com/RichardDawkins/status/1018933359978909696?s=20.

16. Gad Saad (@GadSaad), "Dear Richard: Arabic is my mother tongue. When properly translated, 'Allahu Akbar' means 'we love all people but hold a special fondness for Jews, women, and gays.' Don't worry. It's a message of love, tolerance, and liberalism," Twitter, July 16, 2018, 3:09 p.m., https://twitter.com/GadSaad/status/1018935568162582528?s=20.

17. Gad Saad, "My Tweet to Richard Dawkins Heard around the World" *THE SAAD TRUTH* 703, July 17, 2018, YouTube video, https://www.youtube.com/watch?v=VxKvcVFnRhk.

18. Gad Saad (@GadSaad), "No way Donald. @AOC is a woman of color in Trump's MAGA country. She faces much greater daily threats than those Holocaust survivors ever did," Twitter, June 22, 2109, 1:05 p.m., https://twitter.com/GadSaad/status/1142478696940527621?s=20.

19. The 20 Worst Quotes of 2018: http://archive.vn/k1sSo. See quote #7. I recount this glorious satirical blindness on the part of PJ Media in *THE SAAD TRUTH* 815: "My SARCASTIC Quote Listed in the Top 20 Worst Quotes of 2018!" December 31, 2018, YouTube video, https://www.youtube.com/watch?v=SLGdPoZGpw4.

20. Gad Saad (@GadSaad), "To all Noble Undocumented 'immigrants': We apologize for our bigotry and racism. It is Nazism to not allow you to vote in our elections. After all, national borders is Nazism. Nationhood is Nazism. In a just world, everyone should get to vote in any district. #WeApologize," Twitter, November 6, 2018, 1:21 p.m., https://twitter.com/GadSaad/status/1059873450104369152?s=20.

21. Cristina Lopez, "The Joe Rogan Experience Disproportionately Hosts Men," April 15, 2019, MediaMatters, https://www.mediamatters.org/legacy/joe-rogan-experience-disproportionately-hosts-men.

22. Elizabeth Gibney, "What the Nobels Are—and Aren't—Doing to Encourage Diversity," *Nature*, September 28, 2018, https://www.nature.com/articles/d41586-018-06879-z#correction-0.

23. http://www.scientistsmarchonwashington.com. It is no longer active.

24. Graeme Hamilton, "Quebec Deputy Minister Gets Pushback after Questioning Place of Indigenous 'Traditional Knowledge,'" *National Post*, March 27, 2018, https://nationalpost.com/news/canada/

quebec-deputy-minister-gets-pushback-after-questioning-place-of-indigenous-traditional-knowledge.

25. Gad Saad, "Death of the West by a Thousand Cuts," *THE SAAD TRUTH* 511, September 25, 2017, YouTube video, https://www.youtube.com/watch?v=Y0a_gtYojus.

26. Tristin Hopper, "Law Professor Argues in UBC Human Rights Complaint That Indigenous Scholars Shouldn't Have to Publish Peer-Reviewed Research," *National Post*, January 24, 2016, https://nationalpost.com/news/canada/b-c-aboriginal-scholar-wins-bid-for-rights-hearing-after-shes-denied-tenure-in-part-over-lack-of-research.

27. Ludwig von Mises, *Human Action: A Treatise on Economics* (Auburn, Alabama: Ludwig von Mises Institute, 1998), 76.

28. Jörg Guido Hülsmann, *Mises: The Last Knight of Liberalism* (Auburn, Alabama: Ludwig von Mises Institute, 2007), 668.

29. Gad Saad, "My Chat with Economist Mark Perry," *THE SAAD TRUTH* 1007, January 28, 2020, YouTube video, https://www.youtube.com/watch?v=QaRsexsT3Qk; Mark Perry, "More on My Efforts to Advance Diversity, Equity, and Inclusion and End Gender Discrimination in Michigan," AEIdeas, American Enterprise Institute, May 17, 2018, http://www.aei.org/publication/more-on-my-efforts-to-advance-diversity-equity-and-inclusion/.

30. Frederick L. Oswald *et al.*, "Predicting Ethnic and Racial Discrimination: A Meta-Analysis of IAT Criterion Studies," *Journal of Personality and Social Psychology* 105, no. 2 (2013): 171–92.

31. Mike Noon, "Pointless Diversity Training: Unconscious Bias, New Racism and Agency," *Work, Employment and Society* 32, no. 1 (2018): 198–209.

32. Tom Bartlett, "Can We Really Measure Implicit Bias? Maybe Not," *Chronicle of Higher Education*, January 5, 2017, https://www.chronicle.com/article/Can-We-Really-Measure-Implicit/238807.

33. "Equity, Diversity and Inclusion (EDI) Statement FAQs," Office of Equity, Diversity and Inclusion, UCLA, September 5, 2019, https://ucla.app.box.com/v/edi-statement-faqs.

34. Francis S. Collins, "Time to End the Manel Tradition," National Institutes of Health, June 12, 2019, https://www.nih.gov/about-nih/who-we-are/nih-director/statements/time-end-manel-tradition.

35. Simon Baron-Cohen (@sbaroncohen), "Scientists and other academics should follow this excellent example & refuse to speak on all male panels in conferences/scholarly meetings. This includes as keynote speakers or in

round table discussions. A change in gender diversity has to happen quickly," Twitter June 14, 2019, 6:39 p.m., https://twitter.com/sbaroncohen/status/1139663554850807809?s=20.

36. Christopher F. Cardiff and Daniel B. Klein, "Faculty Partisan Affiliations in All Disciplines: A Voter-Registration Study," *Critical Review* 17, no. 3–4 (2005): 237–55.

37. Mitchell Langbert, Anthony J. Quain, and Daniel B. Klein, "Faculty Voter Registration in Economics, History, Journalism, Law, and Psychology," *Econ Journal Watch* 13, no. 3 (2016): 422–51.

38. Adam Bonica *et al.*, "The Legal Academy's Ideological Uniformity," *Journal of Legal Studies* 47, no. 1 (2018): 1–43.

39. Mitchell Langbert, "Homogeneous: The Political Affiliations of Elite Liberal Arts College Faculty," *Academic Questions* 31, no. 2 (2018): 186–97.

40. Thomas Sowell, "Random Thoughts," *Jewish World Review*, July 31, 1998, http://www.jewishworldreview.com/cols/sowell073198.html.

41. Samuel Abrams, "Think Professors Are Liberal? Try Administrators," *New York Times*, October 16, 2018, https://www.nytimes.com/2018/10/16/opinion/liberal-college-administrators.html.

42. Jerry O'Mahoney, "Students, Faculty, Administration Respond Following National Publication of SLC Professor's Op-Ed," *Sarah Lawrence Phoenix*, October 18, 2018, http://www.sarahlawrencephoenix.com/campus/2018/10/18/students-faculty-administration-respond-following-national-publication-of-slc-professors-op-ed.

43. Yoel Inbar and Joris Lammers, "Political Diversity in Social and Personality Psychology," *Perspectives on Psychological Science* 7, no. 5 (2012): 496–503.

44. Jeremy A. Frimer, Linda J. Skitka, and Matt Motyl, "Liberals and Conservatives Are Similarly Motivated to Avoid Exposure to One Another's Opinions," *Journal of Experimental Social Psychology* 72 (September 2017): 1–12.

45. Andy Kiersz and Hunter Walker, "These Charts Show the Political Bias of Workers in Each Profession," *Business Insider*, November 3, 2014, https://www.businessinsider.com/charts-show-the-political-bias-of-each-profession-2014-11.

46. "Democratic vs. Republican Occupations," Verdant Labs, 2016, http://verdantlabs.com/politics_of_professions/index.html; Ana Swanson, "Chart: The Most Liberal and Conservative Jobs in

America," *Washington Post*, June 3, 2015, https://www.washingtonpost.
com/news/wonk/wp/2015/06/03/why-your-flight-attendant-is-probably-
a-democrat/?noredirect=on&utm_term=.ad03ace18140.

47. Rani Molla, "Tech Employees Are Much More Liberal Than Their
Employers—at Least as Far as the Candidates They Support," Vox,
October 21, 2018, https://www.vox.com/2018/10/31/18039528/
tech-employees-politics-liberal-employers-candidates.

48. Lars Willnat and David Weaver, "The American Journalist in the Digital
Age: Key Findings," School of Journalism, Indiana University, 2014,
http://archive.news.indiana.edu/releases/iu/2014/05/2013-american-
journalist-key-findings.pdf.

49. Eitan D. Hersh and Matthew N. Goldenberg, "Democratic and
Republican Physicians Provide Different Care on Politicized Health
Issues," *Proceedings of the National Academy of Sciences of the United
States of America* 113, no. 42 (2016): 11811–16.

50. Margot Sanger-Katz, "Your Surgeon Is Probably a Republican, Your
Psychiatrist a Democrat," *New York Times*, October 7, 2016, https://
www.nytimes.com/2016/10/07/upshot/your-surgeon-is-probably-a-
republican-your-psychiatrist-probably-a-democrat.html.

51. Ronald Reagan, "Encroaching Control," March 30, 1961, YouTube
video, 42:41, https://www.youtube.com/watch?v=8gf9Y7UgGi0. See
also Robert Mann, *Becoming Ronald Reagan: The Rise of a
Conservative Icon* (Lincoln, Nebraska: Potomac Books, 2019), 119.

Chapter Four
Anti-Science, Anti-Reason, and Illiberal Movements

1. Steven Pinker, *The Blank Slate: The Modern Denial of Human Nature*
(New York: Viking, 2002).

2. John B. Watson, *Behaviorism* (London: Kegan Paul, Trench, Trubner,
1924), 82.

3. Ibid.

4. Ibid., 75.

5. I originally recounted this anecdote here: Gad Saad, "Applying
Evolutionary Psychology in Understanding the Representation of Women
in Advertisements," *Psychology & Marketing* 21, no. 8 (2004):
593–612.

6. Gad Saad, "My Chat with Psychologist Jordan Peterson," *THE SAAD TRUTH 265*, October 11, 2016, YouTube video, https://youtu.be/Bpim_n0r0z0.

7. Gad Saad, "Full Testimony at the Canadian Senate," *THE SAAD TRUTH 421*, May 11, 2017, YouTube video, https://youtu.be/4WqryoEJqZg.

8. Bradford Richardson, "California First-Grader Sent to Principal's Office for Misgendering Classmate," *Washington Times*, August 23, 2017, https://www.washingtontimes.com/news/2017/aug/23/california-parents-feel-betrayed-transgender-revea/.

9. Olivia Petter, "JK Rowling Criticized over 'Transphobic' Tweet about Menstruation," June 7, 2020, https://www.independent.co.uk/life-style/jk-rowling-tweet-women-menstruate-people-transphobia-twitter-a9552866.html; Julie Mazziotta, "Transgender Activist Freebleeds to Show Men Can Menstruate Too: It's 'Harmful to Equate Periods with Womanhood,'" *People*, July 25, 2017, https://people.com/bodies/transgender-activist-freebleed-men-can-menstruate/; Helena Horton, "Boys Can Have Periods Too, Children to Be Taught in Latest Victory for Transgender Campaigners," *The Telegraph*, December 16, 2018, https://www.telegraph.co.uk/news/2018/12/16/boys-can-have-periods-schoolchildren-taught-latest-victory-transgender/.

10. Julian Castro (@JulianCastro), "Thank you, Charlotte! Last night I misspoke - it's trans men, trans masculine, and non-binary folks who need full access to abortion and repro healthcare. And I'm grateful to ALL trans and non-binary folks for their labor in guiding me on this issue," Twitter, June 27, 2019, 4:29 p.m., https://twitter.com/JulianCastro/status/1144341924821852160?s=20.

11. Gad Saad (@GadSaad), "Dear @JulianCastro, I'm a trans woman looking to conduct a cervical exam. Do you know of a good gynaecologist that you might be willing to recommend?" Twitter, June 27, 2019, 12:02 a.m., https://twitter.com/GadSaad/status/1144093679969275905?s=20.

12. Megan Fox, "Clown World: Canadian Cancer Society Claims Men without Cervixes Can Get Cervical Cancer," PJ Media, September 11, 2019, https://pjmedia.com/trending/clown-world-canadian-cancer-society-claims-men-without-cervixes-can-get-cervical-cancer/.

13. Douglas Ernst, "Elizabeth Warren Vows: Transgender Child Must Approve of Secretary Of Education Nominee," *Washington Times*,

January 30, 2020, https://www.washingtontimes.com/news/2020/jan/30/elizabeth-warren-vows-transgender-child-must-appro/.

14. Leonid Rozenblit and Frank Keil, "The Misunderstood Limits of Folk Science: An Illusion of Explanatory Depth," *Cognitive Science* 26, no. 5 (2002): 521–62.

15. David P. McCabe and Alan D. Castel, "Seeing Is Believing: The Effect of Brain Images on Judgments of Scientific Reasoning," *Cognition* 107, no. 1 (2008): 343–52; J. D. Trout, "Seduction without Cause: Uncovering Explanatory Neurophilia," *Trends in Cognitive Sciences* 12, no. 8 (2008): 281–82; Deena Skolnick Weisberg *et al.*, "The Seductive Allure of Neuroscience Explanations," *Journal of Cognitive Neuroscience* 20, no. 3 (2008): 470–77; Deena Skolnick Weisberg, Jordan C. V. Taylor, and Emily J. Hopkins, "Deconstructing the Seductive Allure of Neuroscience Explanations," *Judgment and Decision Making* 10, no. 5 (2015): 429–41; Justin Garcia and Gad Saad, "Evolutionary Neuromarketing: Darwinizing the Neuroimaging Paradigm for Consumer Behavior," *Journal of Consumer Behaviour* 7, no. 4–5 (2008): 397–414; Gad Saad and Gil Greengross, "Using Evolutionary Psychology to Enhance the Brain Imaging Paradigm," *Frontiers in Human Neuroscience* 8 (2014): 452, https://www.ncbi.nlm.nih.gov/pmc/articles/PMC4064664/.

16. Gordon Pennycook *et al.*, "On the Reception and Detection of Pseudo-Profound Bullshit," *Judgment and Decision Making* 10, no. 6 (2015): 549–63.

17. Mike Springer, "John Searle on Foucault and the Obscurantism in French Philosophy," *Philosophy*, July 1, 2013, http://www.openculture.com/2013/07/jean_searle_on_foucault_and_the_obscurantism_in_french_philosophy.html.

18. Anthony Barnes, "Blank Canvas: London Gallery Unveils 'Invisible' Art Exhibition," The Independent, May 19, 2012, https://www.independent.co.uk/arts-entertainment/art/news/blank-canvas-london-gallery-unveils-invisible-art-exhibition-7767057.html.

19. Alan D. Sokal, "Transgressing the Boundaries: Toward a Transformative Hermeneutics of Quantum Gravity," *Social Text* 46/47 (Spring/Summer 1996): 217–52. See also Alan Sokal and Jean Bricmont, *Fashionable Nonsense: Postmodern Intellectuals' Abuse of Science* (New York: Picador, 1998).

20. Gad Saad, "Death of Common Sense Will Spell the End of Free Societies," *Psychology Today*, May 5, 2010, http://www.

psychologytoday.com/blog/homo-consumericus/201005/
death-common-sense-will-spell-the-end-free-societies.

21. Gad Saad, "How the Social Construction of the Penis Affects Climate
    Change," *THE SAAD TRUTH* 433, May 20, 2017, YouTube video,
    https://www.youtube.com/watch?v=lMv8-uPqZ5M.

22. Retraction statement regarding the paper in question: Jamie Lindsay and
    Peter Boyle, "The Conceptual Penis as a Social Construct," *Cogent
    Social Sciences*, May 19, 2017, https://www.cogentoa.com/
    article/10.1080/23311886.2017.1330439; Scott Jaschik, "How the Hoax
    Got Published," *Inside Higher Ed*, May 25, 2017, https://www.
    insidehighered.com/news/2017/05/25/
    publisher-explains-how-article-about-viewing-male-organ-conceptual-
    got-published.

23. Gad Saad, "The Grievance Studies Exposé" *THE SAAD TRUTH* 739,
    October 4, 2018, YouTube video, https://youtu.be/bZ6VyiwpHZg; Gad
    Saad, "The Grievance Studies Papers Are Fantastic!—Part I," *THE
    SAAD TRUTH* 742, October 7, 2018, YouTube video, https://youtu.be/
    iUxBJtx_3Y8; Gad Saad, "The Grievance Studies Papers Are
    Fantastic!—Part II," *THE SAAD TRUTH* 743, October 8, 2018,
    YouTube video, https://youtu.be/435ZCqFpx7M.

24. Katherine Mangan, "Proceedings Start against 'Sokal Squared' Hoax
    Professor," *Chronicle of Higher Education*, January 7, 2019, https://
    www.chronicle.com/article/Proceedings-Start-Against/245431.

25. Alex Ballinger, "Rachel McKinnon Becomes First Transgender Woman
    to Win Track World Title," *Cycling Weekly*, October 17, 2018, https://
    www.cyclingweekly.com/news/latest-news/
    rachel-mckinnon-becomes-first-transgender-woman-win-track-world-
    title-397473.

26. Gad Saad (@GadSaad), "Dear Dr. @rachelvmckinnon: I appreciate your
    desire to fight for fairness when it comes to transgender rights. Do you
    think though that the biological women who lost against you have a
    right to feel aggrieved when a biological male beats them in a women's
    competition?" Twitter, October 14, 2018, 6:11 p.m., https://twitter.com/
    GadSaad/status/1051596279720087553; Gad Saad (@GadSaad), "Or do
    you think that the behavioral, anatomical, physiological, morphological,
    and hormonal advantages that men possess over women in such
    competitions are mere social constructions imposed by the transphobic
    patriarchy? I'd be happy to chat with you on my show THE SAAD

TRUTH," Twitter, October 14, 2018, 6:11 p.m., https://twitter.com/GadSaad/status/1051596281456529409?s=20.

27. Gad Saad, "Entering World Judo Championship as a TransGravity and TransAgeist Competitor," *THE SAAD TRUTH 755*, October 18, 2018, YouTube video, https://www.youtube.com/watch?v=DoTeh8EWEP8.

28. "Dutch Man, 69, Who 'Identifies as 20 Years Younger' Launches Legal Battle to Change Age," *The Telegraph*, November 7, 2018, https://www.telegraph.co.uk/news/2018/11/07/dutch-man-69-identifies-20-years-younger-launches-legal-battle/.

29. Gad Saad (@GadSaad), "What gives the right of my physician to use antiquated notions of weight to determine that I need to lose weight. Real scientists now know that a given weight scale reading is not fixed but rather fluid. Plus what about those who wish to be weightless? Don't they have rights?" Twitter, December 5, 2017, 2:05 p.m., https://twitter.com/GadSaad/status/938122074283003904?s=20.

30. Claire Toureille, "Trans Woman Files Human Rights Complaint against Canadian Spa That Refused to Wax Her," PinkNews, May 21, 2018, https://www.pinknews.co.uk/2018/05/21/trans-woman-human-rights-complaint-canada-spa/.

31. Douglas Quan, "'Not for Men Sorry': Transgender Woman Denied a Brazilian Wax by Spa Files Human Rights Complaint," *Canadian National Post*, August 22, 2018, https://nationalpost.com/news/canada/not-for-men-sorry-transgender-woman-files-human-rights-complaint-after-being-denied-brazilian-wax.

32. Tristan Hopper, "Canada's Oldest Rape Crisis Centre Stripped of City Funding for Refusing to Accept Trans Women," *Canadian National Post*, March 19, 2019, https://nationalpost.com/news/canada/canadas-oldest-rape-crisis-centre-stripped-of-city-funding-for-refusing-to-accept-trans-women.

33. Gad Saad (@GadSaad) "Dear @CydZeigler: I'm currently watching you on @foxnews. Do you not think that transwomen (biological males) exhibit physiological, anatomical, morphological, and hormonal differences as compared to biological females? As an evolutionary behavioral scientist who," Twitter, February 18, 2019, 10:58 p.m., https://twitter.com/GadSaad/status/1097706973297025024?s=20; Gad Saad (@GadSaad), "has researched evolutionary-based sex differences, I was under the impression that sex differences exist. Perhaps you'd like to come on my show and educate me?" Twitter, February 18,

2019, 10:58 p.m., https://twitter.com/GadSaad/status/109770697418621 7473?s=20.

34. PinkNews (@PinkNews), "Trans women are women. So trans women's bodies are women's bodies. So trans women's penises are women's penises," Twitter, February 19, 2019, 6:45 p.m., https://twitter.com/ PinkNews/status/1098005566268547072?s=20. Incidentally, a few months earlier I had satirically suggested that if one gave oral sex to a trans woman (a biological male) it would constitute cunnilingus. Gad Saad, "TransCunnilingus—My Prophetic Satire Strikes Again," *THE SAAD TRUTH* 796, November 28, 2018, YouTube video, https://www. youtube.com/watch?v=OXmMvetnTTU.

35. Pat Eaton-Robb, "Transgender Sprinters Finish 1st, 2nd at Connecticut Girls Indoor Track Championships," *Washington Times*, February 24, 2019, https://www.washingtontimes.com/news/2019/feb/24/ terry-miller-andraya-yearwood-transgender-sprinter/.

36. Lisa Littman, "Rapid-Onset Gender Dysphoria in Adolescents and Young Adults: A Study of Parental Reports," *PLOS ONE* 13, no. 8 (August 16, 2018), https://journals.plos.org/plosone/article?id=10.1371/ journal.pone.0202330.

37. Colleen Flaherty, "Journal Looking into Study on 'Rapid-Onset Gender Dysphoria,'" *Inside Higher Ed*, August 31, 2018, https://www. insidehighered.com/quicktakes/2018/08/31/ journal-looking-study-rapid-onset-gender-dysphoria.

38. Chelsea Ritschel, "Charlize Theron Says She Is Raising Her Child as a Girl: 'It's Not for Me to Decide,'" The Independent, April 19, 2019, https://www.independent.co.uk/life-style/charlize-theron-children- transgender-jackson-age-girl-boy-a8878686.html.

39. The three tweets in question: Gad Saad (@GadSaad), "So brave, so stunning, so progressive. Well done @CharlizeAfrica. I raised my children as non-arboreal multicellular carbon-based agents. I did not impose a species on them. It's for them to decide whether they wish to be part of Homo sapiens or not," Twitter, April 20, 2019, 4:53 p.m., https:// twitter.com/GadSaad/status/1119705660365651969?s=20; Gad Saad (@ GadSaad), "I'm following the lead of the parental heroism of @ CharlizeAfrica. I've advised my non-arboreal multicellular carbon-based agents (children) that they do not need to call my wife and I 'mom' and 'dad' respectively. We are gender-neutral non-binary caregivers 1 and 2," Twitter, April 20 2019, 4:59 p.m., https://twitter.com/GadSaad/status/11 19707205530472449?s=20; and Gad Saad (@GadSaad), "I don't want

my children to be restricted to viewing themselves as carbon-based. This is why I am now immersing them in the fluidity of the Periodic Table. I've asked them to look at all elements and decide which ones they self-identify with (in terms of their building blocks)," Twitter, April 20, 2019, 5:15 p.m., https://twitter.com/GadSaad/status/111971131843566796 9?s=20.

40. Sara B. Johnson, Robert W. Blum, and Jay N. Giedd, "Adolescent Maturity and the Brain: The Promise and Pitfalls of Neuroscience Research in Adolescent Health Policy," *Journal of Adolescent Health* 45, no. 3 (2009): 216–21.

41. Madeline Fry, "Lowering the Voting Age to 16 Is a Crazy Idea," *Washington Examiner*, May 18, 2020, https://www.washingtonexaminer.com/opinion/lowering-the-voting-age-to-16-like-nancy-pelosi-wants-is-a-crazy-idea.

42. Chuck Weber, "Teacher's Refusal to Supervise Transgender Student in Locker Room Sparks Debate," ABC6 News, December 15, 2018, https://abc6onyourside.com/news/nation-world/teachers-refusal-to-supervise-transgender-student-in-locker-room-sparks-debate; Joy Pullman, "School Punishes Male Teacher for Refusing to Watch a Naked Girl in the Boys' Locker Room," The Federalist, November 14, 2018, https://thefederalist.com/2018/11/14/florida-school-district-gags-p-e-teachers-telling-parents-girl-watching-naked-sons/.

43. Adapted from: Peter Glick and Susan T. Fiske, "The Ambivalent Sexism Inventory: Differentiating Hostile and Benevolent Sexism," *Journal of Personality and Social Psychology* 70, no. 3 (1996): 491–512. The scale is found on page 512.

44. Gad Saad, "The Acronym for Benevolent Sexism Is BS: The Linguistic Irony Is Delicious," *Psychology Today*, January 7, 2009, https://www.psychologytoday.com/ca/blog/homo-consumericus/200901/the-acronym-benevolent-sexism-is-bs-the-linguistic-irony-is-delicious; Gad Saad, "Exploring the Items Used to Measure Benevolent Sexism," *Psychology Today*, January 8, 2009, https://www.psychologytoday.com/ca/blog/homo-consumericus/200901/exploring-the-items-used-measure-benevolent-sexism.

45. "Why Women Receive Less CPR from Bystanders," American Heart Association, November 5, 2018, https://www.sciencedaily.com/releases/2018/11/181105105453.htm; Emma Teitel, "When It Comes to Life-Saving CPR, Men Are Too Worried about Touching Women:

Teitel," *Toronto Star*, November 14, 2017, https://www.thestar.com/news/canada/2017/11/14/women-will-consent-to-life-saving-first-aid-teitel.html.

46. Gad Saad, "Is Toxic Masculinity a Valid Concept?" *Psychology Today*, March 8, 2018, https://www.psychologytoday.com/ca/blog/homo-consumericus/201803/is-toxic-masculinity-valid-concept.

47. Christina Hoff Sommers, *The War Against Boys: How Misguided Feminism Is Harming Our Young Men* (New York: Simon & Schuster, 2001).

48. Anthony Gockowski, "Schools Offer 'Safe Spaces' to Combat 'Toxic Masculinity,'" Campus Reform, January 16, 2017, https://www.campusreform.org/?ID=8645.

49. "Can Fashion End Toxic Masculinity?" Events, Cornell University, May 1, 2019, http://events.cornell.edu/event/can_fashion_end_toxic_masculinity; "Men's Cuddling Group Aims to Redefine Masculinity and Heal Trauma," News and Events, Lehigh University, March 26, 2019, https://ed.lehigh.edu/news-events/news/men's-cuddling-group-aims-redefine-masculinity-and-heal-trauma.

50. Kathleen Elliott, "Challenging Toxic Masculinity in Schools and Society," *On the Horizon* 26, no. 1 (2018): 17–22.

51. Breanne Fahs and Michael Karger, "Women's Studies as Virus: Institutional Feminism and the Projection of Danger," *Multidisciplinary Journal of Gender Studies* 5, no. 1 (2016): 929–57.

52. Anastasia Salter and Bridget Blodgett, *Toxic Geek Masculinity in Media: Sexism, Trolling, and Identity Policing,* (New York: Palgrave Macmillan, 2017).

53. Mari Kate Mycek, "Meatless Meals and Masculinity: How Veg* Men Explain Their Plant-Based Diets," *Food and Foodways* 26, no. 3 (2018): 223–45; Anne DeLessio-Parson, "Doing Vegetarianism to Destabilize the Meat-Masculinity Nexus in La Plata, Argentina," *Gender, Place & Culture: A Journal of Feminist Geography* 24, no. 12 (2017): 1729–48.

54. Lisa Wade, "The Big Picture: Confronting Manhood after Trump," Public Books, October 26, 2017, http://www.publicbooks.org/big-picture-confronting-manhood-trump/.

55. Suzannah Walters, "Why Can't We Hate Men?" *Washington Post*, June 8, 2018, https://www.washingtonpost.com/opinions/why-cant-we-hate-men/2018/06/08/f1a3a8e0-6451-11e8-a69c-b944de66d9e7_story.html?noredirect=on&utm_term=.af070edc055d.

56. Hillary Clinton, "First Ladies' Conference on Domestic Violence, San Salvador, El Salvador," Web Archive, November 17, 1998, https://web. archive.org/web/20010726225357/http://clinton3.nara.gov/WH/EOP/ First_Lady/html/generalspeeches/1998/19981117.html.

57. Jos Boys, "Is There a Feminist Analysis of Architecture?" *Built Environment* 10, no. 1 (1984): 25–34; Emily Martin, "The Egg and the Sperm: How Science Has Constructed a Romance Based on Stereotypical Male–Female Roles," *Signs* 16, no. 3 (1991): 485–501; Whitney Stark, "Assembled Bodies: Reconfiguring Quantum Identities," *Minnesota Review* 88 (2017): 69–82; Ágnes Kovács, "Gender in the Substance of Chemistry, Part 1: The Ideal Gas," *HYLE—International Journal for Philosophy of Chemistry* 18, no. 2 (2012): 95–120; Ágnes Kovács, "Gender in the Substance of Chemistry, Part 2: An Agenda for Theory," *HYLE—International Journal for Philosophy of Chemistry* 18, no. 2 (2012): 121–43; Geraldine Pratt, "Feminist Geography," *Urban Geography* 13, no. 4 (1992): 385–91; Leone Burton, "Moving Towards a Feminist Epistemology of Mathematics," *Educational Studies in Mathematics* 28, no. 3 (1995): 275–91; Mark Carey *et al.*, "Glaciers, Gender, and Science: A Feminist Glaciology Framework for Global Environmental Change Research," *Progress in Human Geography* 40, no. 6 (2016): 770–93.

58. Charlotte Perkins Gilman, *Women and Economics* (New York: Cosimo Classics, 2007), 74.

59. Gina Rippon, *The Gendered Brain: The New Neuroscience That Shatters the Myth of the Female Brain* (London: The Bodley Head, 2019). Two other academic proponents of this view recently penned an opinion article in the *New York Times*: Daphna Joel and Cordelia Fine, "Can We Finally Stop Talking about 'Male' and 'Female' Brains?" *New York Times*, December 3, 2018, https://www.nytimes.com/2018/12/03/ opinion/male-female-brains-mosaic.html.

60. Gad Saad, "I'm Getting a Giraffe as a House Pet!" *THE SAAD TRUTH* 862, March 4, 2019, YouTube video, https://www.youtube. com/watch?v=W13POJw2KyA.

61. Amber N. V. Ruigrok *et al.*, "A Meta-Analysis of Sex Differences in Human Brain Structure," *Neuroscience and Biobehavioral Reviews* 39 (February 2014): 34–50; Stuart J. Ritchie *et al.*, "Sex Differences in the Adult Human Brain: Evidence from 5216 UK Biobank Participants," *Cerebral Cortex* 28, no. 8 (2018): 2959–75.

62. Lise Eliot, "Neurosexism: The Myth That Men and Women Have Different Brains," *Nature*, February 27, 2019, https://www.nature.com/articles/d41586-019-00677-x.

63. Gad Saad, "Women's Studies and Diversity: Where Are the Men?" *THE SAAD TRUTH* 319, December 23, 2016, YouTube video, https://youtu.be/qLx_be6ZoF8.

64. John Phelan, "Harvard Study: 'Gender Wage Gap' Explained Entirely by Work Choices of Men and Women," Foundation for Economic Education, December 10, 2018, https://fee.org/articles/harvard-study-gender-pay-gap-explained-entirely-by-work-choices-of-men-and-women/.

65. Kirsten Gillibrand (@SenGillibrand), "Here's an idea: If you win 13–0—the most goals for a single game in World Cup history—you should be paid at least equally to the men's team. Congratulations, #USWNT!" Twitter, June 11, 2019, 4:59 p.m., https://twitter.com/SenGillibrand/status/1138551389783810049?s=20.

66. Tara Golshan, "How the U.S. Women's Soccer Team 13–0 World Cup Win against Thailand Became about Pay Equity," Vox, June 11, 2019, https://www.vox.com/culture/2019/6/11/18661914/women-soccer-team-world-cup-win-thailand-pay-gap.

67. United Nations (@UN), "1 male soccer player makes almost double as much as the combined salaries of all players in the top 7 women's soccer leagues. During the #WomensWorldCup2019, join @UN_Women in demanding equal pay for #WomenInSport," Twitter, June 23, 2019, 6:03 p.m., https://twitter.com/un/status/1142915986993164293?lang=en.

68. Roger Gonzalez, "FC Dallas Under-15 Boys Squad Beat the U.S. Women's National Team in a Scrimmage," CBS Sports, April 4, 2017, https://www.cbssports.com/soccer/news/a-dallas-fc-under-15-boys-squad-beat-the-u-s-womens-national-team-in-a-scrimmage/; James Benge, "Australian Women's National Team Lose 7–0 to Team of 15-Year-Old Boys," *Evening Standard*, May 2, 2016, https://www.standard.co.uk/sport/football/australian-womens-national-team-lose-70-to-team-of-15yearold-boys-a3257266.html.

69. Stephen Kiehl, "'I Think We're Getting Hijacked,'" *New York Daily News*, September 10, 2006, https://www.nydailynews.com/bs-xpm-2006-09-10-0609100034-story.html.

Chapter Five
Campus Lunacy: The Rise of the Social Justice Warrior

1. Edward Schlosser, "I'm a Liberal Professor and My Liberal Students Terrify Me," Vox, June 3, 2015, https://www.vox.com/2015/6/3/8706323/college-professor-afraid.

2. William McKinley, *Speeches and Addresses of William McKinley: From His Election to Congress to the Present Time* (New York: D. Appleton and Company, 1893), 393.

3. See also Bradley Campbell and Jason Manning, *The Rise of Victimhood Culture: Microaggressions, Safe Spaces, and the New Culture Wars* (New York: Palgrave Macmillan, 2018).

4. Bertrand Russell, "The Superior Virtue of the Oppressed," in *Unpopular Essays* (New York: Routledge, 2009).

5. Valerie Richardson, "Attack by White Mob on Gay Asian Journalist Upends Left's Identity-Politics Script," *Washington Times*, July 2, 2019, https://www.washingtontimes.com/news/2019/jul/2/andy-ngo-antifa-attack-upends-liberals-identity-po/.

6. Steve Stankevicius, "Intellectually Sterile Universities Are Causing Idea Allergies," The Daily Banter, March 8, 2016, https://thedailybanter.com/2016/03/intellectually-sterile-universities-are-causing-idea-allergies/.

7. Jennifer Billing and Paul W. Sherman, "Antimicrobial Functions of Spices: Why Some Like It Hot," *Quarterly Review of Biology* 73, no. 1 (1998): 3–49; Paul W. Sherman and Geoffrey A. Hash, "Why Vegetable Recipes Are Not Very Spicy," *Evolution and Human Behavior* 22, no. 3 (2001): 147–63.

8. Mark Schaller and Lesley A. Duncan, "The Behavioral Immune System: Its Evolution and Social Psychological Implications," in *Evolution and the Social Mind,* eds. Joseph P. Forgas, Martie Haselton, and William von Hippel (New York: Psychology Press, 2007), 293–307.

9. Pavol Prokop and Jana Fančovičov, "Preferences for Spicy Foods and Disgust of Ectoparasites Are Associated with Reported Health in Humans," *Psihologija* 44, no. 4 (2011): 281–93.

10. Gad Saad, "My Chat with Twitter Co-Founder Jack Dorsey," *THE SAAD TRUTH* 843, February 5, 2019, YouTube video, https://www.youtube.com/watch?v=U7u2oJ_HX3U.

11. Bruce J. Lanser *et al.*, "Current Options for the Treatment of Food Allergy," *Pediatric Clinics of North America* 62, no. 6 (2015): 1531–49.

12. Scott O. Lilienfeld, "Microaggressions: Strong Claims, Inadequate Evidence," *Perspectives on Psychological Science* 12, no. 1 (2017): 138–69.

13. Gad Saad, "Trigger Warning: I Am about to Critique Trigger Warnings," HuffPost, February 5, 2015, https://www.huffpost.com/entry/ trigger-warning-i-am-abou_b_6604686.

14. "What Is Exposure Therapy?" PTSD Guideline, American Psychological Assocation, July 2017, https://www.apa.org/ptsd-guideline/patients-and-families/exposure-therapy.

15. Izzy Gainsburg and Allison Earl, "Trigger Warnings as an Interpersonal Emotion-Regulation Tool: Avoidance, Attention, and Affect Depend on Beliefs," *Journal of Experimental Social Psychology* 79 (November 2018): 252–63.

16. Benjamin W. Bellet, Payton J. Jones, and Richard J. McNally, "Trigger Warning: Empirical Evidence Ahead," *Journal of Behavior Therapy and Experimental Psychiatry* 61 (December 2018): 134–41.

17. Mevagh Sanson, Deryn Strange, and Maryanne Garry "Trigger Warnings Are Trivially Helpful at Reducing Negative Affect, Intrusive Thoughts, and Avoidance," *Clinical Psychological Science* 7, no. 4 (2019): 778–93; See also Payton J. Jones, Benjamin W. Bellet, and Richard J. McNally, "Helping or Harming? The Effect of Trigger Warnings on Individuals with Trauma Histories," preprint, submitted July 10, 2019, https://osf.io/axn6z/.

18. W. A. Oldfather, C. A. Ellis, and Donald M. Brown, "Leonhard Euler's Elastic Curves," *Isis* 20, no. 1 (1933): 76.

19. Eric L. Charnov, "Optimal Foraging, the Marginal Value Theorem," *Theoretical Population Biology* 9, no. 2 (1976): 129–36.

20. "Mission, Values, Strategic Vision," About, Palo Alto University, https:// www.paloaltou.edu/about/strategic-vision-statement.

21. Hans H. Toch and Albert H. Hastorf, "Homeostasis in Psychology: A Review and Critique," *Psychiatry* 18, no. 1 (1955): 81–91; John M. Fletcher, "Homeostatis as an Explanatory Principle in Psychology," *Psychological Review* 49, no. 1 (1942): 80–87; Nathan Maccoby and Eleanor E. Maccoby, "Homeostatic Theory in Attitude Change," *Public Opinion Quarterly* 25, no. 4 (1961): 538–45.

22. Fletcher, "Homeostasis as an Explanatory Principle," 86.

23. Robert A. Cummins, "The Theory of Subjective Wellbeing Homeostasis: A Contribution to Understanding Life Quality," in *A Life Devoted to Quality of Life,* ed. Filomena Maggino, Social Indicators Research Series

60, (Switzerland: Springer International Publishing, 2016), 61–78; Alex C. Michalos, "Multiple Discrepancies Theory (MDT)," *Social Indicators Research* 16 (1985): 347–413.

24. Jan-Benedict E. M. Steenkamp and Hans Baumgartner, "The Role of Optimum Stimulation Level in Exploratory Consumer Behavior," *Journal of Consumer Research* 19, no. 3 (1992): 434–48; Roland Helm and Sebastian Landschulze, "Optimal Stimulation Level Theory, Exploratory Consumer Behavior, and Production Adoption: An Analysis of Underlying Structures across Product Categories," *Review of Management Science* 3, no. 1 (2009): 41–73.

25. Philip M. Parker and Nader T. Tavassoli, "Homeostasis and Consumer Behavior across Cultures," *International Journal of Research in Marketing*, 17, no. 1 (2000): 33–53.

26. Gerald J. S. Wilde, "Risk Homeostasis Theory: An Overview," *Injury Prevention* 4, no. 2 (1998): 89–91.

27. Steven Robbins and Edward Waked, "Hazard of Deceptive Advertising of Athletic Footwear," *British Journal of Sports Medicine* 31, no. 4 (1997): 299–303.

28. David E. Levari *et al.*, "Prevalence-Induced Concept Change in Human Judgment," *Science* 360, no. 6396 (2018): 1465–67, https://doi.org/10.1126/science.aap8731. Many thanks to Greg Gutfeld of Fox News for having alerted me to this highly relevant paper.

29. Many thanks to my good friend Andrew Ryder, a professor of psychology at my university, for having alerted me to Haslam's paper (after I had shared with him my theory about the homeostasis of victimology).

30. Nick Haslam, "Concept Creep: Psychology's Expanding Concepts of Harm and Pathology," *Psychological Inquiry* 27, no. 1 (2016): abstract, 1.

31. Joanna Smith, "Conservative Motion to Label ISIS Actions Genocide Fails as Liberals Vote Against," CBC Canada, June 14, 2016, https://www.cbc.ca/news/politics/isis-genocide-tory-motion-1.3635632; Brian Lilley, "LILLEY: Trudeau Lets Canada Down with Genocide Comment," *Toronto Sun*, June 7, 2019, https://torontosun.com/opinion/columnists/lilley-trudeau-lets-canada-down-with-genocide-comment; Jonathan Kay, "The Ultimate 'Concept Creep': How a Canadian Inquiry Strips the Word 'Genocide' of Meaning," Quillette, June 3, 2019, https://quillette.com/2019/06/03/

the-ultimate-concept-creep-how-a-canadian-inquiry-strips-the-word-genocide-of-meaning/.

32. "'Lorne Grabher's License Plate Is Not Offensive or Dangerous,' States Expert Report," Justice Centre for Constitutional Freedoms, October 25, 2018, https://www.jccf.ca/lorne-grabhers-license-plate-is-not-offensive-or-dangerous-states-expert-report/.

33. "Lorne Grabher's Licence Plate Dispute Headed Back to Court," CBC News, March 9, 2020, cbc.ca/news/canada/nova-scotia/lorne-grabher-appeal-licence-plate-1.5490889.

34. Alice Lloyd, "College Dean Ousted for Saying Title of Book," *Weekly Standard*, June 3, 2016, https://www.weeklystandard.com/alice-b-lloyd/college-dean-ousted-for-saying-title-of-book.

35. Michelle McQuigge, "Carleton University Faces Backlash Removing Scale from Athletic Facility," *Maclean's*, March 14, 2017, https://www.macleans.ca/society/carleton-university-faces-backlash-removing-scale-from-athletic-facility/.

36. Jaime Johnson, "Waitrose to Rename 'Sexist' Sandwich after Protest by Feminist Campaigner," *The Telegraph*, October 17, 2018, https://www.telegraph.co.uk/news/2018/10/17/waitrose-rename-sexist-sandwich-protest-feminist-campaigner/.

37. Anita Sarkeesian, "How to Be a Feminist" panel, All About Women Festival, Sydney, Australia, March 9, 2015, YouTube video, 32:37, https://www.youtube.com/watch?v=Jzcs4ti_bdI.

38. Gad Saad, "Long List of Cases of White Supremacy," *THE SAAD TRUTH 538*, November 4, 2017, YouTube video, https://www.youtube.com/watch?v=HU5U_qDmgec. I've since expanded this ever-growing list.

39. Gad Saad, "Munchausen by Proxy: The Dark Side of Parental Investment Theory?" *Medical Hypotheses* 75, no. 6 (2010): 479–81.

40. Gregory Yates and Marc D. Feldman, "Factitious Disorder: A Systematic Review of 455 Cases in the Professional Literature," *General Hospital Psychiatry* 41 (July–August 2016): 20–28; Gregory Yates and Christopher Bass, "The Perpetrators of Medical Child Abuse (Munchausen Syndrome by Proxy)—A Systematic Review of 796 Cases," *Child Abuse & Neglect* 72 (October 2017): 45–53.

41. Gad Saad, "Gad Saad on Hysteria and 'Collective Munchausen' around Donald Trump, Speaking Out as an Academic, and Evolutionary Psychology 101," Areo Magazine, January 23, 2017, https://

areomagazine.com/2017/01/23/gad-saad-on-hysteria-and-collective-munchausen-around-donald-trump-speaking-out-as-an-academic-and-evolutionary-psychology-101/; "'Collective Munchausen': Dr. Gad Saad on What Drives the 'Fake Hysteria Associated with Trump,'" The Blaze, February 25, 2019, https://www.theblaze.com/glenn-beck-podcast/dr-gad-saad-collective-munchausen.

42. Wilfred Reilly, *Hate Crime Hoax: How the Left Is Selling a Fake Race War*, (Washington, D.C.: Regnery Publishing, 2019).

43. Scott Greer, "SJWs Are Putting Politics Back into the Bedroom," The Daily Caller, December 8, 2017, https://dailycaller.com/2017/12/08/sjws-are-putting-politics-back-into-the-bedroom/.

44. Gad Saad, "Help Me…My Marriage Is Transphobic!" *THE SAAD TRUTH* 408, April 26, 2017, YouTube video, https://youtu.be/h_eNsrEk7H4.

45. Dave Quinn, "Lena Dunham Says the Oberlin College Food Court Serving Sushi and Banh Mi Is Cultural Appropriation," *People*, July 15, 2016, https://people.com/food/lena-dunham-oberlin-food-court-cultural-appropriation/.

46. Frances Watthanaya, "This Chef Wants to Reclaim Bone Broth,"*VICE*, October 23, 2018, https://www.vice.com/en_us/article/9k774d/meet-the-woman-decolonizing-bone-broth.

47. Mehera Bonner, "Katy Perry Admits She's Been Appropriating Black and Japanese Culture," *Marie Claire*, June 12, 2017, https://www.marieclaire.com/celebrity/news/a27674/katy-perry-cultural-appropriation/.

48. Samantha Schmidt, "'It's Just a Dress' Teen's Chinese Prom Attire Stirs Cultural Appropriation Debate," *Washington Post*, May 1, 2018, https://www.washingtonpost.com/news/morning-mix/wp/2018/05/01/its-just-a-dress-teens-chinese-prom-attire-stirs-cultural-appropriation-debate/?noredirect=on&utm_term=.526b0f6ce1d9.

49. Julee Wilson, "Katy Perry Apologizes for Cultural Appropriation, Rocking Cornrows," *Essence*, June 14, 2017, https://www.essence.com/hair/katy-perry-apologizes-cultural-appropriation/.

50. Erin Jensen, "Vogue Apologizes for Kendall Jenner Photo with 'Afro': We 'Did Not Mean to Offend,'" *USA Today*, October 23, 2018, https://www.usatoday.com/story/life/entertainthis/2018/10/23/vogue-kendall-jenner-photo-afro-apology/1738143002/.

51. Hailey Branson-Potts, "San Francisco State Investigating Confrontation over Man's Dreadlocks," *LA Times*, March 29, 2016, https://www.

latimes.com/local/lanow/la-me-ln-sf-state-dreadlocks-20160329-story.
html.

52. "University of Ottawa Yoga Class Cancelled over 'Oppression' Concerns
    Resumes—with Indian Teacher," *Canadian National Post*, January 26,
    2016, https://nationalpost.com/news/canada/
    university-of-ottawa-yoga-class-cancelled-over-concerns-about-
    oppression-resumes-with-indian-teacher.

53. Scott Jaschik, "Hoop Earrings and Hate," *Inside Higher Ed*, March 15,
    2017, https://www.insidehighered.com/news/2017/03/15/
    pitzer-students-debate-free-speech-student-safety-and-cultural-
    appropriation.

54. Lynne Bunch, "Opinion: Eyebrow Standards Makes Women Feel
    Ostracized, Ridiculed," *L.S.U. Daily Reveille*, January 25, 2017, http://
    www.lsureveille.com/daily/opinion-eyebrow-standards-makes-women-
    feel-ostracized-ridiculed/article_180863ea-e2ad-11e6-afa8-
    335d23e10243.html.

55. Conor Friedersdorf, "The New Intolerance of Student Activism," *The
    Atlantic*, November 9, 2015, https://www.theatlantic.com/politics/
    archive/2015/11/
    the-new-intolerance-of-student-activism-at-yale/414810/.

56. Gad Saad, "Get Your Lebanese-Jewish Cultural Appropriation
    Clearance Here!" *THE SAAD TRUTH 465*, June 15, 2017, YouTube
    video, https://www.youtube.com/watch?v=aTIDS0sRBTc.

57. Gad Saad, "I've Received Global Cultural Appropriation Clearances!"
    THE SAAD TRUTH 464, June 14, 2017, YouTube video, https://www.
    youtube.com/watch?v=F5AYrLZXXqA.

58. Sarah Boesveld, "Becoming Disabled by Choice, Not Chance:
    'Transabled' People Feel Like Impostors in Their Fully Working Bodies,"
    Canadian National Post, June 3, 2015, https://nationalpost.com/news/
    canada/becoming-disabled-by-choice-not-chance-transabled-people-feel-
    like-impostors-in-their-fully-working-bodies; Tom Midlane,
    "Psychologist Blinds Woman with Drain Cleaner—Because She Wanted
    to Be Disabled," *The Mirror*, October 1, 2015, https://www.mirror.
    co.uk/news/real-life-stories/psychologist-blinds-woman-drain-
    cleaner-6552282; Anna Sedda and Gabriella Bottini, "Apotemnophilia,
    Body Integrity Identity Disorder or Xenomelia? Psychiatric and
    Neurologic Etiologies Face Each Other," *Neuropsychiatric Disease and
    Treatment* 10 (2014): 1255–65.

59. Hillel Fendel, "Heb. U. Paper Finds: IDF Has Political Motives for Not
    Raping," Israel National News, Decmber 23, 2007, http://www.
    israelnationalnews.com/News/News.aspx/124674#.Ve20vmC_vdt; Hen

Mazzig, "An Israeli Soldier to American Jews: Wake up!" Times of Israel, October 10, 2013, http://blogs.timesofisrael.com/an-israeli-soldiers-call-to-american-jews/.

60. Anisa Rawhani, "Overt to Covert: What Spending 18 Days Covered with a Hijab Taught Me about Racism and Stereotyping," *Queen's University Journal*, March 14, 2014, https://www.queensjournal.ca/story/2014-03-14/features/overt-covert/.

61. Matthew M. Hessel and Scott A. McAninch, "Coral Snake Toxicity," in *StatPearls* (Treasure Island, Florida: StatPearls Publishing, 2019). Available from https://www.ncbi.nlm.nih.gov/books/NBK519031/.

62. Gad Saad, "Why Do Social Justice Warriors Have Colored Hair?" *THE SAAD TRUTH 505*, September 10, 2017, YouTube video, https://youtu.be/ZwATG95Irfk.

63. Emanuel J. Gonçalves *et al.*, "Female Mimicry as a Mating Tactic in Males of the Blenniid Fish *Salaria Pavo*," *Journal of the Marine Biological Association of the United Kingdom* 76, no. 2 (1996): 529–38.

64. Mark D. Norman, Julian Finn, and Tom Tregenza, "Female Impersonation as an Alternative Reproductive Strategy in Giant Cuttlefish," *Proceedings of the Royal Society of London. Series B: Biological Sciences* 266, no. 1426 (1999): 1347–49.

65. Culum Brown, Martin P. Garwood, and Jane E. Williamson, "It Pays to Cheat: Tactical Deception in a Cephalopod Social Signalling System," *Biology Letters* 8, no. 5 (2012): 729–32.

66. Aaron Sell, John Tooby, and Leda Cosmides, "Formidability and the Logic of Human Anger," *Proceedings of the National Academy of Sciences of the United States of America* 106, no. 35 (2009): 15073–78; Michael Bang Petersen *et al.*, "The Ancestral Logic of Politics: Upper-Body Strength Regulates Men's Assertion of Self-Interest over Economic Redistribution," *Psychological Science* 24, no. 7 (2013): 1098–103; Michael E. Price *et al.*, "Is Sociopolitical Egalitarianism Related to Bodily and Facial Formidability in Men?" *Evolution and Human Behavior* 38, no. 5 (2017): 626–34; Michael Bang Petersen and Lasse Laustsen, "Upper-Body Strength and Political Egalitarianism: Twelve Conceptual Replications," *Political Psychology* 40, no. 2 (2019): 375–94.

67. Richard Sosis, "Why Aren't We All Hutterites? Costly Signaling Theory and Religious Behavior," *Human Nature* 14, no. 2 (2003): 91–127. Another religious ritual that serves as a costly signal is male circumcision.

68. Karl Popper, *The Open Society and Its Enemies,* rev. ed. (New York: Routledge, 2002), 668.
69. For a discussion of the self-flagellants of the Western world, see Pascal Bruckner, *The Tyranny of Guilt: An Essay on Western Masochism* (Princeton, New Jersey: Princeton University Press, 2010).
70. Incidentally using the term *illegal alien* in New York City could result in a $250,000 fine. Christopher Brito, "New York City's Anti-Discrimination Policy Warns against Terms Like 'Illegal Alien,'" October 1, 2019, https://www.cbsnews.com/news/new-york-illegal-alien-city-law-fine-hatred-freedom-of-speech/.
71. Daniel Victor, "'Reparations Happy Hour' Invites White People to Pay for Drinks," *New York Times,* April 26, 2018, https://www.nytimes.com/2018/05/26/us/reparations-happy-hour-portland.html.
72. Regina Jackson and Saira Rao, "White Women: Let's Talk about Your Racism and Your Complicity," Mission, Race2Dinner.com, https://race2dinner.com.
73. "Undoing Whiteness," Rainier Beach Yoga, https://www.rainierbeachyoga.com/undoing-whiteness/.

Chapter Six
Departures from Reason: Ostrich Parasitic Syndrome

1. George R. R. Martin, *A Game of Thrones: Book One of a Song of Ice and Fire* (New York: Bantam Books, 2019), 105, 222, 647.
2. Isaac Asimov, *The Gods Themselves* (New York: Bantam Books, 1990), 239.
3. Bandy X. Lee, *The Dangerous Case of Donald Trump: 27 Psychiatrists and Mental Health Experts Assess a President* (New York: St. Martin's Press, 2017), 273. Interestingly, the psychiatrist in question appears to suffer from Collective Munchausen when it comes to Donald Trump.
4. Ullica Segerstråle, *Defenders of the Truth: The Sociobiology Debate* (New York: Oxford University Press, 2001).
5. Dominique Lecourt, *Proletarian Science? The Case of Lysenko* (London: NLB, 1977); Valery N. Soyfer, *Lysenko and the Tragedy of Soviet Science* (New Brunswick, New Jersey: Rutgers University Press, 1994).
6. Gad Saad, "My Chat with Infectious Diseases Specialist Paul Offit," *THE SAAD TRUTH* 1030, April 9, 2020, YouTube video, https://

youtu.be/xY_oO31Gfuo; Paul A. Offit, *Deadly Choices: How the Anti-Vaccine Movement Threatens Us All* (New York: Basic Books, 2011); Paul A. Offit, *Autism's False Prophets: Bad Science, Risky Medicine, and the Search for a Cure* (New York: Columbia University Press, 2008); Paul A. Offit, *Bad Advice: Or Why Celebrities, Politicians, and Activists Aren't Your Best Source of Health Information* (New York: Columbia University Press, 2018).

7.   Christina Korownyk *et al.*, "Televised Medical Talk Shows—What They Recommend and the Evidence to Support Their Recommendations: A Prospective Observational Study," *British Medical Journal* 349, no. 7346 (2014).

8.   Gad Saad, "The Narcissism and Grandiosity of Celebrities," *Psychology Today*, June 15, 2009, https://www.psychologytoday.com/ca/blog/homo-consumericus/200906/the-narcissism-and-grandiosity-celebrities.

9.   Sander L. van der Linden, Chris E. Clarke, and Edward W. Maibach, "Highlighting Consensus among Medical Scientists Increases Public Support for Vaccines: Evidence from a Randomized Experiment," *BMC Public Health*, 15, no. 1207 (2015), https://bmcpublichealth.biomedcentral.com/articles/10.1186/s12889-015-2541-4.

10.   Richard W. Byrne and Andrew Whiten, ed., *Machiavellian Intelligence: Social Expertise and the Evolution of Intellect in Monkeys, Apes and Humans* (Oxford: Clarendon, 1988); Andrew Whiten and Richard W. Byrne, eds., *Machiavellian Intelligence II: Extensions and Evaluations* (Cambridge, United Kingdom: Cambridge University Press, 1997).

11.   Robert L. Trivers, *Social Evolution* (Menlo Park, California: Benjamin/Cummings, 1985); Robert L. Trivers, *The Folly of Fools: The Logic of Deceit and Self-Deception in Human Life* (New York: Basic Books, 2011).

12.   Sigmund Freud, *The Interpretation of Dreams*, rev. ed., trans. James Strachey (1955; repr., New York: Basic Books 2010), 596.

13.   Thomas L. Webb, Betty P. I. Chang, and Yael Benn, "'The Ostrich Problem': Motivated Avoidance or Rejection of Information about Goal Progress," *Social and Personality Psychology Compass* 7, no. 11 (2013): 794–807; Niklas Karlsson, George Loewenstein, and Duane Seppi, "The Ostrich Effect: Selective Attention to Information," *Journal of Risk and Uncertainty* 38, no. 2 (2009): 95–115; Dan Galai and Orly Sade, "The 'Ostrich Effect,' and the Relationship between the Liquidity and the Yields of Financial Assets" *Journal of Business* 79, no. 5 (2006): 2741–59.

14. Gad Saad, "Most Dangerous Global Virus: Ostrich Parasitic Syndrome," *THE SAAD TRUTH* 104, December 6, 2015, YouTube video, https://www.youtube.com/watch?v=1eXGj_RnGS4.

15. Albert-László Barabási, *Linked: How Everything Is Connected to Everything Else and What It Means for Business, Science, and Everyday Life* (New York: Plume, 2002).

16. Jeffrey Travers and Stanley Milgram, "An Experimental Study of the Small World Problem," *Sociometry* 32, no. 4 (1969): 425–43. See also Duncan J. Watts, *Six Degrees: The Science of a Connected Age* (New York: W. W. Norton, 2003).

17. Edwin Wang, ed., *Cancer Systems Biology* (Boca Raton, Florida: CRC Press, 2010).

18. "Chaos at Fifty," *Physics Today*, May 1, 2013, https://physicstoday.scitation.org/doi/10.1063/PT.3.1977?journalCode=pto.

19. Bill Nye, "Bill Nye The Science Guy Explains the Connection between Climate Change and Terrorism in Paris," HuffPost, December 1, 2015, https://www.facebook.com/HuffPostLive/videos/834171176702548/?fref=nf.

20. Abraham Kaplan, *The Conduct of Inquiry: Methodology for Behavioral Science* (San Francisco: Chandler Publishing Company, 1964), 28.

21. Abraham Maslow, *The Psychology of Science: A Reconnaissance* (New York: HarperCollins, 1966), 15.

22. Robert J. Sternberg and Elena L. Grigorenko, "Unified Psychology," *American Psychologist* 56, no. 12 (2001): 1069–79.

23. The *Forbes* writer changed the culprit from "toxic masculinity" to "unconscious bias" (yet another nonsensical cause) after undoubtedly receiving a lot of blowback. Here is the original archived link: http://archive.is/lvNem. The internet never forgets.

24. Salim Mansur, "Evidence," Standing Committee on Citizenship and Immigration, House of Commons Canada, October 1, 2012, http://www.ourcommons.ca/DocumentViewer/en/41-1/CIMM/meeting-51/evidence.

25. Miller McPherson, Lynn Smith-Lovin, and James M. Cook, "Birds of a Feather: Homophily in Social Networks," *Annual Review of Sociology* 27 (2001): 415–44.

26. Jason D. Boardman, Benjamin W. Domingue, and Jason M. Fletcher, "How Social and Genetic Factors Predict Friendship Networks," *Proceedings of the National Academy of Sciences of the United States of America* 109, no. 43 (2012): 17377–81.

27. Christina Payne and Klaus Jaffe, "Self Seeks Like: Many Humans Choose Their Dog Pets Following Rules Used for Assortative Mating," *Journal of Ethology* 23, no. 1 (2005): 15–18; Michael M. Roy and Nicholas J. S. Christenfeld, "Do Dogs Resemble Their Owners?" *Psychological Science* 15, no. 5 (2004): 361–63.

28. Min Zhou, "Intensification of Geo-Cultural Homophily in Global Trade: Evidence from the Gravity Model," *Social Science Research* 40, no. 1 (2011): 193–209.

29. The Religion of Peace, https://www.thereligionofpeace.com.

30. Gad Saad, "50+ Reasons to Explain Terrorism in 67 Countries," *THE SAAD TRUTH* 103, December 5, 2015, YouTube video, https://www.youtube.com/watch?v=ZX2ORcaJ_wQ.

31. Liam Stack, "A Brief History of Deadly Attacks on Abortion Providers," *New York Times*, November 29, 2015, https://www.nytimes.com/interactive/2015/11/29/us/30abortion-clinic-violence.html.

32. Darío Fernández-Morera, *The Myth of the Andalusian Paradise: Muslims, Christians, and Jews under Islamic Rule in Medieval Spain* (Wilmington, Delaware: ISI Books, 2016); See also "My Chat with Dario Fernandez-Morera, Improved Audio," *THE SAAD TRUTH* 461, June 9, 2017, YouTube video, https://youtu.be/Y-9oPo-brl8.

33. Gad Saad, "The Holy 3M of Apologia: Mistranslated, Misinterpreted, and Misunderstood," *THE SAAD TRUTH* 192, June 9, 2016, YouTube video, https://youtu.be/XH9WAMvsE50.

34. Meagan Fitzpatrick, "Trudeau Retracts 'Barbaric' Remarks," CBC, March 15, 2011, https://www.cbc.ca/news/politics/trudeau-retracts-barbaric-remarks-1.985386.

35. Stefan Collini, *That's Offensive! Criticism, Identity, Respect* (London: Seagull Books, 2010), 46–47.

36. *Reliance of the Traveller: A Classic Manual of Islamic Sacred Law*, ed. and trans. Nuh Ha Mim Keller (Beltsville, Maryland: Amana Publications, 1994), 584, 590. The original in Arabic is *Umdat al-Salik* by Ahmad ibn Naqib al-Misri (1368).

37. George Orwell, *Animal Farm: A Fairy Story* (London: Secker & Warburg, 1945).

38. Mike Royko, "Jesse Jackson's Message Is Too Advanced for Most," *Baltimore Sun*, December 3, 1993, https://www.baltimoresun.com/news/bs-xpm-1993-12-03-1993337169-story.html.

39. Martin Daly and Margo Wilson, *Homicide* (New York: Aldine de Gruyter, 1988).

40. Gad Saad, "Our Brains Have Evolved the Ability to Discriminate," *Psychology Today*, August 11, 2013, https://www.psychologytoday.

com/ca/blog/homo-consumericus/201308/
our-brains-have-evolved-the-ability-discriminate.

41. Gad Saad, "In Some Instances, Profiling Is Adaptive and Rational," *Psychology Today*, March 8, 2012, https://www.psychologytoday.com/ca/blog/homo-consumericus/201203/in-some-instances-profiling-is-adaptive-and-rational.

42. Evan Sayet, *KinderGarden of Eden: How the Modern Liberal Thinks and Why He's Convinced That Ignorance Is Bliss* (CreateSpace Independent Publishing Platform, 2012), 11.

Chapter Seven
How to Seek Truth: Nomological Networks of Cumulative Evidence

1. Harry G. Frankfurt, *On Bullshit* (Princeton, New Jersey: Princeton University Press, 2005), 1.

2. Hugo Mercier and Dan Sperber, *The Enigma of Reason* (Cambridge, Massachusetts: Harvard University Press 2017), 8.

3. Leon Festinger, Henry W. Riecken, and Stanley Schachter, *When Prophecy Fails* (Minneapolis, Minnesota: University of Minnesota Press, 1956), 3.

4. See David P. Schmitt and June J. Pilcher, "Evaluating Evidence of Psychological Adaptation: How Do We Know One When We See One?" *Psychological Science* 15, no. 10 (2004): 643–49; Gad Saad, "On the Method of Evolutionary Psychology and Its Applicability to Consumer Research, *Journal of Marketing Research* 54, no. 3 (June 2017): 464–77, and references therein.

5. Juan Miguel Campanario, "On Influential Books and Journal Articles Initially Rejected Because of Negative Referees' Evaluations," *Science Communication* 16, no. 3 (1995): 304–25; Juan Miguel Campanario and Erika Acedo, "Rejecting Highly Cited Papers: The Views of Scientists Who Encounter Resistance to their Discoveries from Other Scientists," *Journal of the American Society for Information Science and Technology* 58, no. 5 (2007): 734–43; Juan Miguel Campanario, "Rejecting and Resisting Nobel Class Discoveries: Accounts by Nobel Laureates," *Scientometrics* 81, no. 2 (2009): 549–65.

6. Max Planck, *Scientific Autobiography and Other Papers* (New York: Philosophical Library, 1949), 33–34.

7. Frederick R. Schram, "Anatomy of a Controversy," *American Zoologist* 32, no. 2 (1992), 357.

8. Dean Ornish, "The Power of Science," HuffPost, January 5, 2012, https://www.huffpost.com/entry/the-power-of-science_b_1179584.

9. Heiner Evanschitzky *et al.*, "Replication Research's Disturbing Trend," *Journal of Business Research* 60, no. 4 (2007): 411–15; Stefan Schmidt, "Shall We Really Do It Again? The Powerful Concept of Replication Is Neglected in the Social Sciences," *Review of General Psychology* 13, no. 2 (2009): 90–100; Matthew C. Makel, Jonathan A. Plucker, and Boyd Hegarty, "Replications in Psychology Research: How Often Do They Really Occur?" *Perspectives on Psychological Science* 7, no. 6 (2012): 537–42. See also the Reproducibility Project (Center for Open Science).

10. Gad Saad, "The Effects of Dysphoria on Sequential Choice Behavior," Working paper, Concordia University, Montreal, Quebec, Canada (1998).

11. Gad Saad, "On the Method of Evolutionary Psychology and Its Applicability to Consumer Research," *Journal of Marketing Research* 54 (June 2017): 464–77. See Figure 3, p. 468 for the relevant references.

12. But, for recent evidence that questions this link, see Douglas T. Kenrick, "The Hourglass Figure Is Not a Sign of Fertility and Health," *Psychology Today*, June 17, 2019, https://www.psychologytoday.com/ca/blog/sex-murder-and-the-meaning-life/201906/the-hourglass-figure-is-not-sign-fertility-and-health. This highlights the provisional nature of scientific knowledge, namely an honest scientist must always be open to contrary evidence.

13. Paul Thagard, "Explanatory Coherence," *Behavioral and Brain Sciences* 12, no. 3 (1989): 435–502.

14. Gary L. Brase, "Behavioral Science Integration: A Practical Framework of Multi-Level Converging Evidence for Behavioral Science Theories," *New Ideas in Psychology* 33 (April 2014): 8–20.

15. Edward O. Wilson, *Consilience: The Unity of Knowledge* (London: Abacus, 1998).

16. Gad Saad, "On the Method of Evolutionary Psychology and Its Applicability to Consumer Research," *Journal of Marketing Research* 54, no. 3 (2017): 464–77. See Figure 2, p. 467 for the relevant references.

17. Marcelo Nepomuceno *et al.*, "Testosterone & Gift Giving: Mating Confidence Moderates the Association between Digit Ratios (2D4D and rel2) and Erotic Gift Giving," *Personality and Individual Differences* 91 (2016): 27–30; Marcelo Nepomuceno *et al.*, "Testosterone at Your Fingertips: Digit Ratios (2D:4D and rel2) as Predictors of Courtship-Related Consumption Intended to Acquire and Retain Mates," *Journal*

of Consumer Psychology 26, no. 2 (2016): 231–44; Eric Stenstrom *et al.*, "Testosterone and Domain-Specific Risk: Digit Ratios (2D:4D and *rel2*) as Predictors of Recreational, Financial, and Social Risk-Taking Behaviors," *Personality and Individual Differences* 51 (2011): 412–16.

18. Recall that all of the citations corresponding to the toy example can be found in Gad Saad, "On the Method of Evolutionary Psychology and Its Applicability to Consumer Research," *Journal of Marketing Research* 54, no. 1 (2017): 464–77. See Figure 2, p. 467 for the relevant references.

19. Brenda K. Todd *et al.*, "Sex Differences in Children's Toy Preferences: A Systematic Review, Meta-Regression, and Meta-Analysis," *Infant and Child Development* 27, no. 2 (November 2017): e2064, https://doi.org/10.1002/icd.2064.

20. Gad Saad, "Katie Holmes Is Taller Than Tom Cruise: This Proves That Men Are Not Taller Than Women…No It Doesn't!" *Psychology Today*, April 13, 2009, https://www.psychologytoday.com/ca/blog/homo-consumericus/200904/katie-holmes-is-taller-tom-cruise-proves-men-are-not-taller-women-no.

21. Lee Ellis *et al.*, *Sex Differences: Summarizing More Than a Century of Scientific Research* (New York: Psychology Press, 2008).

22. David M. Buss, "Sex Differences in Human Mate Preferences: Evolutionary Hypotheses Tested in 37 Cultures," *Behavioral and Brain Sciences* 12, no. 1 (1989): 1–49.

23. Lingshan Zhang *et al.*, "Are Sex Differences in Preferences for Physical Attractiveness and Good Earning Capacity in Potential Mates Smaller in Countries with Greater Gender Equality?" *Evolutionary Psychology* 17, no. 2 (2019), https://doi.org/10.1177/1474704919852921.

24. Jonathan Gottschall *et al.*, "Sex Differences in Mate Choice Criteria Are Reflected in Folktales from around the World and in Historical European Literature," *Evolution and Human Behavior* 25, no. 2 (2004): 102–12.

25. See David P. Schmitt (Table 1.1 for a summary of relevant studies), "Evaluating Evidence of Mate Preference Adaptations: How Do We Really Know What *Homo sapiens sapiens* Really Want?" in *Evolutionary Perspectives on Human Sexual Psychology and Behavior*, ed. Viviana A. Weekes-Shackelford and Todd K. Shackelford (New York: Springer, 2014), 3–39.

26. Gad Saad, "Nothing in Popular Culture Makes Sense Except in the Light of Evolution," *Review of General Psychology* 16, no. 2 (2012): 109–20; Gad Saad, "The Darwinian Roots of Cultural Products," chap.

5 in *The Evolutionary Bases of Consumption* (Mahwah, New Jersey: Lawrence Erlbaum, 2007), Ch. 5; Gad Saad, "Cultural Products: Fossils of the Human Mind," Ch. 6 in *The Consuming Instinct: What Juicy Burgers, Ferraris, Pornography, and Gift Giving Reveal About Human Nature* (Amherst, New York: Prometheus Books, 2011).

27. Don A. Monson, "Why Is *la Belle Dame sans Merci*? Evolutionary Psychology and the Troubadours," *Neophilologus* 95, no. 4 (2011): 523–41.

28. Martin Brüne, "De Clérambault's Syndrome (Erotomania) in an Evolutionary Perspective," *Evolution and Human Behavior* 22, no. 6, (2001): 409–15.

29. Robert L. Trivers, "Parental Investment and Sexual Selection," in *Sexual Selection and Descent of Man: 1871–1971*, ed. Bernard Campbell (Chicago, Illinois: Aldine, 1972), 136–79.

30. Marcel Eens and Rianne Pinxten, "Sex-Role Reversal in Vertebrates: Behavioural and Endocrinological Accounts," *Behavioural Processes* 51 (2000): 135–47.

31. Jeffry A. Simpson and Steven W. Gangestad, "Individual Differences in Sociosexuality: Evidence for Convergent and Discriminant Validity," *Journal of Personality and Social Psychology* 60, no. 6 (1991): 870–83.

32. David P. Schmitt, "Sociosexuality from Argentina to Zimbabwe: A 48-Nation Study of Sex, Culture, and Strategies of Human Mating," *Behavioral and Brain Sciences* 28, no. 2 (2005): 247–75.

33. Russell D. Clark III and Elaine Hatfield "Gender Differences in Receptivity to Sexual Offers," *Journal of Psychology & Human Sexuality* 2, no. 1 (1989): 39–55.

34. Bruce J. Ellis and Donald Symons, "Sex Differences in Sexual Fantasy: An Evolutionary Psychological Approach, *The Journal of Sex Research* 27, no. 4 (1990): 527–55.

35. Laura L. Betzig, *Despotism and Differential Reproduction: A Darwinian View of History* (Hawthorne, New York: Aldine, 1986).

36. Joseph Henrich, Robert Boyd, and Peter J. Richerson, "The Puzzle of Monogamous Marriage," *Philosophical Transactions of the Royal Society B: Biological Sciences* 367, no. 1589 (2012): 657–69.

37. Heather A. Rupp and Kim Wallen, "Sex Differences in Response to Visual Sexual Stimuli: A Review," *Archives of Sexual Behavior* 37, no. 2 (2008): 206–18.

38. Gad Saad, Aliza Eba, and Richard Sejean, "Sex Differences When Searching for a Mate: A Process-Tracing Approach," *Journal of Behavioral Decision Making* 22, no. 2 (2009): 171–90.

39. Gad Saad and Tripat Gill, "The Framing Effect When Evaluating Prospective Mates: An Adaptationist Perspective," *Evolution and Human Behavior* 35, no. 3 (2014): 184–92.

40. Brad J. Sagarin *et al.*, "Sex Differences in Jealousy: A Meta-Analytic Examination," *Evolution and Human Behavior* 33, no. 6 (2012): 595–614.

41. Gad Saad and Tripat Gill, "Sex-Specific Triggers of Envy: An Evolutionary Perspective," *Human Behavior and Evolution Society Annual Conference*, Austin, Texas, June 2005.

42. For relevant references, see David M. Buss and David P. Schmitt, "Mate Preferences and Their Behavioral Manifestations," *Annual Review of Psychology* 70 (2019): 87.

43. I presented earlier versions of this nomological network at several venues including the Global Forum on Countering Violent Extremism (November 2016) and LogiCal-LA (January 2017).

44. Brian J. Coburn, Bradley G. Wagner, and Sally Blower, "Modeling Influenza Epidemics and Pandemics: Insights into the Future of Swine Flu (HINI)," *BMC Medicine* 7, no. 30 (2009), https://doi.org/10.1186/1741-7015-7-30; Klaus Dietz, "The Estimation of the Basic Reproduction Number for Infectious Diseases," *Statistical Methods in Medical Research* 2, no. 1 (1993): 23–41.

45. Samuel P. Huntington, "The Clash of Civilizations?" *Foreign Affairs* 72, no. 3 (1993): 22–49. Quotes come from pages 31 and 35.

46. "Most Wanted Terrorists," Federal Bureau of Investigation, https://archive.is/CH4Pb.

47. Stuart Winer, "UK Police: London Attacker Acted Alone, Motive May Remain a Mystery," *Times of Israel*, March 26, 2017, https://www.timesofisrael.com/uk-police-london-attacker-acted-alone-motive-may-remain-a-mystery/.

48. Bill Warner, "Statistical Islam," Center for the Study of Political Islam, http://www.cspipublishing.com/statistical/pdf/Statistical_Islam.pdf.

49. Eric Schmitt and Somini Sengupta, "Thousands Enter Syria to Join ISIS despite Global Efforts," *New York Times*, September 26, 2015, https://www.nytimes.com/2015/09/27/world/middleeast/thousands-enter-syria-to-join-isis-despite-global-efforts.html.

50. "Currently Listed Entities," National Security, Public Safety Canada, May 7, 2019, https://archive.is/PnSJ9.

51. "This Day in History," The Religion of Peace, July 19, 2019, https://archive.is/Qwzrl.

52. Erin Miller, "Global Terrorism in 2017," National Consortium for the Study of Terrorism and Responses to Terrorism, July 2018, https://www.start.umd.edu/pubs/START_GTD_Overview2017_July2018.pdf.

53. "Foreign Terrorist Organizations," Bureau of Counterterrorism, U.S. Department of State, https://www.state.gov/j/ct/rls/other/des/123085.htm. (Archived at https://archive.is/2SMv2).

54. "Views of Religious Groups," Mixed Views of Hamas and Hezbollah in Largely Muslim Nations, Pew Research Center, February 4, 2010, https://www.pewglobal.org/2010/02/04/chapter-3-views-of-religious-groups/.

55. "An Index of Anti-Semitism," Anti-Defamation League, https://global100.adl.org/map.

56. "The Global Divide on Homosexuality," Pew Research Center, June 4, 2013, https://www.pewglobal.org/2013/06/04/the-global-divide-on-homosexuality/.

57. Max Bearak and Darla Cameron, "Here Are the 10 Countries Where Homosexuality May Be Punished by Death," *Washington Post*, June 16, 2016, https://www.washingtonpost.com/news/worldviews/wp/2016/06/13/here-are-the-10-countries-where-homosexuality-may-be-punished-by-death-2/.

58. "The Global Gender Gap Report," World Economic Forum, 2018, http://www3.weforum.org/docs/WEF_GGGR_2018.pdf.

59. Juan Pina and Emma Watson, "World Index of Moral Freedom," Freedom Press, July 2018, http://www.fundalib.org/wp-content/uploads/2018/07/World-Index-of-Moral-Freedom-2018.pdf.

60. Abby Ohlheiser, "There Are 13 Countries Where Atheism Is Punishable by Death," *The Atlantic*, December 10, 2013, https://www.theatlantic.com/international/archive/2013/12/13-countries-where-atheism-punishable-death/355961/.

61. "Number of Countries with Very High Restrictions and Hostilities Went Down in 2014," Pew Research Center, June 23, 2016, https://www.pewforum.org/2016/06/23/number-of-countries-with-very-high-restrictions-and-hostilities-went-down-in-2014/.

Chapter Eight
Call to Action

1. For a discussion on the various versions of this quote, see Harold Marcuse, "Versions in Niemoller's Publications," UC Santa Barbara faculty page, last updated July 14, 2020, http://www.history.ucsb.edu/faculty/marcuse/niem.htm#versions.

2. Martin Luther King Jr. "Beyond Vietnam," King Institute, April 4, 1967, https://kinginstitute.stanford.edu/king-papers/documents/beyond-vietnam.

3. Danuta Kean, "'Show Me the Money!': The Self-Published Authors Being Snapped Up by Hollywood," *The Guardian*, May 15, 2017, https://www.theguardian.com/books/2017/may/15/self-published-authors-hollywood-andy-weir-the-martian-el-james; Lynn Neary, "'The Martian' Started as a Self-Published Book," NPR, February 27, 2016, https://www.npr.org/2016/02/27/468402296/-the-martian-started-as-a-self-published-book.

4. Lisette Voytko, "Joe Rogan—Controversial Backer Of Bernie Sanders—Is the Top-Earning Podcaster, Making $30 Million a Year," *Forbes*, February 3, 2020, https://www.forbes.com/sites/lisettevoytko/2020/02/03/joe-rogancontroversial-backer-of-bernie-sandersis-the-top-earning-podcaster-making-30-million-a-year/#358f07a049c4.

5. Charles Stewart, *Haud Immemor: Reminiscences of Legal and Social Life in Edinburgh and London 1850-1900* (Edinburgh, Scotland: William Blackwood & Sons, 1901), 33.

6. Gad Saad, "Judging Those Who Never Judge," *Psychology Today*, August 20, 2014, https://www.psychologytoday.com/ca/blog/homo-consumericus/201408/judging-those-who-never-judge.

7. "Non-judgmental," *Cambridge Dictionary*, https://archive.is/1E6yy.

8. All four quotes are from the *New International Version (NIV)*, https://www.biblestudytools.com/niv/.

9. William Lane Craig and Sam Harris, "Is the Foundation of Morality Natural or Supernatural? The Craig-Harris Debate," Reasonable Faith with William Lane Craig, April 2011, https://www.reasonablefaith.org/media/debates/is-the-foundation-of-morality-natural-or-supernatural-the-craig-harris-deba/.

10. Amotz Zahavi and Avishag Zahavi, *The Handicap Principle: A Missing Piece of Darwin's Puzzle* (New York: Oxford University Press, 1997).

11. I discuss such rites of passage (including the bullet ant example) as sexual signals in Ch. 9 of my book *The Consuming Instinct* (2011).

12. Claire Brownell, "Canada's First World War Sacrifice by the Numbers," *Maclean's*, October 4, 2018, https://www.macleans.ca/news/canada/canadas-first-world-war-sacrifice-by-the-numbers/.

13. "What You Wanted to Know: Champions League Penalties," UEFA.com, February 20, 2019, http://archive.is/Uu58W; and Richard A. Fariña *et al.*, "Taking the Goalkeeper's Side in Association Football Penalty Kicks," *International Journal of Performance Analysis in Sport* 13, no. 1 (2013): 96–109.

14. See for example: Gad Saad (@GadSaad), "This idiot @mzemilycain came after me because she apparently hates Jews from the Middle East (people of color) who are war refugees. Clearly, she hates Jews and arabs. [I will always win the game of Oppression Olympics.] @jack: Please protect me against this racist white woman," Twitter, September 9, 2018, 12:26 a.m., https://twitter.com/GadSaad/status/1038644843013132289?s=20.

15. Gad Saad (@GadSaad), "I apply biology & evolutionary psychology in the behavioral sciences (including consumer behavior), you retarded degenerate," Twitter, September 27, 2017, 8:30 p.m., https://twitter.com/GadSaad/status/913199211503607810?s=20; Joshua of the Cheesecake Factory Bar (@CellBioJosh), "So not actual science. An ableist and a homophobic slur, nice. I also like that you've confirmed that you're not a legal or medical expert," Twitter, September 27, 2017, 8:30 p.m., https://twitter.com/CellBioJosh/status/913199960442601472?s=20.

16. Joshua of the Cheesecake Factory Bar (@CellBioJosh), "Imagine supporting a professor that actively harasses & bullies students online to the point of defamation. @Concordia @ConcordiaUnews https://twitter.com/GadSaad/status/913200126356807680," Twitter, September 28, 2017, 12:20 a.m., https://twitter.com/CellBioJosh/status/913256996580626432?s=20.

17. Scott Kelly (@StationCDRKelly), "One of the greatest leaders of modern times, Sir Winston Churchill said, 'in victory, magnanimity.' I guess those days are over," Twitter, October 7, 2018, 12:05 p.m., https://twitter.com/StationCDRKelly/status/1048967485821599744?s=20.

18. Scott Kelly (@StationCDRKelly), "Did not mean to offend by quoting Churchill. My apologies. I will go and educate myself further on his atrocities, racist views which I do not support. My point was we need to

come together as one nation. We are all Americans. That should transcend partisan politics," Twitter, October 7, 2018, 7:22 p.m., https://twitter.com/StationCDRKelly/status/1049077517208838144?s=20.

19. Gad Saad (@GadSaad), "Stop apologizing. Stop compromising your positions for fear that you might offend the perpetually offended. Grow a pair. Stand tall. Be confident in your personhood. Know which side of the track truth is to be found. Stop the cowardice. Stop it @ StationCDRKelly," Twitter, October 8, 2018, 10:15 p.m., https://twitter.com/GadSaad/status/1049483473294118915?s=20.

20. Daniel McGraw, "Ideology and Facts Collide at Oberlin College," Quillette, June 20, 2019, https://quillette.com/2019/06/20/ideology-and-facts-collide-at-oberlin-college/.

21. Talal Ansari, "Ohio Bakery Awarded $44 Million in Libel Case against Oberlin College," *Wall Street Journal*, June 14, 2019, https://www.wsj.com/articles/ohio-bakery-awarded-44-million-in-libel-case-against-oberlin-college-11560528172.

22. Evan Gerstmann, "Judge Slashes the Verdict against Oberlin College— an Appellate Court Might Reduce It Further," *Forbes*, July 1, 2019, https://www.forbes.com/sites/evangerstmann/2019/07/01/judge-slashes-the-verdict-against-oberlin-college-an-appellate-court-might-reduce-it-further/#78e06f07650d.

23. Mark J. Brandt *et al.*, "The Ideological-Conflict Hypothesis: Intolerance among Both Liberals and Conservatives," *Current Directions in Psychological Science* 23, no. 1 (2014): 27–34.

24. Scott Jaschik, "U Chicago to Freshmen: Don't Expect Safe Spaces," *Inside Higher Ed*, August 25, 2016, https://www.insidehighered.com/news/2016/08/25/u-chicago-warns-incoming-students-not-expect-safe-spaces-or-trigger-warnings.

25. "The Plan for Dartmouth's Freedom Budget: Items for Transformative Justice at Dartmouth," March 2014, Dartblog, http://www.dartblog.com/Dartmouth_Freedom_Budget_Plan.pdf. See also Gad Saad, "The All-Time Greatest Social Justice Warriors," *THE SAAD TRUTH 59*, September 9, 2015, YouTube video, https://www.youtube.com/watch?v=rSqz0ZBKjbo.

26. Gad Saad, "I'll Have Large Fries, a Hamburger, a Diet Coke, and an MBA. Hold the Pickles," *Psychology Today*, January 28, 2009, https://www.psychologytoday.com/ca/blog/

homo-consumericus/200901/i-ll-have-large-fries-hamburger-diet-coke-and-mba-hold-the-pickles.

27. Stuart Rojstaczer, "Recent GPA Trends Nationwide Four-Year Colleges and Universities," GradeInflation.com, March 29, 2016, http://www.gradeinflation.com.

28. Colleen Flaherty, "Grades: Don't Ask, Don't Tell," *Inside Higher Ed*, September 13, 2018, https://www.insidehighered.com/news/2018/09/13/cornell-mba-students-vote-grade-nondisclosure-recruitment.

Index